Katherine, It's Time

Katherine, It's Time

An Incredible Journey into the World of a Multiple Personality

Kit Castle and Stefan Bechtel

1817

HARPER & ROW, PUBLISHERS, NEW YORK
Grand Rapids, Philadelphia, St. Louis, San Francisco
London, Singapore, Sydney, Tokyo, Toronto

To my wife, Kay, with love, admiration, and thanks

—S.B.

. . . to those who are many, and to those who are one, the abused and the abusers . . .

—K.C.

Photographs follow page 176.

FIRST EDITION

Designed by Cassandra J. Pappas

Library of Congress Cataloging-in-Publication Data

Castle, Kit.
  Katherine, it's time: an incredible journey into the world of a multiple personality / Kit Castle and Stefan Bechtel. — 1st ed.
      p.   cm.
  Includes index.
  ISBN 0-06-015926-X
  1. Castle, Kit—Mental health. 2. Multiple personality—Patients—United States—Biography. I. Bechtel, Stefan. II. Title.
RC569.5.M8C37 1989
616.85'236'0092—dc20   89-45028
[B]

---

89 90 91 92 93 AI/HC 10 9 8 7 6 5 4 3 2 1

Acknowledgments

N ow that this enormous project is done, I would like to send out my thanks to many different people, for many different reasons. First, I would like to send my thanks to "the others" for their compassion and strength. To Stefan and Kay, for their trust and their time, but most of all for their love. To Terry, Andy, and Ray, my little family—they taught me how to love, and taught me what it means to be needed. To the Zenns, who accepted and loved me even when they weren't quite sure who they were accepting and loving. To Joanie and Jerry, who let me be the boss—sometimes! To Jeff A., my first friend; to Gib, my gentle friend; and to Isabell, whom I love from a distance and who remains in my heart. To C.A.K., who through her own circumstances taught me courage. To Sherry and G.W.—there are not enough words to thank you for your continuing support as this adventure continues to unfold. To Millie and Ed, who gave me a second home in the way of good food and socialization, and who didn't ask questions. To Teresa and Ed, my young sweethearts. To the nice lady who transcribed the tapes of our many hours of interviews. To Ralph and Walt, who have my never-ending love and respect. And, of course, to Michael. There are not enough words—but then he knows. He always knows.

—K.C.

I would like to thank our long-suffering agent, Connie Clausen, who believed in this project from the very start and whose tenacious and insightful editing helped shape it into a real book. My great thanks also go to John Michel, our editor at Harper & Row, whose ideas for restructuring the manuscript greatly improved its readability. Dr. Ralph Walton is central to the entire story, and his support for the project has been invaluable. I would also like to thank everyone who consented to be interviewed for the book, whether or not the interviews were actually included here. And, of course, I'd like to thank my loving family, without whose support and forbearance this book would not have happened.

—S.B.

Foreword

As Kit Castle's psychiatrist, I would like to greet the reader with a confession. During the process of gathering the history on this most remarkable young woman, I knew her story had to be told. Yet I procrastinated—her case never was presented in the psychiatric literature.

In retrospect, I believe my lack of action may well be typical of my professional colleagues' response when it comes to the complex phenomenon of multiple personality disorder. Psychiatry is a fairly young discipline, currently struggling with its own identity crisis. As a stepchild of modern medicine, greater "legitimacy" is sought by an editorial policy within the mainstream journals that encourages "hard, scientific" data characteristic of the other medical specialties. A case such as that of Kit Castle certainly challenges the usual notion of what is "scientific." My feeble attempts to render her case history into a format suitable for a scientific presentation so distorted the reality of her life as I had come to perceive it that I eventually gave up trying. I now realize that the most appropriate way to share this powerful story is to have Kit tell it.

It would be easy to label what transpired in our therapy as a manifestation of psychopathology. The case could (and almost certainly will) be made that Kit's behavior represented the histrionics of a gifted patient with multiple personality disorder; that she experienced fugue states; that Michael, her "spirit guide," is "just an Inner Self-Helper"; that she has a borderline personality disorder; and so on. Such labeling of Kit would, I believe, minimize, distort, and ultimately destroy understanding. Having stated this, I would also like to point out that as a fairly traditional "mainstream" psychiatrist, I fully believe that psychiatric nosology is necessary. In this particular case, however, I came to feel it was inappropriate and would detract from rather than enhance our understanding of this very special story.

The experience of therapy with Kit raised questions for me not only about human identity, but forced me to confront fundamental metaphysical issues of reality. Events that transpired during our hours of therapy quite literally sent shivers down my spine, raised goosebumps on my skin, and more often started me thinking about developments in modern physics than psychiatry. For example, I believe that the confluence of spin, energy, and identity, as outlined in Kit's description of the "final farandola"—the high-velocity spin that she maintains completed her transformation into a whole, unified personality—to an astounding degree mirrors some of the recent developments in quantum mechanics and theoretical physics, which indicate that the ultimate nature or identity of the universe is very much related to the concept of spin.

Indeed, I find her account of the "farandola" no more remarkable than Stephen Hawking's contention that the fundamental particles of the universe, with a spin of one-half, do not look the same if one turns them through just one revolution, but that two complete revolutions are required for identity. In order to understand the universe as perceived by Einstein or Hawking, one must be willing to expand one's horizons beyond the teachings of Euclid and Newton—and indeed abandon "common sense" notions of reality. It is my hope that the reader can look upon the material presented here in a similar light.

RALPH G. WALTON, M.D.
Chairman, Department of Psychiatry
Western Reserve Care System
Youngstown, Ohio

A Note to the Reader

This book is based largely upon forty hours of interviews I conducted with Kit Castle during January 1988. At the time of these intense and emotionally exhausting sessions, a year and a half had elapsed since the remarkable event she still refers to as her "birth." (Psychiatrists would prefer to call it integration.) Prior to this event, her body had been occupied by seven alter personalities. Afterward, these seven alters had vanished and Kit Castle—an apparently whole, unified personality—had emerged.

Kit adamantly insists that she is distinct and separate from these seven others, and it is for this reason that this book is written in the third person. To Kit, the events described here occurred not to her, but to "them." She can recall their life histories, often in astonishing detail. In her mind's eye, she can picture their comings and goings. Their memories are stored in her brain like a library of videocassettes. But their love affairs, their foolish decisions, their great aspirations—these do not belong to her. They belong to Kitty Rosetti, Penny Lavender, Jess, Liz, Me-Liz, Little Andrea, and Little Elizabeth. After all, at the time the events described in this book occurred, Kit Castle did not yet exist.

It's important for the reader to bear in mind that, *at the time it was happening,* all the personalities except Kitty Rosetti (and, to some extent, Jess) were entirely unaware of the existence of the others. Each of their individual memories were filled with inexplicable blanks. It was only slowly, during the months after Kit Castle was "born" in June 1986, that she was able to gain access to all of their memories, and for the first time begin piecing together the story that had never been entirely clear in any of their minds except Kitty's. In effect, this book is an attempt to lay together the seven different life stories that Kit retains in her memory, rather like lining up the differently colored overlays of the human body in an anatomy textbook.

The others were all terribly confused about time, and some of the confusion is still reflected in this book. Through medical records, legal documents, and other corroborating evidence, I've attempted to piece together the time sequence of their lives as accurately as possible, but some gaps remain. Kit is still not entirely sure of her physical age, for instance, since she has no birth certificate and no memory of where or when she was born. If some small discrepancies concerning dates and ages remain, I beg the reader's forgiveness.

Although I have done my best to corroborate the physical facts of this story, I have done nothing to alter the distorting lens of the others' perceptions. Unlike most other books about multiple personality disorder, this one is written from *their* point of view, not that of a psychiatrist or an outside observer. What they saw and felt and believed, whether or not it was "real" to anyone else, was as real to them as life and death. I've attempted here to be faithful to their memories and perceptions, not to some arbitrary notion of my own about what constitutes reality and what does not.

Occasionally, the main narrative is interrupted by the voice of Kit Castle, speaking directly, looking back on the others' lives from her vantage point in the present time. It was my feeling that her insights and observations about the others' behavior were so fascinating, and added such an important new dimension to the story, that they demanded inclusion.

To help convey the great, doomed drama of the others' lives, I've taken the liberty of recreating dialogue, adding color and detail to scenes, and so forth. In doing so, however, I've done my best to remain truthful to the substance of what occurred, as well as it can be documented. Many names and locations have been altered to protect the privacy of those who may not wish to be identified.

⋆   ⋆   ⋆

As if the drama of this tale were not enough, one—no, two—final dramas were destined to unfold in the last days before this book went to press. The day I completed the final revisions on the manuscript, quite by accident, my wife came across a children's book published in 1973 called *A Wind in the Door*, by Madeleine L'Engle. The story was captivating, having to do with a great metaphysical conflict that takes place within the cells of an ailing boy genius; it was full of dragons and demons and rips in the galaxy and, as in all of L'Engle's books, a sense of the glorious strangeness and wonder of life. But what I found distressing beyond words was that two terms that are central to L'Engle's story are also central to Kit Castle's tale of the final integration of "the others." How was it possible, I wondered, that a pair of words as exotic as "farandola" and "mitochondria" would be so pivotal to both stories, if the "others" had not, consciously or unconsciously, borrowed from L'Engle's fictional tale? Although L'Engle's use of these terms is actually quite different from Kit's use of them, the similarities had the appearance of plagiarism, or worse. (In L'Engle's book, the "farandola" is not used to describe a whirling circular dance. But the creatures she calls "farandolae"—bizarre microscopic entities that live within the cells—do perform a wild spinning dance at the climax of the book.)

When I angrily demanded an explanation, Kit seemed shocked. She tearfully denied ever having read the book or even having heard of the author; she added that she had no recollection of any of the others ever having read the book either. In fact, her distress quickly surpassed my own. She had always believed that the crowning event of her integration, the transforming experience that made her whole, was an event she called the "final farandola." If that was *not* the way she was born— if it were in fact merely something one of the other personalities had borrowed from a children's book—what *were* the circumstances of her integration?

For help in understanding what might have happened, I turned to several eminent psychiatrists who are also leading authorities in multiple personality disorder: Richard Kluft, M.D., of Philadelphia; and Cornelia Wilbur, M.D., whose most famous case was described in *Sybil*, the 1973 book by Flora Rheta Schreiber.

First of all, Dr. Wilbur explained, though Kit may not consciously remember having read Madeleine L'Engle's book, it wouldn't be at all surprising that one of the alter personalities *did* read it, was powerfully moved by it—and remembered the phrases but forgot the source. "Source amnesia," as this is called, is common among normal people as well as multiples. After all, Dr. Wilbur explained, amnesia is one of the multiple's most basic defense mechanisms. Subjected to unbearable abuse, the child "splits off" or dissociates from the self that is having the experience—in effect, using amnesia as a wall to block off the experience from the rest of the self (and in so doing creating an entirely new self). It's easy to understand how a book, no matter how powerful, could be lost in this maze of forgetfulness.

But according to Kit's account, the knowledge of the farandola was presented to her through a series of encounters with a mysterious, difficult-to-describe "guide" by the name of Michael. Visible only to Kit, Michael was her lifelong friend and protector, whom she looked upon as a kind of benevolent guardian angel. While I initially had some difficulty accepting the idea of Michael, I came to accept him as a presence in Kit's life. However, this new discovery raised the question, if the "final farandola" was something borrowed from a book, what does this say about who or what Michael may be?

Both Dr. Kluft and Dr. Wilbur believe Michael is probably an ISH, or "Inner Self-Helper," a type of entity often found in multiple personality patients. Who or what these ISHs are is still a matter of some controversy—whether they are another alter personality, some other entity of the subconscious, or even, perhaps, something that comes from outside the self entirely.

Dr. Kluft believes the ISH (including Michael) is simply another alter personality. Michael, he suggests, had access to the memories of all the other alters, and when one of them read L'Engle's book as a child, he remembered the story (though the one who read it forgot). Later, Michael may have used these alluring and lyrical images as a *metaphor* for helping the others understand the process of integration. It is, he says, not at all uncommon that an ISH will create a myth or metaphor to communicate to the other alters; Michael may have used the idea of the farandola simply as a way of helping them vividly envision a process they could not otherwise comprehend.

Does this mean that the farandola was not really "real"? Not at all, says Dr. Kluft. "The healing virtue of stories, myths and metaphors is very profound—in fact, Ericksonian hypnotherapy uses metaphors and stories as a major healing tool." It could be that the "final farandola" was a self-created myth of extraordinary power and drama, a dream desperately believed in. To the others, nothing could have been more real. (It could also be—who can say?—that the farandola was something else entirely, something we know not of.)

Still, these answers raised more questions in my own mind about the mysterious figure of Michael, who would often appear to the lonely, troubled alter personalities wearing a dark coat and a dark hat. If he was another alter personality, how was it possible for the others to see him as clearly as if he were standing in the room?

"It's not uncommon for multiples to be able to see the ISH," Dr. Wilbur said. "Being able to visualize the ISH is a way of preserving its integrity, its separateness. It's a way of saying, 'This [ISH] has nothing to do with me, it is someone completely outside of me, helping me. I am helpless and powerless, but [the ISH] is benevolent and all-powerful.'

"I don't believe it's necessary to postulate a 'spirit guide' to explain the ISH," Dr. Wilbur adds. "They are alter personalities, though they may not appear to be at first. They know everything about the patient, but they don't have emotional reactions to the horrible things the alters have lived through; they just record the memories, very accurately and completely. Often they assist the therapist in integration, and they're very useful."

However, some other psychiatrists are willing to entertain the possibility that the ISH may be what it says it is—some kind of guardian angel or spirit guide. Ralph Allison, M.D., another specialist in multiple personality disorder (and the one who first coined the term ISH) is receptive to this view. To him, the ISH does not appear to be a true alter because it has no "date of birth." Many (but not all) alter personalities remember being born as a result of a specific, traumatic incident, but ISHs (including Michael) often claim to have been present since the patient's birth. Then there's the eerie content of what the ISHs actually *say*. Often, Dr. Allison explains, the ISH denies being an alter, instead describing itself as a kind of spiritual guardian—"a conduit for God's healing power and love." It speaks in an emotionless, somewhat stilted fashion, "in the manner of a computer repeating programmed information." And often the ISH will make bizarre claims about itself—that it has been in training "two hundred years or more" for the job of looking after this particular multiple, for instance, or that reincarnation is a fact.

Very often there is a hierarchy of ISHs surrounding the patient, not just one, Dr. Allison says. Each one is higher, more spiritual, and harder to reach, "and the highest ISH often speaks of being next to God. I have found it difficult to summon this type of ISH; it seems almost as though the therapist is not worthy of such contact." Still, he adds, in therapy "I always try to get to the highest helper that I can."

Dr. Allison is not surprised by Kit's ability to "see" Michael, either:

xiii

many of his multiple patients are able to do so, and one even made him a copper wall plaque with portraits of her pantheon of ISHs.

Interestingly enough, Dr. Allison does not believe that the ISH is unique to multiples. In his view, based upon what these entities have told him, even healthy individuals have one, two or three of them—it's just that we can't see them.

"Do I believe all this?" Allison asks. "Look, I can only describe what I have encountered in my practice. There are limits to what you can prove. All this stuff [the ISHs] will tell you about reincarnation, for instance—they never give you any information you can check. But more to the point, I don't feel it's my job as a therapist to doubt or even to theorize; it's my job to help the patient."

Curious about what Michael might have to say about *himself*, I attempted to "interview" him directly not long after we began this project. I sent Kit written questions by mail, and according to her account, she sat at the typewriter while Michael dictated long, rather eerie-sounding answers to each one. (He would not speak to me directly, nor has anyone else ever "seen" him.)

"Can you describe who and what you are?" I asked.

"I am Michael. I am created by my creator, who is your creator. I am created by the same force that created all that you can see and all that you cannot see. I am a healer. Some will see me as an enabler, although this is a misconception . . ."

"Are you a part of Kit, or is Kit a part of you?"

"I am both one with Kit, and yet not one with Kit. She is both one with me, and yet not one with me. The explanation is that I reside not only in this plane, but in the many, many parallel dimensions that exist . . ."

"What is your purpose?"

"I am created specifically as guardian and healer of this child. I cannot tell you if I have been gifted with all knowledge. I can tell you that when a question arises, the answer is provided, for me as well as for her. She is of her creator and therefore self-knowing, but is also of this world, so is also self-denying. My function is to create balance . . ."

And on and on it went.

After talking with the various specialists, seeking an explanation for the *Wind in the Door* incident, I relayed what I had learned to Kit. But she still seemed disconsolate and confused.

"I have no explanation for any of this," she said for the tenth time.

"All I know is that the farandola *exists,* whether you call it the farandola or the can-can," she said. "It exists whether or not it's in somebody else's book. And the farandola existed for the others, too, the same way it exists for me. I don't think they could have been integrated without their faith in the farandola.

"I am not able to give up my faith in Michael, either," she added. "Whether he is another alter personality, an ISH, a spirit guide, or whatever, all I know is that he is Michael. I am not going to hate the one person who loved the others and never stopped—the one person who loved me, too. *He* taught me to be honest and to be a good human being. *He* showed me how to become whole. How could I ever betray him, after he loved me like that?"

Kit's confusion and anxiety were understandable, because, at the same time we were investigating this latest development, yet another drama had come to light—and this one made the first one seem almost pedantic.

A few weeks before our discovery of the L'Engle book, as part of her own personal research on multiple personality disorder, Kit had made contact with another of the country's leading authorities on MPD (who has asked not to be identified). They'd had a face-to-face meeting in which Kit told the psychiatrist some of the details of her own case. Not long after this first meeting, after Kit had returned home, Michael came to her and asked if he could speak to the psychiatrist alone. She agreed. After she got the therapist on the phone, she told him about Michael's request, and then she let Michael speak through her. For the first time since her integration, Kit said later, she "lost time"; she has no memory of what Michael told the therapist. But the therapist later relayed to her the important part.

"There are others," Michael told him. "And they are in desperate need."

Almost three years after the "final farandola," out of which Kit Castle emerged as an apparently whole person, an entirely new layer of alter personalities had emerged. So far, Kit knows almost nothing about these new alters, except that they appear to be children. And she knows still less about the terrible secrets they surely keep. It has only recently come to light (in a paper Dr. Kluft published in 1984) that some multiples will develop more than one layer of alter personalities. A patient may successfully fuse one layer of personalities through therapy, believe him- or herself healed—and then, months or years later, discover a whole new strata of selves lying beneath the first. This "extremely

xv

clever strategy," as Dr. Wilbur calls it, hides the most severely abused personalities, and the most painful memories, in the deepest, most impenetrable layer.

(One note: Both Dr. Kluft and Dr. Wilbur said that the very fact that Michael survived integration is proof that the integration was not complete. Very likely, Dr. Wilbur said, Michael will stay to help with this new round of therapy—and then he, too, will be integrated into Kit.)

As of this writing, Kit is about to enter therapy. She does not know what this will force her to face—or even if she herself, and not some as-yet-undiscovered new personality, will emerge from the process. She is brave but frightened. Her earnest belief that she was whole is now exposed as just another parting veil, just another half-finished truth. There is much more work to be done; even now, the story seems far from over. In the hall of mirrors that is multiple personality disorder, the truth always seems to be something distantly glimpsed, but never seized.

—*STEFAN BECHTEL*
April 1989

Prologue

When Elizabeth Katherine Castle burst into his storefront medical office that afternoon of May 8, 1985, Dr. Walter Scott's first impression was that she might actually be in a state of clinical shock. Her skin and lips were gray. Her whole body was shaking. She was sobbing. She stood in the doorway wringing her hands over and over, as if she were freezing to death. She was a pretty, small-boned young woman in her late thirties, with clear blue eyes and a great tumble of curly, reddish-brown hair. Her hands were the hands of a child. But suddenly she looked very old, very small, and very sick.

"Liz! What's the matter?" Dr. Scott asked, his face rapidly shifting from surprise to fear. "Are you OK?"

He crossed the empty waiting room in three steps, threw his arm around her, and helped her into a chair. She collapsed into it, then hunched down over her hands, rubbing them over and over, feverishly, desperately, like a madwoman.

"Liz? Are you all right?" Dr. Scott asked again.

But she didn't answer. How could she describe what was going on inside her? Her guts were exploding—a poisonous mushroom cloud was just blowing it all apart, everything, all of it. The whole thing was

1

coming violently undone. She remembered that neighborhood! She'd grown up there! When the pictures came on the TV, it was as if she'd been magically transported back to that place she had fled so long ago, back to the house on Ontario Street. Back to those gloomy, secluded rooms, back to that . . . that smell . . . too awful to remember. Back to that bathroom with the yellow tiles. The yellow tiles! The yellow tiles! In the roar of the explosion, debris from the blast—pictures, stories, and images from things she never even knew had happened to her—lifted up in slow motion and turned end over end in the air.

"Walt, I—I just . . ."

"Try to calm down, Liz," Dr. Scott said soothingly, handing her a tissue. "Relax. Take a deep breath."

"Walt," she whispered finally, "What's happening to me? *What's happening to me?* Do you think I'm going to die? Is that what this is all about? Am I going to die now?"

Dr. Scott could hardly believe what he was seeing. Over the past nine months, he had been through the seven rings of hell with this patient, and he'd never seen her like this. He thought he'd seen everything, and now this. She'd sailed through life-threatening medical emergencies and major surgery with her reserves of strength and good humor intact. She'd endured enough medical tests to support a small hospital—since last summer, hardly a week had gone by that Liz Castle was not in his office, or in the hospital, for one reason or another. Yet still she was plagued by the strangest array of symptoms he'd ever seen—wave upon wave, like assault troops: disturbing neurological problems, seizures, weird rashes on her face and hands, crippling abdominal pains, neck pain, hallucinations, blackouts.

She'd suddenly develop crippling back pain, and then lose control of her bladder and bowels. He'd rush her to the hospital for a CT scan of the lumbar spine, it would show nothing out of the ordinary—and then the problem would spontaneously resolve. It would just disappear, like a ghost. This kind of thing happened over and over. Ghosts! For months, he felt as if he'd been chasing ghosts!

One by one, tests had ruled out nearly every disease syndrome he could think of: lupus erythematosis, multiple sclerosis, endometriosis, rare enzyme disorders. He'd begun to consider increasingly exotic possibilities: Mediterranean familial fever? Mono? Hyperlipidemia with pancreatitis? Two or three different, overlapping disorders? He was reaching for the stars. How many times had he sifted over the medical evidence in her case, obsessively, like an archeologist sifting the dust of a lost civilization,

2

hoping to spot the glint of bone fragment or painted shard, the revelation, that would explain it all?

Finally, he'd had to admit, he really had no idea what was going on with this woman, and neither did any of the specialists to whom he'd sent her. He was left with a clinical picture that simply did not make sense. Something was missing; the pieces just didn't fit.

Even the things she'd told him about her past didn't fit together—they were just disconnected stories, scattered across the United States like pamphlets dropped from a plane. She'd lived all over the place, she said: Minnesota, North Carolina, Virginia, Arizona. She and her third husband, Jeff, had only recently moved to Aurora, this tiny town in rural New York State. She had a very long and complicated medical history, involving multiple admissions to hospitals and neurological wards all over the country. She'd been raised in foster homes in Texas, she said, and had no idea who her parents were. Her first husband and three kids had been killed in a car wreck. In some ways, he thought, she really had no past at all.

"Liz," Dr. Scott said again, softly, as if he were trying to rouse her from sleep. "Liz. Can you talk now?"

Slumped in the chair, she rocked and rocked. Then she began to mumble in a dazed, slightly mechanical voice, as if she were talking to herself.

". . . I'm sitting there in front of the TV and I'm watching this news broadcast, and they're showing these aerial shots of this neighborhood in Houston, and I just . . . I just . . . I recognized that neighborhood! I think I lived there! And then it was like I was flashing back . . . back and back . . . I saw a bathroom, a yellow bathroom . . . yellow tiles . . ."

She choked back sobs.

". . . And then somebody was on top of me. He was grabbing me from behind, and he was hurting me . . . It hurt! It hurt! I was struggling to get away, and I couldn't. He was . . . raping me . . . but I couldn't get away! I couldn't get away!"

"This was a memory?" Dr. Scott asked. "A childhood memory?"

"It was like a memory, except it was so real. It was like I was really there, and I couldn't do anything about it. I was just bouncing around in my chair in front of the TV, trying to get away from this guy, and I couldn't! I couldn't!"

"Who was it?"

"It was . . ." her voice trailed off. She stared at him.

3

"Were you abused, sexually abused, as a child?" he asked her suddenly.

"Yes," she said in a tiny voice. "Walt, am I crazy? Am I nuts? Is that what's the matter with me?"

He shook his head, but didn't answer.

No, he thought. No. More than once, on consult sheets from other specialists who had seen her, they'd suggested the problem might be premenstrual syndrome, hysteria, or Munchausen's syndrome—code words for "it's all in her head." But he kept fighting that conclusion. For one thing, if there was an organic problem behind all this, it was his job to find it—he was an internist, after all, not a psychiatrist. For another thing, he couldn't find anything in her personality to suggest he was dealing with anything other than neck pain, belly pain, and funny rashes. To him, this was still a straightforward, though perplexing, medical problem. She didn't seem depressed, agitated, psychotic, delusional, or anything like that. She was lucid, alert, and very bright, brilliant, in fact. He'd come to believe her IQ was genius or near-genius level. He was no dummy himself, but he had to admit that her intellectual equipment was probably of a higher order than his own: she was fine stuff, top drawer. This was not some ordinary nut case.

Still, sometimes he had to wonder. Last winter, she and Jeff would sometimes stop by Dr. Scott's house on Cayuga Lake on Thursday nights, and during one of those visits, she had begun hinting darkly about things in her past that were "too terrible to even talk about." She'd told him about her "spirit guide," Michael, who kept her safe and sometimes took her on trips to other dimensions. She told him about hearing voices in the air. About visitations from little "beings of light." She'd told him about these things with such conviction she almost had him believing it— especially at eleven o'clock at night, with an arctic wind off the lake gabbling and whispering in the eaves.

As she sat huddled in front of him now, a little leaf storm of other memories suddenly drifted into his mind. There were things about her that would make anybody wonder. A few months ago, she'd had a partial hysterectomy. The day after the operation, he stopped by her hospital room to see her. To his bewilderment, it quickly became clear to him that she did not know who he was. Here he was talking to this woman who had been to his house half a dozen times, who knew all kinds of intimate details about his personal life—who clearly did not recognize him at all. It was weird, eerie. He knew very well that she wasn't on enough medication to whack her memory out like that.

"You know, Liz," Dr. Scott said suddenly, "I swear, it's almost like . . . I mean, one day you're talking about hearing voices, the next you don't even recognize me, and now you're having these flashbacks from your childhood. . . ."

Silence. She didn't look up.

"Then here we are burning up your Blue Cross card, ordering every test in the book for symptoms that disappear as soon as we figure out what they are . . . I mean, I don't know. I'm stumped, Liz. I really am. Sometimes I think there really *is* a psychiatric overlay to this whole thing. Maybe this has nothing to do with medicine at all. Maybe it never did."

She looked up at him then, her eyes rimmed with tears.

"What are you trying to tell me, doc?"

"I don't know. Maybe you're a multiple personality or . . . something. Like Sybil."

When he said this, he was as startled as she.

For a long moment, neither of them spoke. It was strange—almost unimaginably so—but in a weird way, it fit. Finally, something fit. Her mind seemed to have turned to stone. She was staring over his shoulder at the black filing cabinet behind him. She couldn't think. In front of her, everything had turned into a film clip running in slow motion and without sound.

"Look," Dr. Scott said suddenly, "let me give Gene Jacoby a call. Hmmm? Gene's a good guy, friend of mine; maybe I can even get you in to see him this afternoon. He's a . . . shrink, you know. Down in Ithaca."

She saw him pick up the phone and dial. She saw him talking. She saw him motioning for Doris, his wife and office manager, to come out of the back office and get her coat. She saw Doris helping her out the door to the car, saw the streets and buildings drifting past out of town. She saw the high, rolling hills along the eastern shore of Cayuga Lake passing by the window, and she saw the big hawks wheeling on the updrafts off the lake, high up, ascending the towers of the air in great, slow spirals. She heard Doris chatting pleasantly. There was something playing on the radio.

But there were also voices . . . voices of strangers laughing and chattering and crying in her head. How peculiar; they were the voices of strangers, but they sounded so familiar. Where had she heard them before? They sounded happy and sad, confused and frightened and relieved all at once. There seemed to be hundreds of them. There were children's voices, laughing and chattering in childish, broken sen-

5

tences. There was a young man's voice speaking loudly and rapidly, explaining, analyzing, diagnosing. He sounded like a doctor. And somewhere a lady had begun to sing: sweetly, sadly.

There was something very strange happening to time . . . as if her whole life were a basket of loose pearls, and they were rolling together, mysteriously linking up and then falling apart, as if a child were making a faltering attempt to string a necklace for the first time. It had always been like this! A life made of loose pearls, pretty little disconnected fragments that she could never quite put together, luminous memories afloat in time, with blank spots in between. Blank spots she'd filled in with lies and stories, because she couldn't remember.

There was so much she'd never told Dr. Scott—so much she'd never told anyone. How could anyone understand waking up in the bathtub to find a fresh surgical scar slashed across her stomach—and having no idea where it came from? Only later did she find out, through Jeff, that she'd just had a partial hysterectomy. A hysterectomy! How could anybody *forget* something like that? What was going on with her? These things didn't happen to other people, did they?

Multiple personality? Multiple personality? What did that even mean? Was this the end? Would she have to die now? Or would she have to go all the way back to the beginning and face the horror of the blank spots? What would she find if she did that? What was there? What was it she couldn't remember? Frightened and faltering, she would have to feed the pearls onto the string, like a jeweler of time and memory, linking together all the pieces that had, somehow, come unstrung.

Part 1

"The Dark Light"

Chapter 1

In the fading late afternoon light, the old Dodge nosed eastward through the crush of afternoon traffic out of downtown Dallas. Faceless interchanges drifted past. Through the bug-pocked windshield, Kitty watched the golden light wince off green expressway signs drifting by overhead: 635 South, Sunnyvale, Next Exit. Garland, Buckingham, 78 East. Cotton Bowl Parking, Keep Right. None of it meant a thing. She had no idea where she was going—just away. Away was the best she could do for now. But it was a miracle that she was even breathing, after *that* fiasco! She was only two hours old, but already she was in full flight from the past.

Her whole body was trembling, she realized suddenly. She was clinging to the steering wheel so hard her knuckles were white, but her arms were still trembling like she had palsy. Well, she'd be all right. She could handle it. The hatchet slash across the back of her left hand wasn't really so bad; it had just bled a lot. Now it was crusting over with a flaky, blackened lace of dried blood. There was no way she was going to lose her marbles now! No way. She was going to make it. Those girls would have wound up dead or psycho if she hadn't stepped in when she did. There was no way she was going to wind up like that!

9

She was in charge of the body now, and she wasn't going to let them mess it up again!

She shook her head and laughed in sadness and in scorn. Hoo-boy! What a bunch of losers those birds were! Liz, especially—that woman had come completely unglued. Bonkers. When Domingo came home and found her with the kids like that, she was absolutely bouncing off the walls. Her brain had turned to mush. She could have out-crazied any fruitcake in any locked ward in the country. No wonder he freaked! All that screaming and the blood and the hatchet and everything! What a pathetic production. What a scene, what a mess!

Suddenly, to her surprise, a great surge of remorse and longing broke over her in a wave, and she stifled a sob. Little Angel and Rita and Ramona—her babies! Liz and Me-Liz and Penny would never see those kids again. Those kids were the only thing they had ever been proud of, the only thing they could ever call their own. And now those kids were gone forever.

What am I going to do now? Kitty wondered, in sudden desperation to change the subject. *My God, what am I going to do now?* She glanced around her, taking stock of her resources: one 1956 Dodge Coronet with a crumpled fender; one white patent leather purse, contents unknown; two grime-encrusted baby seats; one ripped-open paper sack half-filled with cloth diapers; scattered over the back seat, an assortment of sticky plastic weapons, toys, pacifiers, beheaded dolls, bottles; and the clothes she wore—pale corduroy slacks, white sandals, and a blood-spattered pink, orange, and yellow blouse. God, that blouse was ugly. Who taught Liz to dress, anyway?

Well, it wasn't a lot to build a life on, but it would have to do. She checked the gas gauge: just a hair above empty. It'd be getting cold soon, and dark. At the next available exit, Kitty pulled off the expressway and drove through a little suburban downtown, looking for someplace to park. Finally she stopped behind a supermarket, next to a shabby woods. She got out of the car, opened the back door, and made a bed for herself in the back seat by turning over the baby seats onto the floorboards and covering them with diapers. Then she climbed in, covered herself with diapers, and tried to sleep for the first night of her life.

Unlike any of "the others," Kitty was born knowing the whole pathetic story. She knew all about them—Penny Lavender, Liz, Me-Liz, Little Andrea, Little Elizabeth, and Jess—she had inherited their entire life histories, their conscious and unconscious lives. Her mind and heart

10

bore the scars of everything they had ever experienced, even though none of their experiences were her own. She could remember that gloomy little house at 67 Ontario Street, in Houston, although she was not born there. She remembered the father's shabby shoes and dirty handkerchiefs, his boasting and lies, his terrible stench, even though he was not her father. And she remembered everything that had happened that day outside the bathroom door, when Domingo came home and the girls were screaming and her hands were covered with blood— even though he was not her husband, nor were they her girls.

It was as if Kitty's creation were more a bomb blast than a birth; a blasting away of the walls of amnesia that had sealed the others away from one another all those years. The others lived in a hallway of closets, emerging like sleepwalkers to wander through an empty house and then return to their dark cubicles, entirely unaware that there were other sleepwalkers who emerged from other closets to prowl the house while they were hidden away. But Kitty marched into the hallway and she could see them all coming and going clear as day. Suddenly she woke, created out of the atoms of the moment, and she could see them all moving through their lives like brain-dead zombies. The sight made her shake her head with a poisonous contempt. They were losers, weaklings and losers!

Staring up at the roof of the car, unable to sleep, Kitty watched the others' lives flash before her like the revelations that pass before a drowning man. Strange—so strange! She could remember their lives down to the tiniest detail, but they were not her memories. She was the keeper of the past, the librarian of all their personal histories, but they were not her own. Still, she realized, there was an enormous advantage in that: she could see things that none of them had ever been able to see themselves. Where Liz had stumbled blindly through her days in a fog of confusion and despair, unchastened by her experience or her mistakes, Kitty was the quickest of quick studies. She could see where it had all gone wrong. She could figure things in a flash, and she knew just what to do.

When had it all started going bad with Domingo, she wondered now? Maybe it had happened the moment Liz first spotted him across a crowded room at that Kiwanis Club affair, all those years ago. "Across a crowded room." It was like a bad movie. Liz had always been a sucker for bad movies. Maybe it had started going sour after their ridiculous wedding at the Temple of the Bells, in Austin, not long afterward, or maybe later, after Angel and the twins were born. Maybe it was the fight last Easter, when she threw Jell-O in Domingo's face and he chased her out into the lovely suburban Easter morning and then he bashed her face into the driveway again and again and again. After that, everything had begun to disintegrate completely. That's when she started falling into those black depressions again, and the blank spots in her memory began cracking open and swallowing her whole life alive. Days, weeks, even months just vanished. Her whole life seemed to be spinning wildly out of control, and she couldn't even explain what was wrong.

How could Domingo, or anyone, possibly have understood what was going on with her all those years? How could she possibly have explained it? She didn't even understand it herself. All Liz and Penny Lavender and Me-Liz knew was that, for as long as they could remember, there'd been times when they would seem to simply walk out of a dark room into the world. Suddenly they'd discover themselves standing there talking to someone, or in the middle of something, with no idea how they got there. It was as if they spent their lives walking through rooms in a house, some of which were well lit, familiar, and ordinary, and others of which were utterly dark. More and more, they found themselves emerging out of dark rooms. How often could that happen before they just disappeared altogether—before they didn't come out of the dark rooms at all?

More than once, Liz had considered killing herself. Just taking some pills and going down into the dark stillness forever. But she hadn't: she'd just descended steadily, step by step, down the ladder of poverty and despair. When the marriage finally fell apart, last summer, Liz had taken the kids and moved into a tiny one-bedroom walk-up on the other side of Dallas. The only work she could find was a night-shift job waiting tables in a tacky little beer bar. It was the first time in her life she'd had to take care of her own money, and money, it turned out, was a very mysterious thing: it just vanished. No matter how much she brought home, there was never enough to pay for the rent, gas, food, babysitters, and all the rest of it.

She had no way of knowing that her humble paycheck was supporting more than herself and the three children. Penny Lavender also lived in the apartment with them; she was scornful of the mousy way Liz dressed, and when she came out, she began buying herself the kinds of clothes she felt she had a right to. She loved new fashions; when she saw an outfit she thought she deserved, she just bought it. She wanted to look good. She wanted to meet men. After all, she was a vivacious single woman who was old enough to date—she wasn't a mother or a wife, and she had no intention of becoming one.

12

Penny was the prettiest of all the girls. She imagined herself as a kind of pale, Nordic goddess, with skin so fair and translucent that faint blue veins showed through at the temples. She had droopy, sleepy eyes, and she liked to wear her fine, sumptuous, white-blonde hair either down her back in a long Indian braid, or parted on the side and curling up off her forehead. Perhaps, to an outside observer, Penny's hair was not *really* blonde as wheat, her skin white as porcelain—but when she looked in the mirror of her own mind, that's what she saw. Penny's colors were like a shout of joy: hot pink, sunny yellow, sky blue.

Next to Penny, Liz was a wallflower. Liz imagined herself as a small, thin, childish-looking girl with dull brownish-blonde hair cut short in a pixie, like Peter Pan. She liked sad, drab, earthy colors: the colors of rain-darkened branches and mud and fallen leaves and sorrow. Those colors surrounded her like discolored mist. It was she who took all the pain and sorrow and buried it inside, like radioactive waste. It was she who filled up with guilt and shame. It was she who, in the end, was the first to go completely to pieces.

It was partly Penny's secret clothes-buying sprees that got Liz evicted from the apartment. Liz didn't know where the money went—it just wasn't there on rent day. Liz would make the money, Penny would spend it. Penny was careful to keep her new clothes separate from Liz's clothes, and she made sure that Liz never found them. It wasn't very difficult. Liz was no housekeeper, and Penny knew she'd never look under the bed, where she kept them. Me-Liz had her own secret cache, too, in the linen closet behind the towels, and Liz never found that one, either.

So Liz simply shrugged, in confusion and despair, when she got thrown out of the apartment. She moved the family into another, smaller apartment, a nasty little hovel, but they were evicted from that one, too. There were a series of jobs in taverns and gas stations, and then she was evicted again. Early last winter, she'd moved into a gloomy, dank-smelling little apartment in the rear of a complex of tiny bungalows on a busy highway. The sad furnished rooms, the plastic slipcovers, the smell of someone else's urine in the carpets and the curtains, all reeked of the past, and everything Liz had been trying to escape all those years. But she had no choice. There was no place else to turn.

What bothered Liz most was the way people in the apartment building had started talking about her behind her back. They were checking up on her, trying to peep in her windows. They knew she was crazy.

They knew she was incapable of taking care of those children—she was twenty-two, but she still looked like a teenager—and they were plotting ways to take them away from her. They were going to tell her parents, and then her parents would take them away. She couldn't bear that. If they took her children away, what would she have left?

That's why she never talked to anyone in the building—she didn't want to give them any evidence they could use against her. She stayed inside when she let the children out the back door to play in the cement courtyard behind the building. They were safe back there—the courtyard was surrounded by a chain-link fence, and Angel, though she was only three, was proud and protective of her baby sisters, who were just beginning to walk. She'd taken them under her tiny wing.

"I'll take care of them for you, Mom," she'd sing out, and then Liz would let the three of them out the back door, hand-in-hand.

One morning not long after she'd let them out, she heard someone clattering up the steps to her apartment. When she opened the door, a neighbor lady was standing there with a look of rage and scorn on her face.

"Do you have three little children?" she demanded.

"Yes, I do."

"Well, get your butt outside and take care of them!"

"Why, what's the problem?"

"The one in the middle has the other two by the hand and she's walking across the highway to the playground at the school!"

Liz bolted down the stairs and out to the busy street in front of the apartments. Across two lanes of heavy traffic, she saw Angel just climbing the curb on the other side, her twin sisters grasped firmly by the hand. Liz dodged cars across the highway, knelt on the sidewalk, and scooped them all into her arms. Angel was so proud of herself when she explained what she'd done. She was taking her sisters to the playground, all by herself.

Liz held onto the three of them as tightly as she could, and she cried.

A few weeks later, Liz returned to the apartment with the kids and found an eviction notice stapled to the door. This time, the landlord had locked her out. She didn't have the rent money to get back in, so she couldn't even salvage what little she had inside. All she had was what she and the kids were wearing, the contents of her diaper bag, packed for one day, and her old Dodge. She had no place to turn. She was afraid to let her parents see the babies for fear they'd take them away from her. She'd asked them twice for financial help, and both times they'd refused. She didn't even know where Domingo was.

So she did the only thing she could think of: she moved into the car. For her, moving into the car meant that she was cutting all ties. She was no longer dependent on her parents, or Domingo, or anybody else. She was going to make it on her own.

She developed a little route that she took. There was a McDonald's, a Dairy Queen, and a department store with a lunch counter not far from the apartment. She would go in and order a hamburger to go, and while it was being prepared she'd fill her pockets with packets of ketchup and mustard and creamers and crackers. Then she'd go back out to the car, cut the hamburger in half, give half to Angel and eat the other half herself. She'd feed the twins crackers. Sometimes she'd buy a can of evaporated milk and mix in some ketchup, pour it into the babies' bottles and then set the bottles on the dashboard to heat up in the sun. That would be their tomato soup.

She paid for gas with refunds from pop bottles, thirty or forty cents' worth at a time. At night, she'd park behind a supermarket. Sometimes, when she couldn't find any bottles, she'd just stay there for a day or two. She'd dig through the dumpsters for discarded lettuce and carrots and old bread. Behind the Dairy Queen, she found banana peels from banana splits and she'd peel off the banana meat and feed it to the babies. She'd snitch paper towels out of gas station bathrooms, and she'd use those for diapers.

Sometimes, she'd just put her head down on the steering wheel and pretend she was driving far, far away from there, like she had long ago when she was a child. In the back seat, the babies would be crying and crying. There was nothing she could do. She was overwhelmed and frightened. She was hungry. She didn't know where she was going to go or what she was going to do.

It was hard to tell how long she and the babies lived in that car. Days? Weeks? A month? She didn't know. Time was always a funny thing for her. It was something she would just "wake out of" eventually—and eventually, she did. She didn't even remember how the whole thing came to an end.

It was Me-Liz who had engineered it. When she finally came out, she looked around her in horror at the cramped, filthy car, littered with banana peels and trash and souring milk, and she decided that the only Christian thing to do was to get these children to their father. That was typical of Me-Liz. She had long ago given up the life of the body for the life of the spirit, and she felt it was her duty to God to make sure these children were properly cared for. Me-Liz was the one who had always come to take away the pain and the badness. In a funny way, Liz and Me-Liz were twins. They even looked alike: like Liz, Me-Liz pictured herself as a shy, drab, mousy little thing, except that she liked to wear her hair up in a prim French twist. The difference was that Me-Liz was a good girl, Liz was a bad girl. Liz took the guilt and shame, Me-Liz took it away. Liz was a dark shadow, Me-Liz was a shadow made of light. Long, long ago, when the bad things happened, and Liz felt so full of shame it was like a cold stone in her heart, Me-Liz had always come to atone for her sins and make her feel clean again, so God would love her. Now she had come again.

Somehow, Me-Liz managed to find Domingo's apartment in the Mexican barrio on the other side of town; she marched right in with the kids and laid it on him. Domingo was appalled when he saw them. His daughters were whimpering with hunger, and his wife looked awful. They all smelled like garbage.

"What are you going to do about it?" Me-Liz demanded, her face six inches from his.

"Well, I guess maybe I could make room for you here," he said, helplessly. "Maybe we could try patching things up one last time."

So she and the children moved in immediately.

That was the beginning of the end.

Chapter 2

Kitty lay watching the reflections of headlights crossing and crisscrossing the roof of the car. Unable to sleep, her mind raced, analyzing, planning, remembering. What was she going to do now? How, and with what, would she build a new life? She was determined not to be overwhelmed by the world the way the others had been, determined not to be destroyed, crushed, ripped apart. And she was determined to learn from their mistakes. But their memories of those last days crowded up around her with such a sick, doomed urgency that she felt nauseous.

The apartment that Domingo had found for Me-Liz and the children was a clean, small, two-bedroom place in the Mexican barrio. The apartments were so tightly packed together, and the walls so thin, that there was no escaping the din of other people's lives: family quarrels, in high-pitched, hysterical Spanish; mariachi music; children crying; people coming and going at all hours of the day and night. And everywhere was the smell of tortillas frying in hot grease. In a narrow cement walkway between the buildings, crowded with tricycles, laundry baskets, and trash, fifteen or twenty Mexican mothers would spend the afternoon in lawn chairs with beer and cigarettes, while their children rocketed back and forth on their trikes and Hot Wheels, screaming and laughing in Spanish.

Me-Liz was grateful to have a roof over her head, and to have something other than crackers and ketchup to feed the children. But she was disgusted that this was the best Domingo could do for them. It wasn't much more than a Mexican slum. And the noise was insufferable. What she longed for more than anything was calm and quiet, but here there was none. The hubbub never stopped. It hummed and buzzed in her brain, like a bumblebee that had somehow gotten trapped inside her skull, or a headache that never went away.

It was obvious almost from day one that their newly revived marriage wasn't working. Liz felt shaky and scared most of the time. There were times when she felt daunted by the task of cooking a TV dinner, much less taking care of three small children. What if she just "woke up" somewhere an hour or a day or a week later and the stove was still on? What if she burned the house down? What if she did something really awful . . . to the children? Me-Liz was doing the best she could to hold the family together. She was convinced, rightly, that the children were not being well taken care of. But when Me-Liz came out, as she did more and more often, Liz lost time. She would find herself, hours or days later, walking out of a dark room. She'd blink confusedly in the light, hurriedly trying to figure out where she was, and then simply go on from there. The panic and despair that rose up inside her then she would simply swallow, like a poison pill that didn't kill you right away.

Liz never told anyone about what was going on inside her. She didn't *know* what was going on, but she sensed in a vague sort of way that something was terribly, terribly wrong. It was "her secret." A few times, she tried to confide in Domingo, but by now his resentment had turned to a cold, distant rage, and he would simply withdraw behind his proud, handsome Mexican face. How dare she withhold sex from him, after all he had done for her? He'd taken her in off the street, and now she shuddered at his touch. Where was the big payoff for all his compassion? Domingo could not have understood that the woman who climbed into bed with him each night was not his wife. It was Me-Liz. And Me-Liz had long ago vowed to give her life to God, not to man. It was Liz whom Domingo had married, but it was Me-Liz who was pushing him away.

"All the guys at work are giving me grief because I went back with you," Domingo told her one night as they lay in bed, side by side, not touching. "They think I'm a real retard, a real A-1 sucker. I swear, I don't know what to say to those guys anymore."

"Domingo," she pleaded, "I'm sorry. I'm so sorry. But something is wrong with me. Something is terribly wrong. I don't know what it is. I just . . . I just feel so sad sometimes."

But he didn't seem to be listening. Nobody seemed to be listening.

What a weird, bitter irony, Kitty thought, that Mother's Day, 1971— the day of love and family—turns out to be the day the whole thing falls apart forever. It was the twins' first birthday, a day she would remember for the rest of her life, no matter how hard she tried to forget it.

Liz and Domingo had decided to throw a little birthday party for the twins, and Liz and Me-Liz both pitched in. Liz cleaned up the house and prepared a list of things to buy. Then Me-Liz added things: balloons, party favors, napkins. Me-Liz had sat at the kitchen table and made out little invitations, then gone downstairs and simply handed them out to kids in the walkway, because she didn't know their names. Her hands were shaking, she noticed.

The morning before the party—God, it was only yesterday—she'd woken up feeling dizzy. Just beneath the surface of consciousness, wind moved on dark water. A tempest touched the water's surface, began picking up speed, whirling out of control. When she got up and moved through the house, she discovered she had to hold onto chairs to walk. She felt exhausted and full of vague dread. She knew she had to go shopping for the party, but it seemed like an insurmountable task. It was as if she had to reach down inside herself and physically lift an enormous weight in order to summon the strength. She walked into the kitchen. Baby Angel had helped the twins into their high chairs for breakfast, and now the three of them sat looking up at her expectantly. She turned around and walked out of the room. She couldn't do it, couldn't face them. She couldn't stand it. She walked into the bathroom and stared at herself in the mirror, gripping both sides of the sink as hard as she could. She looked tired, and slightly out of focus.

She walked into the bedroom and sat down on the edge of the bed, held her arms around her waist, and began to rock. She just rocked and rocked and rocked. Out the bedroom window, she could hear mariachi music on a radio. Two women were arguing in Spanish down in the walkway, periodically breaking off the fight to scream at their kids, then picking up where they left off. In the kitchen, she could hear the twins beginning to cry. But she just rocked and rocked.

Finally Me-Liz came out, got up, and fed the children. She got dressed and cleaned up. She fed the children lunch and then put the twins down for a nap. She let Angel go outside on her trike for awhile. Then she sat down at the kitchen table and put her face in her hands. She was sitting that way when her husband walked through the door.

"Hey, what's going on?" he demanded. "What's the matter? You got a birthday party tomorrow and you haven't even been to the store! What's wrong with you, babe? What's the matter?"

She didn't say anything. She got up from the table, walked into the bathroom, locked the door, and sat down on the toilet. For a long time, she just rocked and rocked.

This morning, the morning of the party, she'd gotten up, fed the children breakfast, and herded them into the car. She drove to a Zayre's store. She piled them into a shopping cart. She pushed the cart down the aisle, loading in a package of party favors, balloons, crepe paper, a Pin-the-Tail-on-the-Donkey game. Angel ripped open the party favors and blew one. It made a flat, farting sound, and the twins laughed. But their laughter sounded dreamy and far away, like echoes of laughter in an enormous empty room. She felt faint; she clung to the shopping cart with all her strength so she wouldn't fall over. The big fluorescent lights in the store began to dim and brighten eerily, like strobes. She saw the floor and the shelves stacked with cans begin to heave and ripple. A jolt of fear went through her. Was it an earthquake? Was the roof about to cave in? She came to a dead stop in the aisle, unable to move any farther. She felt dizzy and dreamy, as if she were completely outside of herself and looking down at herself standing frozen in the aisle. In the cart, the children were laughing and playing with the pretty decorations and favors.

Suddenly Angel blew the party favor in her face and she snapped out of it. The floor stopped rippling. The lights steadied. The children laughed. She pushed the cart to the checkout counter, paid for everything, loaded the kids into the car, and got them home. She unpacked the party stuff onto the kitchen table, mechanically, not thinking. She sat the children in their chairs and put soup on the stove. Liz disappeared and Me-Liz fed them lunch. She tried to get them ready for a nap, but they were all wired up and excited about the party. They didn't want to go to sleep. She put them in their beds, walked out of the room, and they started crying and screaming all at once.

Liz came back and walked into the bedroom. She stood looking down at them in their beds. The twins were wailing and trying to climb out of the crib. They wouldn't go to sleep. The noise of their crying was right down inside her head, like bits of broken glass between her brain and skull, and it wouldn't go away, it wouldn't stop. She grabbed her head with both hands and fell down on her knees beside the bed. Something was ripping apart. Something bad, something awful was about to happen. She was afraid she was going to do something very, very bad.

A seasick despair swept over Kitty, lying rigid and unsleeping on the upended baby seats in the back seat of the car. Dawn was rising in the sky, faint and discolored, like dishwater. She could hear birds. How could anyone even imagine doing that to their own children? How could things have gotten that far out of hand? Those girls should have been institutionalized; they shouldn't have been allowed on the streets.

The screams had gone all the way down inside Liz's brain. She raised the hatchet and it went *thunk*. *Thunk, thunk, thunk.* Suddenly, the hatchet glanced off sideways and opened a gash in her hand. Blood had spilled down the white door. Blood spilled on her blouse. At the sight of that blood, Liz shrank away and Me-Liz came out. She was horrified and confused. What was she doing with this axe? What was all this blood? And the children, why were the children—

At that moment, Domingo had come home. He burst in the front door and came bounding up the stairs, and when he saw her standing there dazed and crying in her blood-spattered clothes, holding the hatchet, with the children like that, he stopped dead still. His eyes widened.

"What the hell is going on? *What the hell is going on?* Are you nuts? Are you *crazy?*"

He grabbed the hatchet out of her hand. Me-Liz shrank away in terror at the look on Domingo's face, and then Penny appeared, sleepy and confused. What was going on? Why was he looking at her like that? Why was Ramona so still? Domingo grabbed her and shoved her against the wall.

"You monster! You monster! Get the hell away from here!" he shouted at her. "Get the hell away from here!"

Penny stumbled into the darkened bedroom. She sat down on the edge of the bed and held herself around the waist, and she began to rock. Then Liz came back. She was incapable of comprehending what was going on. She was numb. She couldn't seem to think at all. She just stared down at the blood on her clothes and rocked and rocked and rocked. Something inside her had completely snapped. Finally

21

Domingo came into the bedroom where she sat, shut the windows, and drew the blinds. He stood in front of her in the dark room, and when he spoke his voice was icily calm. But all Liz could hear were those words:

"Murder the children! Murder the children!"

The words howled through her, like a hurricane through a house made of paper and sticks. *Murder the children!* The words ripped the house away, all of it, all the terror and confusion and the screams and the blood. They ripped away Liz and Me-Liz and Penny. And suddenly, sitting quietly on the edge of the bed, sat someone new. Her name was Kitty. She felt calm, almost cold. She crossed her legs, placed her palms on her top knee, and straightened her spine. She knew exactly what had happened—she knew everything. At lightning speed, she was processing her options. She raised her chin, high. The first thing she had to do, she realized, was remove herself from this situation.

"If you try to come back here, I'm going to have you arrested and thrown in prison," Domingo growled.

He handed Kitty her purse. She took it, stood up, walked down the stairs and out the door. She got into the car and turned the key.

Then she drove away.

Chapter 3

It was fully light when Kitty climbed stiffly out of the back seat of the car and stood in the alley behind the supermarket, stretching, pushing her palms straight up toward the sky. Her body felt old and sore, but her heart was racing. Just imagine, creating a whole new life out of thin air! The prospect filled her with wild excitement, an absolutely single-minded determination to succeed, and a deep, icy, dangerous kind of rage. Kitty was furious at what the world had done to Liz and the rest of those poor girls. She hated their parents with a pure, black hate. She hated Domingo Garcia, and everyone else, for making so little effort to understand them. And she vowed never to forgive him, or anyone else, who would let a tragedy like that happen, and then just throw them out onto the street. Those girls could never have survived out here alone. They would have died. They would have wound up in some back ward somewhere with no brain left, or dead in an alley. But she would survive. She was going to make it. She was going to win.

There were a pair of big trash dumpsters in the loading bay behind the store, she noticed. She glanced up and down the alley: nobody was in sight except a couple of vile-looking cats. She leaned into the opened, rear door of the car and gathered up an armload of diapers, walked across the alley to the dumpster, and chucked them in. Then she walked

23

back, hefted out Ramona's baby seat, carried it across the alley, and heaved that in. Then she offloaded Rita's baby seat, the bag of diapers, and handfuls of toys, pacifiers, and bottles. She was not a mother. She wasn't even married. And she certainly had no intention of ever going back to that house.

Kitty closed up the car and walked around to the front of the supermarket, where the parking lot had just begun to fill. Across the highway, she spotted a little coffee shop beneath a blinking neon doughnut, so she scampered across the road through morning traffic, walked in, and ordered herself breakfast. She was ravenous. She scraped the plate clean with her toast and then sat there for a long time nursing a cup of coffee, trying to wake up, trying to think. What now? What was she supposed to do now?

She left her coffee cooling on the counter and slipped into the ladies' room to tidy up. Whatever was coming next would go easier if she didn't look like a bag lady, she thought. But when she caught sight of herself in the full-length bathroom mirror—the first time she'd ever seen herself in her life—Kitty gasped. Liz's eyes had always been rather dull and flat; fearful, suspicious. But the eyes that stared back at her now were savagely intense and determined: they glittered. There was something dazzling and contemptuous and vulgar in them, as if they had a life of their own. And . . . where'd all that red hair come from? Liz's hair was a dull brownish-blonde, but this woman in the mirror had a great extravagance of curly bright-red hair. She was a stunner, a real head-turner. Kitty gave herself a sly, self-satisfied smile. She knew she looked good, and she knew she deserved it. The world owed it to her. Now all she needed was to get this fabulous body out of these ridiculous clothes.

Kitty walked back to the car, drove straight to a shopping mall, found an expensive women's clothing store, and went in to make herself presentable. She bought two new outfits—two pairs of slacks, two sweaters, two shirts, a bra and panties, and a pair of shoes. She bought a new makeup bag and filled it with all the cosmetics she needed. At the checkout counter, she pulled out a checkbook she'd found in the purse, flipped it open to the top check. She knew very well it didn't belong to her—it belonged to Liz—and she felt bad about that. She knew it was wrong. You could get thrown in jail for stuff like this. Besides, what if they were already looking for her? Forging checks in the name of Mrs. Elizabeth Katherine Garcia was like leaving little paper footprints all over town. But how else was she supposed to dress herself? She couldn't go around looking like this. Very carefully, hop-

ing the cashier wouldn't notice she was blushing down to her finger-
nails, Kitty signed the check "Mrs. Elizabeth Garcia." Kitty hadn't
spoken to a soul since she was born less than twenty-four hours before;
she'd never spoken her new name, Kitty, aloud in her life. It never
occurred to her to wonder where that name came from, or why she had
no last name. She just knew, beyond a sliver of a doubt, that that was
who she was.

She closed the checkbook without entering the check (she could
pretty well guess it would bounce), gathered up her bags, and went
directly to the ladies' room to change. By the time she walked out of
the store, Kitty looked like a million bucks. She was ready to handle
whatever life threw her way.

By nightfall, Kitty had landed on her feet, just like she knew she
would. She'd found a place to stay—a clean, spacious, tastefully decorated apartment in Fair Park, near the Cotton Bowl—and she could see
her new life already beginning to take shape before her. She'd stopped
at a taco joint for a burrito and a Coke, and she got to talking to a cute
blonde kid named Steve, who invited her over for dinner. She accepted.
Why not? She could handle herself. She followed him in her car over
to Fair Park, where he and his older brother, Frank, had an apartment
in a place called the Cricket Club. The apartment complex had a sauna
and a pool; these guys lived in nicer digs than the girls had ever lived
in in their lives. Within forty-eight hours, she'd made it to the good
side of town, though the girls had failed to make it there in a lifetime
of trying.

Steve and Frank made her a big, lavish meal and Steve served it
himself in a warm, motherly way, wearing an apron. They were nice
enough guys, earnest and polite, if a little dull. And neither one of
them tried to put the moves on her after they finished their dinner and
sat around sipping a little cheap chardonnay. They also seemed satis-
fied with her vague, throwaway answers to questions about where she'd
come from and what she was doing there.

"I'm new in Texas," she told them. "Just trying to get something
going, you know, looking for work, whatever."

She admitted that she was actually a little short on cash at the moment, so Steve and Frank offered to let her stay in the apartment until
she found a job. She accepted, on the condition that they allow her to
pay them back by cooking and cleaning. Kitty had a curiously formal
yet short-sighted sense of honor—she refused to accept their charity,
yet she thought nothing of writing rubber checks out of Elizabeth Garcia's checking account.

In the days that followed, Kitty would straighten up the apartment after Frank and Steve left for work, and then she'd spend the rest of the day combing the classifieds for a job. She went out looking every day, at furniture stores, clothing stores, a drug store, taverns. It didn't take her long to realize that she had a problem. It wasn't only that she had no particular job skills to speak of; the problem was that she had no past. She didn't even have a last name. She also had no ID—everything in the purse, including a Texas driver's license, a checkbook, and a Sears credit card, were in the name of Mrs. Elizabeth Katherine Garcia. She knew it was morally wrong and also illegal to use phony IDs. But how could she get a driver's license in her own name, knowing what she did about the others' and her own past? She could just imagine trying to explain the whole story to some little zero down at the Department of Motor Vehicles.

All day long, as she bent over the vacuum cleaner or drove around town applying for jobs, Kitty brooded over the problems of her survival in the exterior world. At the same time, she was struggling to resolve even more pressing problems in the other world. What was she going to do about Penny and Liz and Me-Liz, and the babies? They lay there in no-time, in some kind of stunned, shallow sleep, too sad and confused to even understand where they were. Kitty felt sorry for them, she really did. Not one of them clearly remembered what had happened to the kids. Each of them remembered only disconnected pieces of the story, like handfuls of pages ripped out of a book, but none remembered it all. The look on Domingo's face when he came bounding up the stairs. All that blood! Blood on the white door! All that screaming!

"Murder the children! Murder the children!"

The awful thing—the unspeakable thing—was that none of them were absolutely sure they *hadn't* murdered the children. Not one of them knew for sure. The possibility that they might have participated in the murder of three children was so horrifying that they couldn't even seem to wake up. They just lay there in a kind of deep freeze, a semiconscious purgatory in the twilight between the worlds. It wasn't like they were so deeply asleep that Kitty couldn't reach them. By some process she couldn't really understand, she could still reach their minds. She could still tell them things. She could tell them a story, a sad story, about what happened to the kids, so they'd never have to know the truth; they'd never have to be responsible.

Maybe that was it . . . yes, yes . . . maybe it was . . . a car wreck . . . Domingo and the kids were killed in a car wreck. . . . He'd taken them somewhere, to a birthday party, in the car. . . . Some drunk hit them head-on, and they'd all been killed. The police called and told her they'd all been killed. There was a funeral. . . . Then she fled, left town, and never saw any of them again. . . . It was sad, so sad, but it was not her fault and she never saw them again. . . .

Liz, especially, was a fragile thing, delicate as a china cup. If Kitty told her the truth all at once, she'd just go to pieces. Liz couldn't stand it if she thought she was responsible for destroying her own children, the only thing she'd ever really loved. To have failed as a mother, to have done that to them, would mean she was as bad as her own mother and daddy, those people whose hearts were as black as the void. The lie was for everyone's protection, Kitty insisted to herself. It was to keep everyone alive. If Liz found out the truth, she might kill herself— and then it would be over for everybody.

The others just lay there and listened in their confused sleep, until gradually their own terrible, bloody, broken-up memories faded away and all that was left was the car wreck. The police had called. . . . Domingo and the kids had been killed in a car wreck. . . . He'd taken the kids to a party in the car, and they'd all been killed, killed in a car wreck. . . . Stopped at a red light or setting the table, Kitty whispered the story to them over and over, brainwashing them in their sleep. It wasn't a perfect solution, but she was convinced it was best. At least this way, Liz wouldn't kill them all. At least this way, they might eventually learn to live.

An up-front, application-and-ID kind of job search just wasn't going to work, Kitty realized one morning while setting the table for breakfast. Nobody would ever hire her with no experience, references, or identification and only the vaguest sort of story about who she was or where she came from. She'd have to start working the outer fringes of employment, the twilight zone, where everything was strictly cash and nobody asked questions. She thumbed through the morning paper, opened it to the classifieds, and almost at once her eye lit on a tiny ad:

BARMAID WANTED
$800 TO $1,000 A WEEK POSSIBLE
BIRD CAGE LOUNGE, 14445 COLUMBUS AVENUE
APPLY IN PERSON, NO PHONE CALLS

She drove down to the club that afternoon. The place was in a long, low, windowless warehouse on a seedy commercial strip, and when she walked in out of the white afternoon sunlight, she was blind for a moment. The place was dark as a cave. It smelled like beer and piss. As her eyes adjusted to the dark, she could see a brightly lit floor-to-ceiling jukebox, pounding out rock n' roll; a horseshoe-shaped bar at the far end of the big, mostly empty room; and a couple of black men shooting pool under a cone of light. But what riveted her attention was the tall, big-boned blonde woman wearing nothing but a spangly bikini bottom, dreamily dancing up on a small, semicircular stage. The woman had a fabulous body, but the amazing thing was that her breasts hardly moved when she danced; they were immobile as stones. Kitty sank into a chair and stared up at the woman drowsily dancing in the glare of two red spotlights. So this was why $800 to $1000 a week was possible.

Well, she thought. *Well, well, well.*

Finally she got up and walked back to the bar, where two girls in bikinis were lounging against the counter.

"Can I talk to the manager?" she asked.

"Whaddya want?" said an enormous man standing behind the bar. He had a big shovel-shaped beard, a head bald as a cueball, and little, piggy eyes.

"I came about the job in the paper."

He quickly looked Kitty up and down, then hooked his thumb toward a back room. She followed him back to a tiny office, occupied by nothing but an old desk sinking in a sea of papers and a blindingly bright arc lamp, tilted toward her like a gestapo's interrogation light.

"Can you dance?" he asked.

"Sure."

"You old enough to serve beer?"

"'Course."

"Married?"

"No."

"Where you live?"

"Fair Park, up by the Cotton Bowl."

"When can you start?"

"Now."

"Take off your clothes."

Without a moment's hesitation, Kitty did. After all, the money was good, and nobody was asking her for ID.

"You'll do," the man said, when she stood in front of him in the surgical glare of the desk lamp, completely nude. "You're gonna need some costumes—all the girls start out wearing costumes and end up nude. You're gonna need two changes right away—I want you to start tonight at nine. Do good, and I'll letcha work regular."

She was buttoning up her blouse, getting ready to leave, when he reached across the desk and seized her by the elbow.

"I only got a coupla rules," he said, glaring at her unflinchingly. "No dope. No drinking on your shift, or an hour before your shift. No dating customers. And if I ever catch you stealing from me, they'll find you in an alley."

Kitty went home, had something to eat, showered, and put on her makeup. On her way back to the club, she stopped at a K-Mart and bought two bikini bathing suits that looked good and were easy to remove. One was turquoise, with little latches on the sides and one in the center on top; the other was white with black buckles. She got back to the Bird Cage well before nine and took a stool at the bar to look the place over: a beer bar, with a clientele that was about equally mixed, black and white. There were four girls working in shifts, one up on stage while the others, wearing bikinis, served the tables.

"You the new one?" she heard someone say. When Kitty turned around, she saw the big blonde with the stone bust standing behind her.

"Yeah. Hi. I'm Kitty."

"Sunny Day," the blonde said. Her face was beautiful but strangely glossy, as if it had been shellacked. "All I got to say is, don't mess with Buck. Buck be da boss! Got a cigarette?"

"Sure," Kitty said, digging a pack out of her purse and tapping one free. With her head, she motioned back toward the gaunt, hard, unhealthy looking woman up on stage.

"Who's that?"

"That's Jackie." Sunny Day's laughter turned into a cough, and she covered her mouth with one hand, coughing, with the unlit cigarette still poised between her fingers.

"Jackie always looks like that. She shoots up under her hair someplace, so Buck won't find out. Like it's some big secret. I oughta tell him. I really oughta."

"How long are we supposed to dance?"

"Six songs. You pick your own stuff—just punch it up on the jukebox and do your thing. Just so long as you wind up nude, that's all they care about."

Kitty watched Jackie remove her bikini bottom and then slowly undulate around the stage, completely naked, her long, thin, dirty-blonde hair swinging away from her body like old curtains. Kitty glanced around at the men's faces. No one seemed particularly aroused, or even interested. When Jackie gathered up her things and left the stage, no one even seemed to notice. The next dancer, Kathi, was beautiful—she had thick, black, lustrous hair and the figure of a beach queen. She could really dance, too. "What's she doing in this dive?" Kitty wondered, just as Sunny Day gave her a gentle poke in the ribs.

"Better get ready, sugar, you're up next."

Kitty slipped into a little makeshift dressing room and squeezed into her white bikini. Not bad, she thought, checking herself out from all angles in the mirror. Barefoot, she walked out across the big dark room and punched six tunes into the jukebox. There were just a few tunes she liked; she had no idea what you were really supposed to do. She stood there sheepishly until Kathi finished, and then she mounted the stage just as the first piece, *Leyla*, was beginning to play. Standing up there in the red spotlights, she began swaying gently to the sound, but it all seemed so bizarre, so forced—a girl in a bathing suit, dancing on a pedestal, above a hungry sea of men's eyes. *Well*, she thought, *what the hell*. What difference did it make? She could do anything she wanted. And by the time the tune was through, a calm sort of certainty had fallen over her.

When the next tune came up and she gazed down at them all sitting there in the darkness—it was strange, but a special kind of night vision seemed to click in, and suddenly she could see not so much their faces as their colors, or their emotions, or some such thing. She saw the brown, muddy colors of despair. She saw a dark sea of loneliness. She saw fear and pain and anxiety. She sensed their longing, their emptiness, their need. She was touched. She knew about all that. And she felt that she understood these men, in an instant, better than they understood themselves. She began trying to dance the words of the tune, an Al Green love song, for these lonely men, trying to suggest somehow that maybe they weren't the unlovable, lonely lumps they thought they were; that maybe somebody out there might really want to stay with them; that maybe they were worthy of love.

But there was something else going on inside her that the men could not have known or understood. She was dancing for Liz and Me-Liz and Penny Lavender, too. She knew they had never known anything about men, really, except that men caused pain; that they were blind, brutal pigs was all they knew. But Kitty's gift was to have an instinct for reading men, and the capacity to forgive them. Now, by her dancing, she was trying to show the girls what was down there in men's hearts. Somehow she had connected with the great dark well of male feeling in the room, and she shared that with the scared, sleeping beings who inhabited the body with her. She wanted to let them know that men were lonely too sometimes, that sometimes they too felt inadequate and ashamed; they worried, felt despair, and wanted to love and be loved, just like anybody else. For Kitty, this knowledge was her gift to the others. It was to be a balm to their hearts, and the beginning of their healing. Without it, she knew, they could never hope to be whole.

Chapter 4

Kitty moved fast. There was a sense of breathlessness about her from the very beginning, a desperate hunger and a thirst for life. She longed for everything everybody else longs for—to have money and power, to be respected, remembered, and loved. She figured she deserved it, and she was damn well going to have it. If she had to be a stripper in some dive down on Columbus Avenue, fine. She'd become the best stripper these barflies had ever seen. The best. Tops. A real star. What she didn't understand was that the great body that was her ticket to stardom was hers only to borrow, not to own. Six other selves had an equal claim on it, and though they now lay sleeping, they would eventually wake. And they might have other ideas.

Buck was so impressed with Kitty's performance that first night that he told her she could keep on working—for $250 a week, cash, for three nights' work. By her third week at the club, she was making eight hundred dollars a week, plus tips. When Buck started expanding his operation uptown and opened a classy new club in Woodland Hills called Club Pascal, Kitty was hired as the opening star—at one thousand dollars cash for one night's work. She started developing a following, a big black-and-white family of men who were no longer lonely strangers, but fans.

Kitty was a natural. From the very start, she knew where she was headed and just what she was supposed to do. She adjusted to the glittery midnight life of the burlesque circuit as easily as a transatlantic traveler resetting his watch: Waking up at twilight, going to bed at dawn, until her skin took on the pallor of a blind cave fish and midnight seemed like noon. By the time "Miss Kitty" quit six months later, she was pulling down eighteen hundred dollars a week clear and dancing in clubs all over Dallas. She thought of herself as a kind of crossover star. To her, this was not just burlesque, this was Off-Off Broadway. It was legitimate. She was a somebody.

KIT CASTLE: I still wonder so much about the way Kitty was created. How come, when she was born, she just knew how to do everything? It was like she was born in a highly evolved state because she was, in many ways, the sum of six other people. She inherited all of their abilities and knowledge and experience, even though she was as distinctly different from them as anybody could be. She was a sort of superwoman, someone who was literally "larger than life." Yet when I was born (through integration, on June 18, 1986), I actually lost so much! I lost the ability to cook, paint and do quilting, and garden. It was as if my birth was a subtraction, not an addition, like Kitty's was. She had it all!

Kitty's stage specialty was high-speed personality changes. Lots of other strip joints would have to "rent out" girls from other clubs in order to increase the variety of their acts. But Buck valued Kitty because she had a special talent for looking different onstage. She could get up as a redhead, and then come right back as a blonde or a brunette, and she seemed to be a completely different girl. One moment she could be a statuesque long-haired blonde draped in shimmering aquas and purples and fluorescent colors that would glow under the black lights; the next, a redheaded Southern belle in an extravagant yellow hoopskirt covered with lace and frill. She loved becoming whomever she wanted to be up on that stage; she had an instinct for self-transformation and she spent enormous sums on wigs and costumes.

Her costumes themselves became a hit—they were more extravagant by far than anything else on the Dallas burlesque circuit. She hired her own costume maker, a toothless old Chinese lady who began designing and making outfits for her that she beaded and sequined by hand, with linings on the inside, and all kinds of intricate hemming and tucking. Fabulous things, shimmering like scales of a fish made of gold, or extravagantly plumed, or covered with multicolored fur. Kitty would sometimes blow five hundred dollars a week on costumes. She didn't care. She'd always wanted to go first class. Then she started buying wigs in all colors—blonde, brunette, red, black—with cases to match. The wigs never lasted much more than a month or two, because the spotlights were so hot the wigs would get frizzy and then literally start to melt. And, of course, in a matter of weeks they'd start to smell so rank—from sour sweat, cigarette smoke, and beer—that they'd have to be replaced, at one or two hundred dollars a pop. Kitty didn't care about that, either. When she'd go out shopping for clothes, decked out in her wig and made up to beat the band—"coiffed," as she called it— she'd buy whole outfits to suit a redhead, blonde, or brunette. She built entire wardrobes around the personifications of these different hair colors. Variety was her specialty.

She started working out religiously, to develop her figure. She worked out her own music—none of this punching up a few tunes on the jukebox anymore. She brought her own music with her and had it installed in the jukebox. She worked to develop her singing voice, practicing for hours at home, and at night during her show, she started walking down into the audience and singing passages of songs directly into the heart of a particular man. They loved it. Word started getting around, and a new kind of customer started showing up at the Bird Cage—city hall types, businesspeople, family men. Men from the Chamber of Commerce would stop by after meetings to have a drink and get a look at the ladies. Once, when a Chamber delegation was getting ready to go to Africa on a goodwill tour, they asked Kitty what she wanted them to bring back for her. A tusk, she told them. When they came back, they brought her a Hebrew National Salami—the thing was about five feet long—wrapped up in brown paper. Kitty whooped it up, got a knife out of the kitchen and whacked up this salami phallus and served it to everybody in the club. She felt perfectly at home downstage, center.

Later, when Buck sent her out to do the opening act at the Club Pascal, Kitty devoured the place with her eyes: low lights, linen tablecloths, black garters, top hats, and big bills. Uptown: that's where she wanted to be. No more of this beer-and-piss stuff. She was moving up—and she was taking Buck along with her. When she started, the Bird Cage was just a dive; now it was starting to get respectable, becoming a sort of racy nightclub, a Moulin Rouge, and she made sure that Buck knew she knew it. He smiled faintly and gave her more money.

Kitty never entirely forgot about Liz and Me-Liz and the babies during this time, but she didn't really give them much thought. She was too busy with her own life, and enjoying it too much. Besides, she thought, they needed time to recover, time to grieve and rest, and time to fully absorb her big lie about the car wreck. Oh, she'd tell them in a sort of telepathic whisper, it was so terrible, so sad, so unfair! Killed in a car wreck. The police called and said they were all killed in a car wreck! Domingo and the kids were killed! The others just lay there and listened. In their stunned, paraplegic state, there was little else they could do.

One of the bouncers at the Bird Cage was a small-boned, soft-spoken Italian guy named Eric Rosetti, who wore a neat little black waxed moustache in a sort of Three Musketeers style. Kitty was attracted to him immediately. He was kind and intelligent and he loved to read; they'd sit at the bar after her shows and talk and talk. He was a failed stage actor who now managed an appliance store during the day and moonlighted as a bouncer at strip joints at night. Eric often carried a small pearl-handled cane, to disguise the odd little limp he still retained from an old car accident; but he managed to turn that cane into an object of high fashion, twirling and flourishing its flashing length like a stage prop. He was an honorable man whose life had not worked out quite the way he planned it—in addition to his other disappointments, he was now in the midst of an acrimonious divorce. Yet his personal pain had been transformed into real compassion. When Kitty told him about the car wreck that had taken the lives of her husband and three children, and how she had fled her past in a daze of grief and become a stripper because it was the only way she could think of to support herself, his eyes rimmed with tears and he hugged her tight, as if he were taking on her sorrow as his own.

It was only a matter of weeks before Kitty realized Eric was falling in love with her. She could see it in his eyes. She didn't hesitate, or fight him off, or fear it—she fell in love with him, too. At least, she loved him as far as she understood love. Kitty, above all else, was a survivor. Her main intention and purpose was to make it. She had no intention of marrying Eric. She had no intention of losing herself in love, or giving herself up to anyone, because that meant losing control. She knew what it was to lose herself, and she wasn't going to let that happen again.

"Would you ever consider moving in with me?" Eric asked her

one night a few weeks after they met. "I make a mean chicken à la king."

"Gotta do better than that, pal," she said.

"I'd shine your shoes. I'd bring you breakfast in bed. I'd put bonbons in your Cheerios."

"Why should I move in with you? Next thing you know, you'd be proposing."

"I love you, Kitty. I really do."

"Will you tell me that every morning, when you bring me my breakfast in bed?"

"You know I will."

"Look, Eric, hey—I'm not in any big rush to get involved. I'm not looking for some long-term thing. I like my life. I like being free."

"How 'bout if I promise never to propose?" he asked. "At least, not anytime soon?"

She planted a wet smooch on his nose.

"OK, pardner, you got a deal!"

She moved out of Frank and Steve's place and into Eric's small, ex-actor's apartment, with its brick-and-board bookshelves, great stereo, ten-speed bike, and almost nothing else. As a gift to Eric, and a public announcement of her new status as a sort-of-taken woman, Kitty adopted the stage name of "Miss Kitty Rosetti." As her career started taking off and she started bringing home more and more tax-free cash— she was working almost every night, at the Bird Cage, the Club Pascal, and other places—they moved into a swankier place in a high-security building downtown, with potted palms in the lobby. (They needed the security because she often came home late at night with lots of money.) They started buying expensive furniture together. Kitty ordered an enormous yellow custom-built velvet couch, but when it arrived the deliverymen couldn't get it in the elevator or up the stairs—they had to leave it in the lobby, still wrapped in plastic. That night, onstage, she laid her problem on her audience, almost as a joke:

"Hey, fellas, what do you do with a two-thousand-dollar, nine-foot-long, lemon-yellow couch that you can't get in your apartment on the eighth floor because it won't fit in the elevator or go up the stairs?"

After the show, two black men who worked for a crane company told her, "Hey, no problem. Eighth floor? We'll just stick it in the window." The next day they drove a crane loaded on a flatbed truck twenty miles through Dallas to her apartment, wrapped chains around the couch, and lifted it through the sliding glass balcony doors on the eighth floor. They didn't charge her anything. Kitty loved this. She loved being the pampered star. She loved the way they seemed to feel proud and protective of her. And she loved the feeling that these men were her family now. She had a big black-and-white family who loved and respected her. She was successful beyond her wildest dreams, making more money in a week than Liz used to make in three months. She loved the fabulous, glittery, sexy costumes, and being anybody she wanted to be onstage. She felt at home living the midnight life, going out to breakfast after she got off work at 3:00 A.M., or hanging around shooting pool with the black brothers after closing time. They taught her how to play a mean game of eight ball, and she even started hustling a little on the side. She could always make money with a double combination bank shot. In the wee, lightless hours of the morning, still festooned with spangles and furs, she'd take aim over the luminous green velvet. When the ball thunked home and the black brothers whooped, Kitty Rosetti felt terrific. She'd found her place.

One night after Kitty finished up a show at Club Pascal, she wound up with a couple of thousand dollars in cash from the door in her purse. It was too late to drop off the money across town at the Bird Cage, so she just took it back to her apartment. On her way home, she realized she was being followed. She took two or three detours, but each time the headlights stayed on her tail. Everyone at the clubs knew her car—a brand-new lemon-yellow Pinto hatchback with a chrome luggage rack, named Max. It was four in the morning, and she was terrified. She squealed up to the front door of her building, unlocked it, and burst into the lobby. Across the street she saw the car stopped at the curb, waiting.

She immediately called Buck down at the club, and he drove right over to her apartment to get the money. When Eric pressed him, Buck admitted that a lot of scary stuff had been happening lately. This wasn't an isolated incident. The rumors were that somebody—the Mob or somebody like the Mob—was trying to muscle in on the burlesque business all over Dallas. They were trying to threaten and intimidate the owners into getting out; other owners he knew had been harassed, and their girls followed.

Things went downhill fast from there. A few weeks later, on Labor Day, Kitty was working the day shift at the Bird Cage when somebody threw a bottle in the front door. When she went out into the street to investigate, she was grabbed, dragged into the bushes, and beaten up. When she got up and stumbled back into the club, bruised and bleeding but not badly hurt, the black brothers immediately started organizing a lynch mob. Guns appeared out of nowhere. Suddenly the club was packed with armed black men out to protect Miss Kitty and put a big hurt on somebody—even though nobody knew who to hurt, or where they might be. The atmosphere turned nasty and dangerous. Finally Buck came bursting in, towering over the mob like a mountain man, and ordered everybody to get those guns out of there. He didn't want to get busted on a firearms violation. Then he shut the place down for the night, and everybody dispersed, still angry, upset, and excited.

Kitty was scared. This was getting too real. She and Eric started talking at night about getting out of this midnight life, just going somewhere green and peaceful and trying to live like other people—people on TV shows, daylight people. A few nights later, somebody set off a bomb that blew in the back wall of the Bird Cage. Kitty was onstage, just starting her act, when there was a muffled explosion and the cinder-block wall just buckled, and the place filled up with smoke. Weird, menacing phone calls started coming in at the club: "You work for us, or you don't work at all." Click. Rumors started flying around. Stories about other girls getting beat up or knifed as they left clubs late at night; about another bombing, downtown.

Finally Kitty and Eric had had enough. They had saved enough money to get away, they said to each other. They could live somewhere nice, go fishing, go on picnics, and have barbecues in the backyard. They could see daylight, for a change. Eric had lived in Minnesota as a kid, and all he remembered was the green. Maybe that was where they should go. They could just sell all their new furniture, sell Eric's car, dump their clothes in Kitty's Pinto, and split. They could go somewhere sweet and peaceful and innocent.

So they did. The clubs got together and threw them one outrageous going-away party; it lasted two days. Then Kitty Rosetti, Liz, Me-Liz, Jess, Penny Lavender, Little Elizabeth, and Little Andrea got in the yellow Pinto with Eric and headed north, to start over.

Chapter 5

Jess loved it in Minnesota. He loved how green it was, how wild and good the air smelled, and the way the late afternoon light shimmered off the cold, blue-black lakes. But more than anything else, Jess loved going fishing with his big brother Eric. In Eric Rosetti, he'd found a kind, patient teacher and an understanding friend— the pal he'd always longed for.

When the two of them went fishing, they'd make an all-day trip of it. They'd buy minnows at a bait shop the night before, and then early in the morning when there was still mist on the water they'd push out onto Lake Minnetonka in a little rented boat loaded up with tackle boxes, bait buckets, poles, and a picnic lunch, and they'd stay out there fishing and drowsily talking until late afternoon or even dusk. On the water, far from the world of women and civilization and complications, Jess was in his element.

Like all the others, Jess only seemed to grow when he came out. Before he and Eric moved to Minnesota, he hadn't been out in ages, so for the longest time he was just stopped at age eleven. Now he was out nearly every day, and he was growing like a weed. Now he was a gangly, reedy-necked fourteen-year-old kid with a sunburnt nose and a corn-seed cap and a ponytail, unhooking lake trout in the bottm of a boat. He was out fishing with his pal, and there was nowhere else he'd rather be.

For his part, Eric never seemed to have an inkling that his favorite fishing partner was anyone other than his live-in lover and very own burlesque queen, Kitty Rosetti. He seemed impressed that she wasn't the least bit squeamish about cleaning fish; that she actually *relished* it, in fact. When they went out in the boat, she always tied her hair back in a ponytail and wore a cap, and she exuded a sort of boyish new enthusiasm about it all. But that was all right with Eric. He liked her that way sometimes.

Jess was the first one Kitty had let out since that day in the bathroom, almost a year before.

He was the least traumatized, for one thing, since he hadn't even been there that day. For another, he responded to this place; he was like a trout rising to the surface to take the bait. Kitty could hardly restrain him when Eric got ready to go fishing. Besides, since Kitty herself despised fishing, the whole arrangement was wonderfully convenient for her. She'd just let Jess sit out in that dumb rowboat all day; let him come home, clean the fish, and take a shower; and then she'd make her grand re-entry, refreshed and ready for the sack.

Then Jess would slip back inside, to the other world. He had a wonderful, special place where he went there. It was his room. He had an Oriental rug on the floor, a great big desk, and oak bookshelves stuffed with books: Sherlock Holmes, the Hardy Boys, *Gray's Anatomy*, and piles of other grown-up medical books, for when he was to grow up and become a doctor. On the wall was a poster of Albert Einstein. On the desk there was a partly completed application to a Sherlock Holmes club. It was a club to fight evil. And in one corner of the room stood a bright red telescope on a tripod. Jess liked to look through that tripod at other worlds sometimes. He liked to imagine he might see something he'd always been looking for out there.

Someday, he hoped, he might see the woman of his dreams.

After they'd been living in Minnetonka a few months and she felt enough time had passed, Kitty began letting the girls come out, too. She felt it was safe now, because compared to the rhinestone-studded midnight life they'd left behind in Dallas, the life she and Eric had made for themselves in Minnetonka was serene and quiet. She and Eric rented a beautiful house with a wraparound deck near Lake Minnetonka. Eric took a job selling auto parts, until he could find something better, and in the meantime they lived like a quiet, respectable man and wife. They introduced themselves to people as "Mr. and Mrs. Eric Rosetti."

Kitty started letting Penny come out next, and when she did, Penny invariably started painting or drawing. She always signed her name with a picture of a rising sun. Penny was surprised when she came out, but she wasn't traumatized; she had always come and gone as effortlessly as smoke, as wind stirring the leaves. Penny was like that. She had always felt so vaporous and ethereal that she sometimes wondered if people might be able to see right through her. That's why she had such a gift for painting and music: she could just disappear into her pictures or songs like a vanishing trail of mist.

It was in kindergarten, in fingerpainting class, that Penny had first discovered she could go away into her pictures. How she loved it when it was time to tie back her long, white-blonde hair in an Indian braid and put on a man's shirt and make fingerpainting on big sheets of wet paper. She loved the way the wet paper and the paints smelled, and the way they felt on her fingers. She loved the way she could paint a world all her own. It was as if those great, slimy smears of purple and green and yellow opened a secret door out of this world, and she could sail right through it into the sky. She felt misty and almost weightless, as if she had no body at all. She was a thing of the clouds and the air, not a thing of earth or pain. She floated like smoke. She was an angel. She was a bird on the wing. She was a white sheet in the wind.

Penny Lavender had a wonderful place where she went, when she returned to that other world. She understood that she was living at 2220 Wildwood Way, in Minnetonka, Minnesota—but that's not really where she lived. She lived in a little log house beside a pond, surrounded by a meadow strewn with wildflowers. She had a whitewashed wooden room inside the cabin, and a bed where she loved to lay and dream about all sorts of faraway things. The bed had wonderful bedposts that were like four tree trunks growing right up out of the floor. They were covered all over with fantastic carvings that told the story of her life. When she looked at those carvings, in her mind she could see pictures and music and stories of her life.

Kitty was the most careful about letting Liz out.

She recognized that Liz was the sickest of all the girls, mentally and physically. She believed Liz was recovering from a severe, possibly psychotic breakdown, and that it would be months or even years before she was healed. When Liz came out, she was missing so much time she panicked. She didn't know where she was. She knew something awful had happened, that the children were dead, that her husband was dead, but she was still extremely confused. Kitty would let Liz out for an hour or so when Eric was not around, as if she were walking the dog.

When Liz went back inside, the place she went was as different from Penny's cabin by the pond as one could possibly imagine. Liz's place was just a dark hole filled with sadness.

Kitty didn't let the little babies out at all. Little Elizabeth and Little Andrea hadn't been out in years, so they'd never matured beyond infancy. Little Elizabeth was so tiny she could barely talk. She had thin, wispy white hair and round nasty sores on her arms and legs. She was so shocked by fear that she just stayed in there, and she never grew up at all. She was resting; she was safe. Little Andrea, who was four, was still crouched in her warm gray cave that had nothing in it except a brown paper bag. She was still wearing the black-and-white squaw dress she'd been wearing when she was born more than twenty years before.

Me-Liz had a hiding place in the other world, too. It wasn't made of material things at all. It was a holy place, a sort of temple, bathed in a warm pinkish light. In that special place, things would simply appear when she needed them. If she was hungry, food would appear. If she needed to sleep, a bed would appear. It was a place that made her feel warm and safe, and close to God and Michael.

Kitty began letting Me-Liz out in Minnetonka, too, especially when Eric got to talking about her favorite subjects: astral travel and UFOs and life after death. Me-Liz responded to that kind of talk the way Jess responded to fishing. But Me-Liz had her problems, too. She was filled with a terrible, inconsolable grief over the loss of her dear little daughter, Mona. She was the only one of the three children she had ever considered to be her own, and she loved her beyond words. She was a miracle baby, like Jesus. By a process even she could not understand, Mona—the second of the twins to be born—had been born to her. And since she was a virgin, that made Mona a miracle. Hers was a virgin birth. There was no way a child like that could ever be replaced. There was certainly no way she could ever become pregnant again, unless God reached down and planted a divine seed inside her.

Not long after they arrived in Minnetonka, Eric took her to a mental health clinic because he was concerned about her increasingly frequent

42

bouts of depression. The doctor gave her a mood-elevating drug called Mellaril. Unfortunately, he didn't also inform her that the drug can sometimes cause symptoms mimicking pregnancy—morning sickness, tender breasts, cessation of menstruation, and weight gain. When Me-Liz started throwing up in the morning and gaining weight, she realized she must be pregnant. When her period didn't come, she was sure. It had happened: a miracle. God had reached down and touched her with His love! She was speechless, overjoyed. She started buying baby clothes.

It was weeks before she returned to the clinic for a checkup and reported to the doctor that she was pregnant. He ordered a lab test. When the results came back, they showed that the "pregnancy" was just a side effect of the drugs. But Me-Liz refused to accept the results of the test. She refused to let it rest. It was a miracle. She was going to have a baby, to replace the one she had lost. Eric called the clinic, and when he found out that the test was negative, he confronted her.

"Look, Elizabeth, the doctor says it's a false pregnancy. That's what the lab test showed. These guys know what they're talking about."

"Eric, I'm telling you, they *don't* know what they're talking about! Those tests are *always* wrong! We're going to have a baby. And when he comes, I'm going to call that doctor up and tell him myself!"

"Babe, I don't think you're dealing with reality here. *Reality*, you know? As much as you might wish you were pregnant, you're not. Plain and simple. Actually, it's a big load off my mind."

"You don't want a baby?"

He stared at her, incredulous.

"You sure have changed your tune since I first met you, Liz. Nine months ago you were scared to death I was going to propose. Now *I'm* the one who's scared—scared you're going to set suicidal if you don't have a baby. I don't get it, babe."

"But, Eric—aren't you pleased, hon? Aren't you happy? A little baby, all our own? Eric Rosetti, Jr.?"

He smiled faintly, but there was a shadow of sadness and confusion in his eyes.

The weeks and months passed, but her stomach failed to get any bigger. Finally the reality was undeniable. The doctors were right. She wasn't going to have a baby. When Me-Liz finally got that into her head, she grew terribly despondent, worse even than she had been before she started taking the medicine. She felt gray, right down to her bones. Had God favored her, and then punished her? Had He made her pregnant, and then taken that miraculous little seed away? Had she never been pregnant at all? What had she done wrong?

Finally she just went away for awhile.

Eventually, financial pressure forced Kitty to start letting Penny out more and more often. Eric just wasn't bringing home enough to pay the bills, so somebody else had to go to work. Kitty looked, but she couldn't find anything that suited her. It was ludicrous to imagine herself—a thousand-dollar-a-night opening star—working as a clerk in a dime store. That might be all right for one of the others, but *she* was better than that. So in the end it was Penny who found the job, as a clerk in a big downtown hardware store. The store was a regular Disneyland of merchandise, more of a department store than a hardware store, on three full floors in an old building downtown. Every few weeks, a new work schedule would be posted, with clerks being reassigned to different departments. Penny started out in the paint department, where she took great pride in learning to mix colors to match. When she was later rotated to the department filled with clocks and toasters, and then to the art department, with its canvases and acrylics and oil painting kits in skinny wooden boxes, she liked that, too.

Then one morning she was assigned to the sporting goods department. She took the escalator upstairs, and as soon as she turned the corner and walked into that place, she found herself facing a glass case filled with knives. Jackknives, Bowie knives, Swiss Army knives, each with a single blade displayed—two dozen glinting stabs of steel. She spooked. She just went away, like a wisp of smoke, like wind, like rain. In a flash, Jess emerged. And Jess, of course, was born for the sporting goods department with its racks of shotguns and ammo, wading boots, fishing creels, and fly-casting rods.

For weeks afterward, it was he who went to the job for Penny. Penny would get up, get dressed, catch the bus, and the next thing she knew she'd be back in the apartment that night. She'd tell herself she must have "slept in" that day. She never questioned the fact that she had a paycheck in her purse every Friday, even though she hadn't worked. She never questioned how odd it was that she "slept in," all day long, day after day. There were so many things she had learned not to question!

Kitty was deeply impressed by the great reservoirs of compassion Eric seemed to have for other people. He really cared about her—and even seemed to care about people he didn't really know. He joined Big Brothers, and on Saturdays an orphaned eight-year-old boy named Billy would spend the day with them. Sometimes Eric, Billy, and Jess would go out to a Vikings game or go fishing together. Kitty could see what a powerfully positive effect this had on Eric, and it was his example that got her thinking about doing some kind of community work of her own.

For Kitty, this was something new. She had been conceived and born out of a kind of cold rage, simply to survive. Her own survival—never assured—was what motivated all her actions. In the end, she was always looking out for number one. Yet partly due to Eric's example, and partly because something new was happening inside her, she had begun to discover compassion. It was like a counterforce to her anger—as if any energy as powerful as her rage had to be balanced by some opposite force equally strong. She just never knew it was there before.

One day she came across an ad seeking volunteers for a twenty-four-hour crisis intervention hotline called Youth Emergency Services, or YES, and she decided she'd sign up. She genuinely wanted to help people. But she also hungered for the old drama of the spotlight, and she loved the idea of rescuing people. She figured she'd be good at it. She signed up for a series of training sessions at the YES office, in a rundown little apartment over a bar near the University of Minnesota campus. In a matter of weeks, she was manning the phone lines almost every night, taking calls from scared kids in deep water, most of them stoned on drugs and many of them threatening to kill themselves. It was 1973, and the campus was rife with LSD. But what made the situation especially explosive was the recent release of the movie *The Exorcist,* which seemed to be sending people over the edge in droves. Kids would drop acid, go see the movie, and then call up in a suicidal terror, convinced they were possessed and about to kill themselves.

During the day, Penny went to work at the hardware store, and every night Kitty got on the phone to talk people down off the ledge. She was a natural at it. She was so cool and resourceful under stress that she was assigned the midnight shift on weekends—invariably the wildest, scariest time, the maximum stress shift. The phone lines would be flooded with desperate calls, but Kitty was calm and capable, and she learned how to talk people back to safety when their whole world was ablaze and collapsing.

After all, that's where she was born.

Within a few months, Kitty had proved herself so competent at this new line of work that she was assigned to a special crisis team that would be sent out to actually find the person about to commit suicide or jump off a building. The team would be on call for twenty-four-hour shifts. The police would call YES and say, "We've got a jumper," or "We've got a guy with a gun to his head, send over the crisis team." Kitty would get a call, and she'd join the rest of the team in a van, rushing to the scene. In some ways, she only came fully alive when things were in crisis. She responded to the drama. And she knew how to calmly extrapolate from a given set of facts, seeing all the other options available to someone contemplating suicide.

She only lost one person. A young woman who had just seen *The Exorcist* called in, and she told Kitty that she knew her baby was possessed.

"Don't worry about it, though—I took care of it," she said. Then she told Kitty she was about to kill herself. Kitty kept her on the line for over an hour, while the police traced the call to an apartment in downtown Minneapolis. Accompanied by a psychologist and the cops, she drove down to the apartment in a YES van, where they discovered a horrifying scene: the woman had baked the baby in the oven. One of the policemen started throwing up. But Kitty quietly worked on talking the woman back to earth.

Little by little, Kitty started letting Me-Liz and then Liz listen in on her calls. Those poor girls thought they were the only ones in the world with problems! Kitty thought it would help to simply let them know they weren't alone. She'd get a desperate call, talk long enough to make sure the caller wasn't suicidal or in real crisis, and then she'd allow Liz or Me-Liz to listen in. Sometimes they'd even express their feelings to the caller or ask a few questions of their own. They were allowed to give something of value to the caller, and to learn something of value about themselves. Kitty was always firmly in control; she never allowed the girls to intervene in her job, or jeopardize the safety of a caller in crisis.

KIT CASTLE: I don't know how this works, exactly, but somehow Kitty could allow Liz or Me-Liz or Penny to listen in on a call if she wanted them to. They couldn't hear anything if she didn't want them to. But when she wanted them to get in on the conversation, suddenly it was like a conference call, with two people on her end of the line instead of one. The others never took over the body completely; Kitty was always in control.

The girls never asked, "How come I just did ten minutes on the phone at Youth Emergency Services?" either. They were used to it. That kind of thing happened all the time.

Kitty loved the life she'd made for herself in Minnetonka. Slowly, everything had begun to calm down inside her. Enough time had passed that the others had had time to take a rest cure and grieve, and now, one by one, they were creeping out to share the life with Kitty. Little by little, the longer they were out, the more competent they became. Their illness and confusion began to defuse. Kitty loved her work at YES, too—there was nothing like saving a human life to boost your ego, and she needed ego fulfillment, badly. She always wanted to be the best at everything, and she was a real pro at saving lives.

Yet much as she loved her life and her job at YES, she and Eric were still plagued by money problems. He'd taken a better-paying job as a sales rep with the telephone company, but her volunteer work at YES didn't pay anything. She couldn't find any other work that suited her, or paid well—except, of course, going back to the clubs.

"How would you feel if I started checking out a few of the clubs down on Hennepin Avenue?" she asked him one night, as they lay together in bed. "You know, just have a look around?"

"Honey, I don't want you going back to that life," Eric said. "We came up here to get *away* from all that, didn't we?"

"Oh, I don't know. It wasn't so bad."

"Maybe we could just move into a smaller house or something."

"I don't *want* a smaller house," Kitty snapped. "I want a bigger one. Besides, I just feel like I should be contributing more."

"I don't care how much you make at the hardware store. I really don't."

"It's not just the money. I guess it's . . . I guess I just miss it sometimes. I miss the spotlight. I get a big charge out of working the phones down at YES, but I got a big charge out of my act, too. *Plus* bringing down fifteen hundred a week."

"Do you really want to go back to that, Elizabeth?"

"I've been thinking about a new act," Kitty said, suddenly sitting up excitedly. "Picture this: five hot-shit black chicks doing a chorus-line number in the background like the Temptations but wearing black tights and top hats like the Rockettes. Carrying canes maybe, canes with little Day-Glo nubs on the end. We'd do a singing, dancing, bells-and-whistles strip show. Man, oh man! We'd blow this town apart!"

Eric chuckled softly in the dark. But he still said no.

47

By summer's end, he relented.

It was bankruptcy that did it. By then, all the money they'd brought with them from Dallas was gone, and even their combined paychecks weren't enough to pay all the bills. Eric really wasn't much of a salesman; he lacked the killer instinct. And since he was paid strictly on commission, his take-home pay dwindled to a trickle. Penny only made a pittance at the hardware store. Eventually, the two of them went to court to declare personal bankruptcy. They came out of the courtroom debt-free, but broke as ever.

The next morning Kitty got decked out to about a quarter inch past a tramp and took the bus downtown to a place called the Copper Squirrel.

It was back to the midnight life again.

Chapter 6

Funny little girl, lonely little girl,
No place to go, nobody to be.
Take a look at me, fellas!
It's my job you know,
It's my job you see . . .

Standing alone in the spotlight, wearing a shoulder-length red wig, tiny golden slippers, and a sheer, swirling, sequin-spattered harem skirt in lime-green, yellow, and rose, Kitty sang her special song every night at the beginning of her act. She wanted to say something to those men out there. She wanted it known that this was no trash act. She took it seriously. To her, it was never just striptease—the fact that she ended up totally nude was part of what she was trying to convey to her audience. That she could expose herself to them totally. That they could trust her. That she understood them because they, too, were totally exposed to her. To Kitty, it was never an act of submission to stand on that stage nude, it was an act of power.

Kitty was working at the ritziest private club in St. Paul, a place called the Blue Note Lounge. She'd spent a couple of weeks scoping out all the other clubs on the Hennepin Avenue strip in downtown Minneapolis, but none measured up. She'd go there in the afternoon to have a drink and score the material she saw onstage like a gymnastics judge at the Olympics, but in the end she always walked out. She didn't want to find herself up there following some tacky two-stepper with varicose veins. Some corn pone firing rim shots when she took off her top. She wanted to go first class. And she wanted to make absolutely certain that, when she did find a place that was up to her standards, she and she alone was the star. To be anything less was shameful.

Finally, she answered an ad for a new private club in St. Paul, and as soon as she walked into the place she knew this was it: low lights, little brass candles on each table, acres of dark wood and red carpet. The place also had a terrific sound and lighting system, six dressing rooms and a shower backstage, and served food and mixers, not just beer. Kitty liked the owners, too: a young Italian guy named Jimmy Spumoni, who'd made a bundle in the dry cleaning business, and his wife, Sally. It was a real class act—tasteful, pricey, and private. You had to pay $500 to become a member, so that would keep the lowlifes out. No more criminal types, or bombs busting down the back wall.

Or so Kitty thought at the time.

Within a matter of weeks, Kitty Rosetti had started to develop a following, and within a couple of months she was rolling in dough again—sometimes making $250 a night in tips alone. She was doing three and sometimes four shows a night, depending on the crowd. Very often, after her set was finished, they'd insist on an encore, so another girl would go out to do a short set while Kitty changed costumes, wigs, and makeup, and then came back out as somebody else.

KIT CASTLE: To my knowledge, none of the others ever actually came out when Kitty was onstage. She'd never have allowed it—after all, the act was hers. She was proud of it. And if she had let someone out, she might have lost control. I think if Liz had ever come out onstage, she would have absolutely panicked. Me-Liz would have had no way to even understand what was happening—Kitty's strip act didn't exactly fit in with her idea of the spiritual life! Of all of them, Penny would have known how to handle it the best.

Eric was still working at the power company when Kitty started at the Blue Note, but before too long he started working the door in the evenings, and then after a couple of months he quit his job to start working there as a floor manager, full time. Almost before they knew what was happening, both of them had been drawn back into the midnight life again.

For her part, Kitty was glad Eric was now working at the club. She could see more of him, for one thing, and for another, she'd begun to think she needed a bodyguard. Strangers had started pressing backstage to meet her after the show. Cops, lawyers, businessmen, and who knew what. She was a rising star again—admired, lusted after, vulnerable, and exposed. Business boomed. Jimmy and Sally started hiring more girls. The first ladies they hired were four college girls who'd worked in topless go-go bars. They were all fairly decent dancers, but when Kitty got a look at what they wore onstage—skintight cut-off blue jeans and bikini tops—she hit the roof. She wasn't going to have it. No one told her or asked her to become the boss; she just took it upon herself. She had certain standards, and cutoffs were not acceptable, she explained to them. They were going to have to go out and make or buy costumes that measured up to hers. Two of the girls quit immediately, because they couldn't afford to work there as long as Kitty was setting the standards.

Jimmy told Kitty to hire a couple of other dancers, so she went at it with a vengeance. She hired a couple of dance students from the university—gorgeous, talented young girls—and set up mandatory rehearsal sessions. She found them another Chinese lady who could make inexpensive, high-class show costumes. She showed them how to dress and move, how to sequence their music and alter the pace and drama of their acts. And she tried to show them that there was a way all this could be handled so that they could be proud of themselves. They didn't have to be ashamed. They could say something, and give something, to these men. And they could make a couple of hundred in tips a night.

Jimmy was so impressed with Kitty's work that he let her hire and train three or four other girls, until she had a whole retinue of talented young dancers under her wing. To them, she was half madame, half mother hen. She felt entirely responsible for everything that appeared onstage. She was convinced that the place would die without her. Even when she developed phlebitis in one leg and was confined to a wheelchair for more than a month, she still directed the rehearsals, teaching her girls how to put on a show that would—almost—replace her. She'd been flat on her back in the hospital for two weeks, taking a blood-thinning drug that made her gums bleed, but days after she was released and sent home she was having Eric wheel her into the club for rehearsals every afternoon. For four or five hours at a stretch, she'd sit there in her wheelchair imperiously directing everything like some queen mother of burlesque. She was responsible, after all. Everything would have fallen apart if it weren't for her.

Kitty was horrified when she got arrested.

What bothered her more than almost anything was the way they'd torn the wig right off her head—hadn't even let her comb her hair for the mug shot. She looked like a tramp, and she could never forgive them for that.

She'd gotten wind of the rumors weeks before it all came down. There was a big to-do in the papers about cops being paid off in strip joints on the Hennepin Avenue strip, just about the same time she noticed Jimmy handing little envelopes to uniforms coming in. *Hooboy!* she thought, *here we go again.* When the place got raided, Kitty wasn't dancing—she was just standing in the kitchen in her street clothes, eating a cold meatball sandwich. The two girls who were doing their act got popped immediately, and everybody else got booked and sent home.

Next morning, Jimmy called her at home.

"Listen, babe, they got a warrant out for your arrest—'lewd and lascivious behavior on a public stage,' if you can believe that crap."

"You gotta be kidding!"

"I know, I know, babe. They wanna shut me down, they'll try anything."

"What do you think I oughta do?"

"Hey, it's nothing, babe. They got nothing."

"What've they got on *you?*"

"Gotta run, babe."

Click.

She had Eric take her downtown to the station and she turned herself in. She didn't want the cops coming to her house. They fingerprinted her like a street whore, then took her mug shot. That's when the guy ripped off her wig. Some hero! The little creep had been coming into the club for months. He was one of her biggest fans.

She was released on her own recognizance, and a court date was set. The club was closed down for a week. When it reopened, business mysteriously bottomed out. Local business types who liked to bring their paramours and sit in the top tier of seats, where it was dark and private, didn't show up anymore. Everybody, Kitty included, was terrified of getting rounded up in another raid. So she just dropped her budding career on the spot. After she beat the court rap, she never danced there again. There was no way she was going to get messed up in all that! Still, she did feel a lingering sense of responsibility, and a sad, funny longing, so for a long time she'd go down there and stand in back vaguely overseeing everything. It pleased her no end that customers kept complaining that they missed Kitty Rosetti. It just wasn't the same place without Miss Kitty.

It was the end of another one of her six-month cycles: bottom to top to bottom inside of half a year. Things had gone that way down in Dallas, and now the pattern had repeated itself. For the first time in her life, Kitty began to consider the possibility of her own imperfection; a touch of desperation began to creep into her fierce, brassy drive.

Well, screw it, she thought. *Screw it! This whole scene is sorry anyway, always was. Lowlifes and gangsters again. Can't I ever get away from these people?*

It was Kitty's nature to escape from things by burying herself in work, and within days after leaving her life as a burlesque queen, she'd buried herself again. This time, though, she immersed herself in an utterly different world: the world of hospital dayrooms, IV carts, medication schedules, and crushed men in wheelchairs. She'd started working as a volunteer nurse's aide at the local VA Hospital a few months before she left the Blue Note Lounge, but after she quit, she threw herself into this new life full force. For some reason she hungered for this work. She was ravenous to be near men. She wanted to see them, talk to them, touch them, and forgive them; she couldn't seem to get enough of it.

Three or four times a week, Kitty would drive across town to the hospital, where she worked a shift in the dayroom. Most of the men were Vietnam vets, ambulatory or semiambulatory, but they all seemed to be in a sort of daze. Whether it was their medication or combat, they all seemed angry and withdrawn, like closed fists. Kitty wasn't put off by them; she felt she knew just what they needed. She didn't want to waste her time refilling the coffee machine, or emptying ashtrays or playing dominoes or puzzles. She wanted to counsel these men, just like she'd counseled scared, stoned-out kids at YES. She felt so keenly their loneliness and fear and sense of loss. She'd spend hours talking to them, one-on-one, in the dayroom. For them, she became Kitty Rosetti, sharing the dark well of their feeling, but this time she didn't have to take off her clothes.

Somehow, word got up to the director of the hospital and she was given a little medal and a certificate for her work. The medal was brass and blue enamel inscribed with the words "Minneapolis Veterans Administration Volunteer," with a tiny charm with the number "one hundred" suspended underneath. That meant she gave one hundred percent.

Sometimes Kitty would just forget to take off that medal, and she'd wear it around for days.

One day Kitty wandered off down a back ward of the hospital and discovered, to her horror, that there were vets so badly blown apart or burned that many of them were just strange little lumps in beds. Some had tubes going into their stomachs; others had had their faces blown apart and somehow had lived, but were unable to speak or hear. They had no identification. They were John Does. There were a lot of John Does in that ward.

After she finished her duties in the dayroom, Kitty started going to that back ward to work an extra shift, although these men could not even acknowledge her existence. Most of them couldn't speak, or even meet her eyes. Yet she came to realize that just by a change in the way they breathed, they knew that she was there. She sat by their beds and told them stories. She would talk about them and about their feelings, trying to verbalize all the things they were unable to say.

"I know you're scared," she'd say. "I know you can't tell us where your family is. So I'll be your family. You're not going to die alone. I'll be right here with you. I'll be your family for you . . ."

Eric was touched by Kitty's work at the VA Hospital. He'd sometimes go with her on her trips to the back ward. And when she asked how he'd feel about bringing some of these men to their home, he agreed. Even though their combined income was humble—they were living on Eric's small paycheck, plus a dwindling nest egg from Kitty's act—she suggested they start a home-based hospice, rigged up the bathroom with special bars, and fixed up the extra bedroom with all the other equipment that was required. One by one, they began bringing terminally ill men home to care for during their final days. A day nurse from the VA would come in to help from time to time. The nurses taught Kitty how to change colostomy bags and bedpans, and how to give medication (except for injections) when they weren't there.

Despite the financial hardship and the inconvenience of it all, this work made Kitty's heart grow like nothing else she'd ever done. It helped to make her human. It helped to heal the hurt. It deepened the

54

bond of love she had for Eric. And when it all came to an end, she felt that a part of herself had been taken away. The administrators of the VA Hospital began to get nervous about their legal liability if anything should happen to a patient being cared for outside the facility, so Kitty and Eric lost their privileges. That's the way Kitty viewed them: privileges. Something fine and meaningful had been given to her and now, suddenly, it had been taken away.

To her, it was another failure, another humiliation, just like being hauled into court on charges of "lewd and lascivious behavior." First she was arrested and booked like a hooker, now she'd been stripped of her privileges. She was losing control. Or . . . had she ever really been in control? Maybe she was just a loser, just a schmuck like everybody else. Maybe she was kidding herself to think she was a big somebody, some big star or something. She felt tired. Maybe she just needed a rest cure, like the other girls. Maybe she should just go inside for a while and forget about things. So she did. One day Kitty just quit.

Liz woke up in a park. There were leaves all over the ground. It seemed to be fall. Two white swans, heads lifted, drifted across the still water. For a long time she just sat on the bench, hardly daring to look around her, while her eyes filled with tears. She remembered confused little fragments of things here and there—she had a white car now, she was living in Minnesota—but most of what she remembered seemed to be from two or three years ago. How could that happen? She'd lost days before, even weeks sometimes . . . but now it seemed like she'd lost years.

What happened to her baby girls? What happened to Angel and little Rita and Ramona? Something scary and sad. Somebody called. There'd been a car wreck, and the kids were all killed. Killed in a car wreck! Her beautiful babies, their sweet hungry faces, killed in a car wreck! But it all seemed so long ago, so far away, like a dream or a story or something she'd seen on TV. It was like a movie of somebody else's life, lost in a park . . . somebody else's life . . .

She stood up. Did she drive the car here? Did she walk?

How was she going to get home? Where was her home? She wandered dazedly through the drifted leaves toward a parking lot. She found the white car. The keys were under the seat. Suddenly she could visualize the house by the lake, but couldn't remember how to get there.

On the way home, she stopped to get directions by describing the neighborhood where her house was. It was as if she were a tourist from another country.

The others were adrift with Kitty gone. Liz and Me-Liz and Penny Lavender and Jess took turns coming out, but they were all equally confused. It seemed like they'd lost years. For some reason it was Liz, the sickest of them all, who came out most often and stayed out longest now. She felt entirely overwhelmed by vacuuming and laundry, much less by life itself. She was scared to go out of the house. She felt trembly and anxious, and she couldn't sleep. In the night, she'd slip out of bed to go downstairs and pace the living room from one end to the other, like a deranged animal in a cage. She had no appetite and began losing weight again. Her looks went to seed as dirty dishes began piling up in the sink. Eric seemed to grow increasingly frightened and concerned about her; at the same time he drifted further and further away. Rachael and Diane, two nurses who lived next door, told him they thought something was really the matter with her. They'd been concerned about her ever since the false pregnancy, but now they were leaning on him to get her to a hospital.

He talked to her about it, but she refused. She hated hospitals. She was going to be fine.

When the policemen found Liz a few weeks later, she was picking red geraniums out of a cement planter in an alley beside a bank in downtown Minneapolis. She was throwing the flowers away, and very carefully scooping the dirt into a black plastic trash bag. When the officers slipped in beside her, one on each side, she was confused and frightened for a moment.

"Whadja take?" one of them asked, not unkindly. "Downs? Acid?"

She looked up at him dazedly. He had a red moustache and freckles and reminded her of somebody. She couldn't remember how she got there.

"Look, we can run a blood test in about ten minutes. What was it? Reds?"

"No."

"No what?"

"No, I didn't take any dope. I don't do dope."

"She doesn't do dope," the redheaded cop said to his partner, deadpan. "What's your name, then?"

For a second Liz blanked.

"Let's see some ID, honey. Hmmm?"

"Elizabeth. Elizabeth Katherine Rosetti. I mean Garcia. Elizabeth Garcia. I live over by . . ."

The cop smiled gently.

"Listen, I think we're gonna run you on over to the emergency room at Hennepin County. You don't look too good, sweetheart. And I'm sure these people don't appreciate your gardening. OK? Hmmm?"

And they walked her off down the street toward the squad car.

Chapter 7

"PRESENTING ILLNESS: Elizabeth Katherine Rosetti is a twenty-four-year-old white female admitted to Hennepin County General Hospital for the first time on 8/20/73 to try to determine the etiology of some bizarre, amnesic episodes," Dr. M. Ettinger, chief of neurology, noted on his discharge summary of the case. "She reported she was in good health until November of last year at which time she noticed that she began to develop periods in which she experienced strange episodes of doing things and then not being able to recall what she had done. They initially lasted about half an hour, at which time she would do things like get into her car and travel and not know where she had ended up. She would find her way home by asking someone for aid. She noticed that when these episodes came on she would develop severe pain above her left ear. She also noticed the development of some right-sided weakness and some spontaneous shaking movements of her arm and leg that she could not control.

"She experienced one such episode in November and then did not have another until January. She was then free of these episodes until approximately six weeks ago when she began to develop approximately five such episodes a week. One episode found her in an alley with a shovel and a bag of dirt digging up flowers. At that time she was taken to the Crisis

58

Intervention Center and was subsequently referred to the emergency room for evaluation. . . ."

The emergency room was big and cold and yellow. She was administered blood tests and a physical exam on a cold, hard examining table. Two doctors hovered over her like huge bugs, as the girls rippled in and out, taking a peek at the situation, panicking, then fleeing back inside. The blood tests showed she wasn't on drugs, and everything else seemed normal, the doctors said. They told her to go out and sit in the waiting room, but when she turned to go, she faltered a little; one of her legs was dragging slightly. One doctor noticed it immediately, and asked her to walk back and forth across the examining room a couple of times. Then he picked up the phone and called someone, and moments later a nurse helped her into the elevator. When they got out upstairs, the nurse gently guided her toward two imposing glass and steel doors. They reminded her of doors at the zoo.

"What's this?" Liz asked uncertainly.

"This is the neurological ward," the nurse told her. "It's nothing to be afraid of."

But an orderly had to unlock the doors to let them in, and he re-locked the doors behind them. A cold nausea began to curdle in her stomach. It was a locked ward. This was the place they sent you to die. This is where they sent you when you were insane. It was the nut-house, the looney bin. And she knew it for sure when the nurse led her into an enormous room crowded with beds that weren't even divided by curtains: in every bed, there was somebody who looked dead. It looked like a big morgue in there, and it smelled like medicine and rotting flesh.

"Now just take your clothes off and climb into bed, Mrs. Rosetti, and somebody will be with you in just a little while," the nurse said, pulling back the white hospital sheets on a bed pushed into one corner of the room. Liz felt numb. She crawled obediently into bed and stared around her like a frightened mouse.

PHYSICAL EXAMINATION: General appearance was that of a small, friendly female in no acute distress who appeared to be quite nervous during examination. Blood pressure was 117/70, pulse was 88 . . . The Weber and Rinne tests were normal . . . Breasts were small and hard . . . Abdomen was flat, slightly flabby with no organomegaly or masses noted . . . The motor examination showed decreased strength in the right hand, as well as in the right arm . . . Initial impression was

59

that the patient either had temporal lobe epilepsy or that she had a mass lesion [an injury] in the left hemisphere that was causing her to have the right-sided weakness and bizarre episodes.

Had she ever been in an accident that caused a head injury? one of the doctors wanted to know. Kitty told him about the time many years before when her father had been in a collision with a truck in a snowstorm, and the girls were taken to a hospital in Anthony, Oklahoma, and had to wear head bandages for weeks.

HOSPITAL COURSE: The patient was hospitalized in order to perform the diagnostic tests needed in order to determine whether or not she had either temporal lobe epilepsy or a mass lesion. . . ."

Tests and more tests. Pills and more pills. Pushing, poking. Intelligence tests, psychological tests, neurological tests, blood tests. Brain scans, angiograms, doctors gathered around the foot of her bed: big doctors, little doctors, lady doctors, man doctors. All the girls were out in the hospital, including Kitty. They were switching in and out like mad: one would jump out and look around, panic, then jump back in; another would jump out to take her place, then she'd panic too. They were a whirling circle of panic.

Eric brought her a robe and some other things, including a packet of color photographs—photographer's proofs of Kitty Rosetti, topless, doing her burlesque act. Kitty spread the photos out on the bed for the three young doctors who'd been assigned to her case. She was angry; she felt filthy and humiliated and utterly unglamorous in this horrible place. She was tired of doctors and medical students standing around discussing the paradoxes of her case right in front of her—talking about brain tumors and brain operations and epilepsy and cancer—as if she were some dope, as if she were completely nonexistent except as a medical file. She wanted to show them she wasn't just some street urchin. She was a star, and she deserved some respect.

The doctors seemed very interested in the pictures, but not in the way she wanted.

LABORATORY DATA: Urinalysis was normal. EKG was normal. Sed rate was 17. . . . EEG with sleep deprivation and NP leads revealed multiple independent bilateral nasotemporal spikes. This was believed to be compatible with temporal lobe seizure disorder [epilepsy]. . . . MMPI [a standard psychological test] was read as abnormal and was felt

to be compatible with either schizomanic psychosis or paranoid schizo-
phrenia . . ."

Liz woke up one morning to the sound of breakfast carts and the awful scent of death. When she sat up and looked around, she realized that the old lady in the bed next to hers was dead. The orderlies came and wheeled the bed away. It was an affirmation that she had come there to die. Soon her tombstone would be inscribed and dated. Liz wasn't afraid; she was resigned to it. But Penny's response to her situation was to vividly imagine a far, far away place—a humid, fragrant tropical island surrounded by moonlit tropical seas, cut off utterly from this world. One night she drew a picture of it on a chalkboard in the hall by the nurse's station. It was an elaborately detailed scene, subtly shaded, with monkeys swinging from the palm trees and seagulls and volcanoes and orchids and one little lonesome girl on the beach.

It wasn't long before the doctors and nurses were swarming around the chalkboard like the Keystone Cops.

"Look at this! Look at this! Hey, how did you do this?"

The picture was completely upside down. It was a funny little trick she'd always been able to do; she used to read Eric's newspaper upside-down at the breakfast table. Penny stood there in the hallway in her robe and slippers, head hanging, biting her lip so she wouldn't laugh or cry. She was trying to tell them she wanted to be out of there, and also that something was terribly, terribly wrong with her, without explicitly saying so. Within minutes, she was on the elevator downstairs for more tests.

Finally the doctors encircled her bed again and told her that after all the tests, they still believed she might have a brain tumor and that they couldn't rule it out unless they did one final test. It was a scary, dangerous procedure called a pneumoencephalogram. A tiny percentage of people died from it, they said. They had to give her twenty-four hours to think about it, and then she had to sign a consent form. They inserted some kind of flexible tube through the base of her spine all the way up to the base of her brain, withdrew some fluid, and then they put her in a sort of medical carnival ride: a little bucket seat on the end of a mechanical arm that whirled around and around like a centrifuge. Afterward, she felt sick and had to lay flat on her back for days.

But the test didn't tell the doctors much. Finally they admitted they just weren't sure what was going on. Their best guess was that she was having epileptic seizures caused by a lesion on the temporal lobe of her brain. The trouble was, they just couldn't get the lesion to show up on any of their tests. They were going to put her on antiseizure medication and release her, they said. She'd been in the hospital for sixteen days.

DIAGNOSIS: Psychomotor seizure disorder, questionable etiology [cause unknown] . . .
   SECONDARY DIAGNOSIS: Personality disorder . . .
   DISCHARGE ORDERS AND MEDICATIONS: Dilantin 250 mg. per day . . .
   PROGNOSIS: Guarded, as the patient is still strongly suspected of having a mass lesion, which at this time is unable to be detected . . .

She was released, with a bottle of drugs and no answers. All she had was convincing new evidence to support her worst fears. It might be brain cancer. She might be crazy. She might be epileptic. They just didn't know.

Eight days later, she was back in the hospital again. She'd been having what appeared to be drug reactions: double vision, incontinence, hallucinations. She was released two days later with prescriptions for two new drugs: Mysoline and phenobarbital, in addition to Dilantin. The doses were so massive she'd just wander around like a zombie all day long. There were more drug reactions—depression, lack of appetite, crying all the time, the shakes, a kind of galloping paralysis where muscles would go rigid and just shiver—and her doctors would have to readjust the dosage.

What the doctors did not understand, of course, was that they were treating not one patient, but many. And each of them had different drug tolerances. They would adjust the medication for one personality, and it would be too high or too low for the others. At other times, they'd all take their pills in succession: Liz would take her pills, Penny would take hers, Me-Liz would take hers, and they'd all get sick together. Or Kitty would refuse to take any pills at all. Kitty was the only one who knew what was going on—she knew damn good and well that these girls didn't have epilepsy or a brain tumor or any of the rest of that nonsense. It was ridiculous to be taking this medicine.

Slowly, over many months, the same realization began to dawn on the other girls. The drugs hadn't changed their situation at all. They were still missing time like they always had—it was just that now they felt lousy all the time. When they all stopped taking the pills at about the same time, there was an immediate, measurable improvement in the way they felt. But there was no change in the fundamental problem: They were still missing time.

KIT CASTLE: Why didn't Kitty tell any of these doctors she was seeing in the hospital about the real problem—the others? She was seeing these neurologists and nurses and doctors every day, yet she never told anyone about this incredible thing going on inside her. In some ways, this little world inside her had become self-sufficient; they'd all learned to work together as a fairly skillful team. Usually it worked, at least for a little while. Maybe that's why Kitty never told—she figured she had the whole mess under control, and to admit otherwise would be humiliating. Or maybe she just wasn't mature enough at that point. Or maybe she really feared that if she told her secret, that would be the beginning of the end.

If she told, she would have to die.

It was never really clear why, even to Kitty, but shortly after she got out of the hospital she told Eric she had to go home to Dallas, to see her little sister Maryanne. And she had to go alone. In reality, Maryanne, a sister she hadn't seen or even thought about for years, was just an excuse. Suddenly Kitty was full of wild, reckless energy— leaving energy. She was hungry for life, hungry for action, hungry for a new scene. She was sick and disgusted with that fiasco in the hospital; she couldn't get the smell of it off her hands. She wanted to turn her back on the whole humiliating experience, and as long as she was at it, she was prepared to abandon her entire personal history along with it. Just chuck the whole mess overboard and start over.

She borrowed some money from Eric and caught an afternoon flight down to Texas. Maryanne, whom she hadn't seen in years, met her at the airport. They didn't quite know what to say to one another, so they drove back to Maryanne's apartment, dressed to the nines, and went out to a disco bar called Hero's. The moment Kitty walked into that place, filled with the scent of sweat and smoke and unfamiliar cologne, she knew that she was home. She'd had enough of this "Mr. and Mrs. Eric Rosetti" crap. She surveyed the single men lined up along the bar and then she sauntered up beside a lean, bushy-haired guy wearing a Nik-Nik shirt and smoking a cigarette. His name was Matt, he told her, and he worked for the power company scrambling up high-tension lines to do repairs. He had an air of swaggering, physical arrogance about him, like a merchant seaman or a pirate.

When the place shut down, Maryanne went home alone. Kitty went home with Matt.

It was almost a month before Kitty got around to calling Eric, back in Minnetonka. He was distraught. Where on earth had she been? Why hadn't she called? When was she coming back home? She hopped the next flight to Minnesota, but she left all her stuff at Matt's house, where she'd been living since the night she met him.

"So, what? Had a lot of visitors while I was gone?" Kitty asked Eric as soon as she walked into the house. A stranger's presence hung in the air like dust.

"Well, you know. Couple of guys from work stopped by. Rachael and Diane were here for dinner one night."

"Oh really? Been seeing a lot of them?"

"Elizabeth, look, I was worried about you. I was lonely. I wasn't fooling around with Diane."

"Who was it, then?"

"Hey, wait a second. You're the one who disappeared for a month without a word! I missed you, babe. I was worried sick."

"Who was it?"

He tried to stammer something, but suddenly he just stopped. He'd never been any good at lying.

"I called Maryanne and she told me you left that club with some guy," he said. "So . . . so did I."

"What do you mean?"

"I've been seeing someone. A guy. Barry. You know."

"You mean you . . ."

"I'm not going to lie to you, babe. If that's too much for you to handle, I'm sorry."

"I'm being two-timed by some . . . by some *guy?* You've had some *guy* walking around here in his, in his . . . in *our* home?"

"I'm not going to apologize, Elizabeth."

Kitty flipped. She *couldn't* handle it. Besides, it was the perfect excuse to leave him. She screamed, she fumed, she threw things, and then she walked out on the best man who'd ever come into any of their lives.

She never looked back.

Chapter 8

God couldn't have invented a better place for the others than
Parker, Arizona.

It was a place where everybody had a phony story to tell
about where they came from. You listened to the stories, and
you nodded, but you knew they probably weren't telling their real
names or histories, and you didn't care. Your story wasn't true, either.
Everyone was on the lam from something—bad marriages, bad memories, the cops, the IRS, the draft—but as long as you were there, nobody cared. It was as if the day you showed up in Parker was the day
you were born.

Parker was the ultimate party town, dumped in the sun-blasted desert on the shore of the Colorado River, just across the water from California. A desolate moonscape extended outward in every direction from
the outskirts of town. In the center of everything, riding on pontoons
right out on the Colorado, was the incredible floating bar/dance hall,
twenty-four-hour-a-day party called Sundance. The place had a roofed-
over dance floor, without walls and big as a high school auditorium,
that could accommodate three hundred people or more at a time. When
the place was packed on a Saturday night, it rocked like a river raft.
People would dock their powerboats, walk up the pier in their bathing

suits and flipflops, and drink and dance till dawn. Others would arrive by land—the beautiful people, relaxed, lightly stoned, and bronzed as gods, rolling up in vans from Phoenix and Yuma and L.A. They'd party hearty all weekend or all week or all month and then disappear. People came and went like ghosts.

For Kitty and Liz and Me-Liz and Penny and Jess, it was perfect. For the first time in their lives, the burden of trying to remember and understand their own past was lifted; now they could tell any kind of story they wanted to, and nobody cared. They could be anything they wanted. When Matt and Kitty bought a trailer on the river not far from the Sundance compound, they entered a community of strangers who wished to remain anonymous, and they fit right in. The past was either too boring or too embarrassing to mention; here, everyone simply lived in the moment, for as long as it might last.

They'd have "sunrise services" on the riverbank, with baskets of bread and fruit and wine, and then they'd go waterskiing until noon. Noon to three was siesta time—the time everybody got pregnant. Then things would start cranking up at Sundance, and Kitty and Matt would go in to work waiting tables or cooking until the stars came out. Monday through Wednesday, when business was relatively slow, they helped clean the place up and lived something close to a normal life. The energy would start to pick up by Wednesday night, and from then through the wee hours of Sunday morning, it was party time. Then they rested a couple of days and started all over again.

Matt and Kitty's relationship was a long way from love, but it was comfortable just the same. In the six months since they met at the disco bar in Dallas, they'd worked out a sort of sexual friendship, long on physical pleasure and short on talk. Matt liked to drink and party, and Kitty liked to dance and party, and that's what they did. All the sorrows and complications of Kitty's past life—well, for now she'd rather forget them.

There were times, of course, when this fickle little redhead would suddenly become morose and depressed, and convince Matt that she was dying of a brain tumor and only had a few months to live. Other times, she'd be overcome with religious conviction, forcing him to get down on his knees on the living room rug and pray. Sometimes she'd even tie her hair back in a ponytail, slap on a Mets cap, and want to go fishing. Matt had no way of knowing that it was Liz who was convinced she was dying, Me-Liz who felt the need to pray, Jess who wanted to go fishing, and Kitty who wanted to dance till the cows came home.

Nor did he realize it was Kitty who'd convinced him to quit his job with the power company and take off on a trip to Mexico, not long after they first met at Hero's. Matt flung away friends and responsibilities in every direction in a fever of new-found freedom, outfitted a van with air-conditioning, a tiny kitchen, and beds, and the two of them took off for Baja. Screw work. Screw ordinary life. Their attitude was, let's party, for tomorrow we die!

For Kitty, the trip was a lark; but for Liz, it was a death trip. She just wanted to spend her last days in peace beside the sea, before the cancer destroyed her brain and she passed quietly away. Matt and the girls lived on beaches, snorkeling and spearfishing and drinking tequila around the fire—for the first time in her short life, though she'd spent most of it in bars, Kitty discovered alcohol. But there was something menacing about the Baja that seemed to shadow the whole trip. The forlorn, primitive, two thousand-mile peninsula stretching down below the Tropic of Cancer seemed harsh, ugly, inimical to life. Black buzzards circled in the empty sky. The waterless mountains were white as stars, and the sea seemed ominous, rattling the black rocks on the shore. Everything had spines or fangs. Matt seemed anxious, on edge.

Kitty was out almost all the time during the Baja trip, which was all right; it was only during the times she disappeared that there was trouble. One night, she and Matt were camped in the high desert on a remote beach around El Rosario, on the Pacific side of the peninsula. They were in the van, making love, with the doors flung wide onto a rocky, moonlit shore. There was nothing Kitty loved more than good sex, but she was always careful about climaxing with too much abandon, because then she'd lose control and somebody else would pop out to take over the body. There was no telling who it might be—whomever happened to be in position would come rolling down the shoot into the body, like a gumball. On this particular night, it was Liz who came down the shoot. When she woke up in the dark van with a strange man on top of her, apparently trying to rape her, she freaked. She screamed and kicked, trying to throw the man off.

"Whoa, whoa, lady!" Matt exploded. "Whassamatter? Whassamatter with you?"

When she heard his voice, Liz calmed down a little. Oh, yeah. A man named Matt. Power company. Nice eyes. They were in Baja, on a camping trip. She grabbed a handful of clothes and climbed out of the van, wiping away the tears, still shaken. The beach was bathed in moonlight, so bright it seemed surreal. There was nobody around for miles. She heard the van doors close behind her. He'd come out in a minute and comfort her and talk to her, she thought, but right now she needed to be alone. Then the engine started, the lights came on and Liz whirled around in amazement to see Matt simply driving away.

She was abandoned out there, without food or water or even a blanket. She couldn't believe it. Liz's astonishment gave way to panic and then, in an instant, Kitty stepped in. She quickly sized up the situation, began scanning the horizon for help, and then far, far off, she spotted a single light. She followed a dirt road to the highway and from there all the way to the light, two miles or more, where she discovered a little gas station and hardware store, closed for the night. On the ground, run-over but dry, she found a book of matches. She walked back to the campsite and then Jess came out to take charge of building the fire. He was startled when he first came out—for a moment he thought he might be on the moon. Then he realized, no, he couldn't be; he could see the moon in the sky. He must still be in Mexico, he realized. He'd been out once on the trip already, when he and Matt had gone snorkeling around San Felipe. Jess fed tiny sticks into the fire, contentedly watching them flare and crumple.

As the fire steadied and brightened, one by one the girls crept out to warm themselves too. Liz and Me-Liz held their palms up to the fire and glanced fearfully around. Penny Lavender came out, and she sang a mournful song to cover her fear and desolation. Kitty came out, and she spat into the fire in disgust. Thirty-six hours later, when Matt finally returned, they were still there, crouched around the fire like wild animals.

There was no real love in the world, and they knew it.

Matt had friends who owned a place in Parker, and on their way home from Baja, he and Kitty stopped in for a visit. Within a few days, they'd both decided to move there for good. Matt had his own reasons for loving it in Parker, and so did each of the girls. Liz was happy amidst the noise and gaiety and nightlife and lies—she figured this was as good a place to die as any. She didn't know how soon it would happen, but she knew she'd be dying soon. She'd just fade slowly away, like a bad dream. There was something terminally wrong with her brain. Hadn't the doctors in Minnesota told her so? Penny Lavender just liked the chance to get dressed up every night and party. And for the first time in her life, she'd started drinking—not to excess, just to the point of warm, romantic fuzziness.

Kitty Rosetti was born for a place like Sundance. Redheaded and tempestuous, she loved nothing better than to go spinning out onto the dance floor and try to stop the place cold. She was accustomed to the view from center stage, and she wanted to make that clear to the three hundred other people on the floor. Kitty could dance with the best of them, no matter how well-practiced, and she knew she was a looker. She loved to get out there in the glitter and swirl and smoke and become the object in men's eyes. She could feel it when she was being watched, but she didn't realize just how strange, and how special, were the attentions of one particular man..

From his vantage point in the other world—maybe even through the red telescope he'd set up in the window of his secret room—Jess was watching Kitty. He didn't really understand it. He didn't really know who she was. He just knew something new and wonderful was happening inside him. He had found the woman of his dreams. It wasn't that he wanted to have her sexually—he wasn't even sure what that meant. It was just that he wanted to be near her. He wanted to be her younger brother and her friend. He wanted to protect her. He wanted . . . oh, he didn't know what he wanted!

KIT CASTLE: I don't think Jess was ever entirely sure whether Kitty was a real person or some kind of idealized fantasy figure. He wasn't exactly sure who she was or what she was. In some ways she seemed like a composite of all his dreams, the ideal woman. She represented every-thing that was beautiful in a woman to him. He knew that no other woman he ever met could measure up to her, yet he was still not exactly clear about whether she really existed or not.

To me, the very fact that Jess was aware of Kitty, however dimly, shows that he had some knowledge of the others. It was as if, with Jess, the walls of amnesia that separated the personalities were partly permea-ble. With Penny Lavender and Liz and Me-Liz, it was different: they had absolutely no knowledge of one another at all. They just knew there were a lot of blanks in their memory. But with Jess, somehow, on some deep level, he must have known that Kitty and the others were there. I think that's partly why he wanted to be a doctor: he wanted to care for these girls. He knew he had sick people on board.

Me-Liz was attracted to Parker for reasons quite apart from those of all the others. It was the desert she loved. To her, the whole party scene at Sundance was an empty lie. But hanging off the horizon every way she looked out of town, black as coal and shimmering in the heat, were desert mountains as scary and spiritual as anything she'd ever seen. People would wander out there stoned on acid and die sometimes. She respected the desert. She'd wait until twilight when the sand began exhaling heat like a dying animal, and then she'd go out there all alone and just sit on a stone until the stars came out, glistening and near.

Me-Liz had been drawn to the Indians who lived in and around Parker—the town was surrounded by Indian land belonging to the Irwatowa tribe's nation—since the day she arrived. Not knowing exactly how to go about making contact, at first she just started going down to a little bar in town where lots of Indians hung out. It was just one of those nameless Western bars with a Coors sign and pickups parked out front, and Me-Liz felt scared and embarrassed walking in there alone. So Kitty would come out to break the ice and hustle a little pool. Kitty felt at home in bars, and she knew how to make it clear she wasn't cruising. Eventually, she'd get a real conversation going with somebody, and then Me-Liz would emerge.

Me-Liz got to know a couple of Indian women this way, and little by little, she was drawn into a kind of loose network of people living in the desert who shared her interest in traditional Indian culture. And it was in this way, eventually, that she and one other Anglo, a brave and angry Vietnam vet named Jim, were invited to participate in a Native American "naming ceremony." She was told only that she and Jim had been chosen, that the ritual involved seeking a new identity, and that it also involved "spiritual medicine."

One afternoon she, Jim, and ten young Indian men were driven in a van up to the dry, barren Mojave Mountains surrounding Lake Havasu, about twenty-five miles north of Parker on the Colorado. The high country around the lake, actually a widening in the river created by Parker Dam, was an eerie, lifeless landscape considered sacred by the Indians. They were taken to an oddly shaped mountaintop or high bluff, with an enormous natural bowl made of smooth stone set in the top, where they underwent a "cleansing ritual" in a sweat lodge and sipped a strange, bitter tea. By the time Me-Liz and the others emerged from the lodge, it was dark and she felt dim and dreamy. They all gathered around a fire in the center of the great stone bowl, while three elderly Indian men wailed or sang in high, keening, womanly voices. The old men were wearing ceremonial long, white hides painted with earth-colored designs, and three feathers in their hair, splayed outward like three fingers.

Then one of the old men passed around a copper dish containing what looked to Me-Liz like dried banana chips, and they all took one and chewed it, while the old men stood in front of each one of them and recited a long, incomprehensible prayer or chant. The chips tasted nasty and bitter, but Me-Liz, so swept up in the spiritual drama of it all, hardly seemed to notice. The old men began singing another song, this time in English, about leaving this reality behind and searching out the source of personal identity. The only way to do it, they sang, was with fire, wind, and this "spiritual medicine."

An Indian man took her by the elbow and led her away from the fire, and then they walked a long, long way across the starry desert. He sat her down in her spot finally, handed her a little pouch of chips, and disappeared. Me-Liz sat there all night, but for some reason she wasn't afraid. The desert seemed alive. It knew she was there, and it allowed her to stay. For a while she just felt sick. Then—it was strange—there seemed to be a bird who was with her. It looked like a heron or a crane, and it was teaching her to fly. It was as if she were flying into knowledge. She flew through the stony mountains, through the desolate gorges and misty places; she flew through places she thought she'd been before. The bird told her that the wind brings knowledge. That the wind is an intelligence of its own and its reason for being is to spread knowledge all over the world. That this is the way nature communicates with itself. Her name, it said, was Tequehe (Teh-KAY-hee)—Wisdom Flying.

Wisdom Flying! To Me-Liz, this was a glorious revelation. It was her true and secret inner identity. It was a gift from the desert. For months afterward, she cherished her new name like a delicious secret. For a long time, she didn't even tell Matt.

There were a lot of things Matt just didn't seem to understand about the others, but there were a few things they were beginning to understand about Matt. Every month or so, he and his friends would take the van into L.A. for supplies, and lately it had become increasingly obvious that somebody was waiting for him there. Sometimes he'd come back smelling of unfamiliar perfume, or hitching up his collar to hide a hickey. Kitty was disgusted. It was childishly obvious, for one thing, and for another, she was going to have none of it—she'd been faithful to him, and she could find another lover in two seconds if she cared to.

One morning Liz and Matt and their neighbors, Roxanne and Bob, had just come in from waterskiing and were sitting on the dock in front of the trailer. Liz had been trying to ski that morning, but she'd done abysmally. Kitty skiied like a pro, but Liz could never seem to get the hang of it.

"I can't believe you," Matt was saying. "I could teach a poodle to ski faster than I can teach you! One day you know how, the next day I have to start from scratch again!"

"I'm sorry, Matt, I'm a bimbo," Liz whimpered. "I can't get it. It's not in my genes or something."

"Use your brain! Listen to me! Tuck your knees, keep your elbows tight to the body, and concentrate! Don't be such a moron! Just pay attention!"

"I can't do it, Matt. I can't! I don't think I even want to."

"Oh, for God's sake! If you don't want to, what are you wasting everybody's time for then? How come you didn't just say so?"

"I'm sorry, Matt, I don't know, I'm just a mess."

Liz was filling up with humiliation and self-pity, drowning in it, reveling in it, until suddenly Kitty Rosetti had had enough. She burst out, explosively, and the first thing she did was slap Matt flat across the face. The second thing she did was whack him in the mouth with a bunch of grapes she was holding in her hand. Matt staggered back a few steps, incredulous, and then pitched over backward off the dock into the Colorado River.

"You got a lot of nerve calling me names, you two-timing little creep!" Kitty yelled after him, and then she took off running across the highway, into the desert, and stayed there until dark. By the time she came back, hours later, Matt's van was gone. Roxanne told her Matt got so mad he packed up all his stuff and left for L.A.—that he wouldn't be back for a week.

"Good for you!" Roxanne told her. "Matt's been treating you like dirt."

When Matt came back two weeks later, he wasn't alone. He had his new girlfriend with him, and he installed her in a tent in a campground just up the road from the trailer. He apparently intended to shuttle back and forth between the trailer and the tent like a little honeybee that can't make up its mind. But Kitty wouldn't stand for it for a second. When Matt came back from his shift at Sundance that night, he went directly to the tent without even stopping at the trailer. He stayed there until the wee hours of the morning, when Kitty heard him creeping back into the trailer through the kitchen door. When he got to the bedroom, she attacked. He was set upon by a wild animal with red hair. They had a bad, vicious, physical fight, and in the end Matt found himself straddling her on the bed, backhanding her across the face. When he realized what he was doing, he broke down and cried.

"I've never hit a woman before in my life!" he sobbed. "I never hit a woman until I met you! I do not understand you, I cannot live with you, I cannot continue this way! I want out! I can't take this anymore!"

Kitty felt the same way. She took the thousand dollars he offered her—her share of the money they'd spent on the trailer—and moved up the road into a trailer of her own. She'd had it.

Six months later, the girls had turned the trailer into a corporation.

In many ways, "Desert Flower Originals" really was a business venture managed by a board of directors, whose names were Kitty Rosetti, Liz, Me-Liz, and Penny Lavender. The only difference was that, unlike most ordinary companies, Kitty was the only corporate officer who even knew any of the others existed. And if you'd knocked on the door of the trailer, only one person—a small, pleasant young woman with sun-bleached hair, in loose-fitting muslin clothes covered with Indian embroidery—would have opened the door.

The company was a tapestry made of mismatched threads drawn from all the girls' lives. It wove together Me-Liz's fascination with the spirituality and the traditions of the Indians, Penny's creativity and her love of "prettying up," Kitty's all-around competence at running a business—or anything else—and Liz's deathbed desire to be a part of something—anything—that gave her a reason to live.

Me-Liz was the first to notice that the Indian women around town seemed to know how to dress for comfort in a desert climate, by wearing loose, light cottons and other open-weave fabrics. She was fascinated by the way they favored color combinations that were beautiful and at the same time reflected the desert sun. Penny, who was always clever with clothes, noticed it too. Alone in her secret white room on the shore of her imaginary pond, staring at the bedposts that contained the story of her life, she started imagining designs for some high-fashion Indian-style desert clothes of her own. She hitchhiked into L.A. one day, bought some white, unbleached muslin, some thread, and other materials, brought them back to the trailer, and stacked them all neatly on shelves in one corner of the bedroom. Later, when Me-Liz walked in and saw all those lovely materials, she sat down and drew some sketches for patterns. When Penny saw Me-Liz's pictures, she drew some of her own.

What emerged out of this first joint effort was a line of simple, stylish, loose-fitting casual wear made of unbleached muslin or cotton, with inset panels of brightly colored, Indian-style embroidery—a couple of pairs of drawstring slacks and some loose, light-colored tops in white or pastels, with lots of embroidery. In the beginning, when Kitty had a job at a bar and Penny had one at a restaurant (they'd both quit Sundance, to avoid being around Matt), they just made and wore these clothes for their own pleasure. But weekenders started asking them, "Where did you get that outfit? That's very unusual—where could I find one?"

So she took a couple of orders and made some for people. Word started getting around. People on the river started placing orders. Me-Liz came up with the name, Desert Flower Originals, and had labels made. Kitty and Penny quit their jobs, bought a couple of old sewing machines, and hired two people to keep up with the demand. Kitty managed the business; the others, especially Me-Liz and Penny, contributed their creativity. Penny started doing dresses that were like desert clothes for angels—loose, sheer, flowing robes. Women loved them, because when you wore nothing underneath, it felt like you were naked. So Penny's angel dresses became something of a rage on the river. People called them "DFOs."

Then Kitty started her own label. She called it KatydidIt Originals. Naturally, she had her own idea. She liked the whites and pastels, but she liked brilliant, sensational colors better. She took her own hitchhiking trip into L.A. and came back with big bolts of brilliant Hawaiian prints, beads, and sequins, and she started making sarong tops and itty-bitty bikinis, modeled after the outfits she'd worn in her strip shows. She'd never been able to figure out why more bathing suits weren't made with little Velcro tabs like strip costumes were, because they were so convenient, and she incorporated that idea into her designs.

Only Kitty really understood that some of the girls who sat at the sewing machines actually making her outfits were not on the payroll. They were inside her.

Chapter 9

Ever since the Indian naming ceremony, Me-Liz–Tequehe had noticed them: little things, premonitions, visions, fleeting moments when she seemed able to know what was about to happen next. She didn't quite know what to make of it all, and didn't particularly pay it much heed, until that afternoon of June 24, 1976, when something happened that she could never forget. What did it mean? Why had she been chosen? What would God ask her to do with this fearful new power? For years afterward, she wondered about these things. But that morning, it happened so fast she had no time to wonder.

She couldn't put her finger on it, exactly, but all that morning she'd felt a vague sense of uneasiness in the pit of her stomach, anxiety. She experienced a smothery, oppressive feeling, as if the barometer were dropping before a storm.

"I should be happy," she'd thought. "I have a wonderful new love, a beautiful summer day, and we're about to have a great weekend camping out at the Grand Canyon. . . . How come I can't get over this?"

The trip had been a spur-of-the-moment thing, a lark. Her new boyfriend Sandy's crew boss, Mac, had given the guys a day off before they headed up to Colorado for the state fair. After today, they wouldn't be back for two months, maybe longer. So she and Sandy and three other guys on the carnival crew had decided to drive up to the Canyon and camp on the south rim for the night. It was a four-hour drive from Parker, so they'd left the night before in two vehicles and stopped overnight in Williams, a little tourist town about an hour south of the Canyon. They left Williams the next morning, and then they headed north on Route 64, across the desolate tableland called the Coquinino Plateau.

As the monotonous low hills of the high desert passed by outside the window in the hard, flat desert light, she'd glanced over at Sandy, who was sitting at the wheel of the pickup wearing nothing but jeans and a Chicago Cubs cap. He was singing *Moon River* with great happiness and no musical aptitude whatsoever. She couldn't get over how good looking he was. Maybe a little *too* good looking. In a couple of days he'd be gone for two months, she thought—that was almost as long as the entire time she'd known him. It made this trip a little sweeter, a little sadder. They were already talking about getting married when he got back. "Mrs. Elizabeth Lentz." Oh, well. She could live with that.

Was it his gentleness that had attracted her first, Me-Liz wondered? Maybe it was his politeness. "Thank you very much, ma'am." "I do 'preciate that." Maybe it was his North Carolina hill country drawl. The carnival crew would come into Saylor's, the dinner house in Parker where Me-Liz and Penny and Kitty were working as waitresses, and they'd be wearing corn-seed caps and sweat-stained T-shirts and they'd be smudged all over with engine grease, but they would all be polite, and Sandy would be the most polite of all. He treated her with great respect mingled with the faintest trace of raw lust. She loved that.

Sandy was out in Arizona working for summer money on a crew that set up and operated the machinery in a big carnival that traveled through the west during the summer months. He was a journalism student at Guilford College in North Carolina. He would come out here for three or four months in the summer, work himself half to death, and go back home with enough money to pay for the next year of school. The carnival crews would stay in one town a few weeks or months, and then move on. They were living in tents at a campground in Parker, in that awful heat, so Penny had invited him over to her trailer to shower up and have dinner once or twice. He took her out to the movies. Things were sweet between them. He didn't ask a whole

76

lot about her past. Before she knew it, they were living together in her trailer on the river and talking about getting married.

And tomorrow, he'd be gone.

They made it up to the south rim of the Canyon by midmorning, and drove around until they found an empty campsite near park headquarters. Then everybody tumbled out of the trucks, horsing around, hollering, happy to be free for a day. They dumped all their gear out on the ground and went trooping noisily down to the edge of the gorge. But Me-Liz hung back. She was filled with apprehension.

"C'mon, honey!" Sandy laughed, catching her by the elbow. "Hey, it's just a li'l' ole hole in the ground!"

Was it just fear of the Grand Canyon? She edged toward the rim, peering down into that incomprehensible abyss. The feeling of dread got worse. She backed away, but it didn't seem to help. She fought back panic. What was it? The feeling was no longer vague and smothery; it was tangible. It was real. It was as if something awful was about to happen. An earthquake, maybe; a big fire, sweeping across the desert toward them.

"Sandy, I feel really weird," Me-Liz told him. "I feel really strange. I think I've gotta get out of here."

"Aw c'mon, sweetheart! You're not chicken, are you?"

"Babe, I think I've just gotta get out of here."

Sandy flashed her a quick look of annoyance, but he didn't say or do anything. Ten minutes later, she mentioned it again.

"Sandy, I'm sorry, babe, but I feel really strange. I gotta get out of here. I don't know where we have to go, but I think maybe we have to go home. I think I want to go back to Parker."

"You've gotta be joking, Elizabeth!" Sandy said, incredulous. "It took us four hours to get up here! We just *got* here, honey! And now you want to turn right around and go back? I mean, gimme a break, Liz!"

But she insisted.

"Look, Sandy, *please!* I know it doesn't make any sense, but I just have to get away from here. Please, will you do it, just for me? Like . . . now?"

The other guys were chuckling, glancing over at the two of them having their first spit-fight the day before Sandy was supposed to leave. A honeymoon fight. She and Sandy were edging right up into each other's faces. He thought it was absurd. She absolutely insisted. It made him furious that she couldn't even explain it. She didn't care. Finally she threw a tantrum, and finally he gave in. He walked over to tell the others he and Liz were driving back to Parker. She could see him shrugging his shoulders with his palms turned out, and then he came back, fuming and silent, his jaw set. Me-Liz felt awful. She didn't know what she was doing. She just knew she had to get out of there.

They drove back to the campsite, threw their stuff in the back of the truck, and pulled out onto the highway without saying a word. The veins on Sandy's neck were standing out, and he was driving too fast. They took 64 south out of the park, back to Interstate 40, and then turned west toward Kingman. The temperature was probably one hundred two or one hundred three, but it seemed hotter in the cab. When Sandy finally spoke, it was to explain that he was going to take a shortcut, cutting south off I-40 down through Prescott. She didn't say anything. But when they got to the turnoff, Me-Liz panicked again.

"Listen, Sandy, let's not take the shortcut. Please! We gotta go straight down this highway west, toward Kingman."

He glanced at her icily.

"This is getting really outta hand, Liz," he told her. "I mean, this is ridiculous! If I could make this shortcut work for us, it could save us, like, an hour's worth of driving."

"Please don't go that way!"

He didn't. He just got quieter. A fun, funky weekend—their last weekend together for two months—had now turned into stony silence. They continued west on I-40, a two-lane highway that crossed miles and miles of gently rolling nothingness, and neither of them said anything.

LOIS LIRA: My friend Annie and I were going to drive out to California together, just for fun, and we were so excited we just left at two o'clock in the morning. (Laughs.) We couldn't wait. We were both living in Albuquerque. I was twenty-four, not in school, and unemployed. I was kind of . . . directionless. Actually, the day before we left I had taken an oath with the Army, to get GI Bill benefits for college. They swore me in or whatever.

I drove us all the way out to Gallup or Grants or somewhere in the western part of New Mexico and then I started getting real sleepy, so I stopped the car and slept. It was getting light when I woke up, and I ended up driving all the way to Williams, Arizona, just south of the Grand Canyon. By that time it was noon, so we stopped for lunch in Williams. I'd been driving all night, it was hot, and we had no air-conditioning in my little Hornet, so I could barely keep awake. After lunch I let Annie drive. I reclined the seat all the way back, you know, with my seatbelt still on, and I fell asleep.

About a quarter-mile up ahead, Me-Liz noticed a little white car topping the hills, then disappearing into the valleys. The next time it appeared, she noticed it seemed to be weaving a little, wandering over the center line, then jerking back into the right lane. The driver seemed to be drunk, or falling asleep or something. Sandy was still driving too fast; they were gaining on it steadily. She noticed a camper and a big tractor-trailer approaching from the opposite direction, about a mile up ahead. Then, just as the little white car met the oncoming vehicles, it drifted lazily across the center lane and seemed to tap the camper. Then it veered away, hesitated, and drifted back, hitting the tractor-trailer just below the driver's door. It spun around and around, three or four times in a big circle, not end over end, just around and around, until it landed on the shoulder facing the highway. The whole front of the car had caved in, and clouds of steam or smoke drifted lazily into the desert sky.

The moment it happened, Me-Liz realized that this was what her feeling was about. She felt like she was spinning right along with that car, somehow. Then a great calmness fell over her.

"Pull over, right down there on the other side of it," she told Sandy in a voice so full of certainty it surprised even her. "Get on the CB and call an ambulance!"

PHIL NOVAK: We were going back to California after a bicentennial trip to the Grand Canyon in our motor home and I noticed this little white car approaching. It was swerving over to our side of the highway— not weaving out of control, just kind of drifting over, then the driver would pull it back. When it came up on us I pulled the motor home clear on over to the side of the highway as far as I could, hoping it wouldn't hit us, but right at the last second it just turned right into us. It hit the tailgate and just tore off the back quarter of one of the luggage compartments. Directly behind me was a big eighteen-wheeler, and after glancing off us it went right into the eighteen-wheeler.

We stopped immediately, grabbed the first-aid kit, and instructed our four children not to get out of the motor home; then my wife and I ran back there to see what we could do.

Everything was in slow-motion, like a dream. It was as if Me-Liz were watching somebody else get out of the pickup and run down the road toward the wreck. The white car seemed to have turned almost completely black. It was steaming. The front driver's side was completely caved in, and when Me-Liz opened the driver's side door, it just fell off. Inside there was a young girl with short, dark hair and she was . . . severed . . . at about hip level. She'd been impaled by the column of the steering wheel. An impossible amount of blood spilled onto the sand. Me-Liz knelt down and looked into the girl's face. There was nothing there. Felt her pulse. Nothing there. Nothing at all.

Sandy and some other people came up behind her then, and they went around to the passenger side of the car. The door was jammed, so Sandy kicked it open, and there lay another young girl, eyes closed, apparently unconscious, pitched forward in her seat. Her skin was very, very pale, almost blue. She had lots of red freckles and short, curly red hair. Me-Liz smelled burning flesh and looked down in horror to see that the engine, still smoking, was literally sitting in her lap. There was nothing they could do; she was pinned in her seat. Me-Liz felt for a pulse in the girl's neck and found one, faintly throbbing. There was a vertical gash, maybe three inches long, right in the center of her forehead. It was clean and deep, hardly bleeding at all. A little dark blood seeped out of her ears.

"Go back to the truck and get that big jug of water!" she told Sandy. "Call a wrecker to pull this engine off her! And get that trucker out of the road!"

The trucker had pulled off the highway at a crazy angle, almost jackknifed into the road, and now the driver was wandering around dazedly along the center line.

LOIS LIRA: The next thing I remember, we'd come to a dead stop and I woke up. I don't remember the collision at all. I was sitting up. I looked up and I saw that the windshield was missing, so I knew there'd been a wreck. I could see Annie's leg beside me, and I called her name three times, but I got no response. I thought she was either unconscious or dead, I didn't know which. I was afraid to look, for fear of what I might see. I thought I saw a Winnebago-type vehicle across the road, with some people around it, so I started yelling for help. I remember voices. I don't remember faces. Mostly I just kept my eyes shut. I remember feeling like I had to hang on at least long enough to tell people who we were, so I was struggling to stay conscious. *I told someone—I guess it was Elizabeth— my name and Annie's name and how to reach her folks and my folks.*

They were trying to make me as comfortable as possible in there, but midday in the desert in Arizona, in the glaring sun, is pretty unbearable.

I just wanted to get out of the car and lie by the side of the road or something, but they wouldn't let me.

Me-Liz reached down and put her hand on the girl's shoulder, and that's when she saw the colors. She could see colors—jewel colors—everywhere. The girl no longer existed as a human; she existed as colors. They were surrounding her, they were coming from her, they *were* her. The colors lasted only a few seconds—maybe two or three—and then something else happened. Me-Liz could see into the girl's body. She didn't even want to. She could see places that were swollen and bleeding, she could see something awful in her lower back—the way the colors were, she knew that it was very dangerous. There were dark, unhealthy colors surrounding this place in her back. It was a place in her back that had a break in it. She could see organs, soft things that looked like pudding, and she could also see the color around the organs, and the light emanating from them. There was bruising and discoloration in the liver, the spleen, the left lung, the right lung. The lighter, the clearer, the more jewellike the color, the healthier; when the colors became dark, muddy, and gooey- or sticky-looking, that was bad. She could see those dark, dark, gooey colors in her abdomen. She also saw something that was purple in there. It was blood.

LOIS LIRA: When the accident happened, I was lying stretched out with the seat in the reclined position, and my seatbelt on. My body slid forward horizontally, feet first, and the seatbelt slid up around my rib cage. Then the back of my seat was thrown forward from the reclined position. That's what broke my back.

"Hello? Hello? Are you there?"
Me-Liz was shaking the girl's shoulder.
"Hello? Are you awake?"
Then the girl's eyes opened and she looked straight at Me-Liz. It was an amazing look. It said, "I recognize that you are there. I know that I can do nothing to help myself. I am going to die very soon and I know it."
"Can you talk to me?" Me-Liz demanded.
"Yes, I can."
"What is your name?"
"My name is Lois Lira."
"Lois, where do you live?"
"I live in Albuquerque."

"Where does your family live?"

"My father's name is Richard Lira and my father and mother live in Las Cruces, New Mexico."

"Can you tell me where you hurt?"

"I don't hurt."

"Do you want me to call you Lois?"

"No, call me Lu. How is Annie?"

"Annie is doing just fine. I need you to keep talking to me now."

The girl was getting paler by the minute. She seemed to be slipping into shock. Just then a young Mexican-American police officer showed up. Officer Rick Vasquez, of the Arizona Highway Patrol, was working out of Williams when he heard the call come in over the police radio. He glanced into the car. Me-Liz could tell he didn't like what he saw.

"Does anybody here know anything about medicine?" he asked.

"I'm a doctor," Me-Liz said. "I can take care of her, don't worry. Do you have a first-aid kit?"

"Yeah, sure—I'll go get it."

Only much later would she begin to wonder why she said that. The words just seemed to spring out of her mouth. Lu was still talking, mumbling: "My father's name is Richard Lira . . . I have a sister named Jewel . . . My dad works for the water conservation district . . . My father's name is Richard Lira . . ."

The heat was incredible. Flies seemed to appear out of nowhere. When the officer returned with the first-aid kit, Me-Liz washed her hands with water out of Sandy's jug, washed them again with iodine, and then she set to work cleaning out the girl's head wound and wrapping as much gauze around it as she could. When she was done, she pinched the girl on both her legs.

"Do you feel that?"

"No," the girl said.

That made sense to Me-Liz, because of the funny dark space she'd seen in her back. They had to get that engine off her lap and get her to a hospital very, very fast. Officer Vasquez tried to radio for a Medivac helicopter, but none were available; they'd all gone to another bad accident somewhere nearby. An ambulance was on its way, he said, but the nearest hospital was in Williams, twenty or twenty-five minutes away. Traffic had started backing up on the highway. People appeared, gawking into the smashed car. Phil Novak, the driver of the camper, covered Annie's face and the window on her side of the car with a towel and an army blanket. Just as the wrecker pulled up, Me-Liz noticed something she hadn't seen before. Lu appeared to be pregnant.

"Lu, are you going to have a baby?"

"No."

Me-Liz unbuttoned her shirt and then she saw that her belly was swollen not with pregnancy but with blood. She was bleeding into her stomach, and swelling up very fast. She could see the dark, dangerous colors again. The girl was bleeding internally and if she were laid out flat, she would die of drowning. Me-Liz felt sure of this; she didn't know how or why. It was her upright position that was keeping her alive. If they could rig up some kind of a sling, so that she would be suspended upright on the way to the hospital, she might make it.

The coroner, who'd rode out with the wrecker, strolled around the scene snapping pictures with a Polaroid. The wrecker backed his truck up to the smashed car and wrapped cables around the engine, then eased forward enough to lift it away from the girl's legs enough so that Officer Vasquez, Sandy, Phil Novak, Me-Liz, and another man could slip a blanket under her body. Then, after they eased her body out of the car, Me-Liz instructed the men to hold her body up in a sling, like a baby suspended from a stork's bill, with all four corners of the blanket held above her and her legs dangling out of the gaps.

"Well, that's pretty tricky—what happens when the ambulance gets here?" the trucker asked.

"We'll figure that out when we get there!" Me-Liz snapped.

Then, for ten agonizing minutes, until the ambulance arrived, the men stood there holding Lu's dead weight in the breathless heat.

LOIS LIRA: After a while I was having trouble breathing. I remember complaining that I couldn't breathe, and I remember Elizabeth telling me to imagine a peaceful place, to forget everything that was going on out-side, and just to go inside myself to that peaceful place with a cool stream, where it was quiet, and then that was better. That helped a lot: I could breathe.

When the ambulance arrived, two girls still wearing waitress uni-forms jumped out. They unloaded a stretcher and started to lay the girl out on it.

"No, no!" Me-Liz insisted. "Look, I'm a doctor! If you do that, she'll die! Do you have a cross-member or anything we could suspend her from inside the ambulance?"

They did. The storklike apparatus was trussed up and hung from the ambulance roof, with the dying girl inside. Officer Vasquez quickly finished out his accident report, taking dictation from Me-Liz on the girl's condition. Then he passed the report over to one of the ambulance drivers.

"You coming with us?" she asked Me-Liz.

"No, I can't."

"What do you mean, you can't?"

"I can't!" It was funny, but she knew for certain that she shouldn't go. She was not needed anymore. It was over. She'd also begun to wake up to what she'd just done: impersonate a doctor in a life-threatening medical emergency. Was that a crime? She peeked into the ambulance one last time, to see if Lu was still conscious.

"I'm cold," Lu moaned.

Me-Liz ran back to the truck and grabbed a red shirt out of the cab. She ran back to the ambulance, stuck her hand inside the stork rig, and covered up the girl the best she could. Then the ambulance pulled onto the highway, siren screaming, bound for the hospital in Williams.

LOIS LIRA: I don't remember anything about being put into the ambulance, but I do remember it was a rough ride, with the siren wailing, and I remember somebody beside me telling the driver to take it easy. I remember there was a lady doctor there at the hospital in Williams who stitched up my head. I also remember they wanted my husband's name and I was real pissed off they were going to call him, the jerk! So I refused to give them his name.

They put me on an "air ambulance," an airplane, there in Williams, and I was flown down to Phoenix, to the Barrow Institute of Neurology, at St. Joseph's Hospital. They said I nearly died on the way down there in the plane. I remember—it's real funny—I was aware in a detached way that I was on an airplane, and then this was instantly followed by a sense of traveling at an enormous rate of speed through some kind of tube or tunnel, a very long tunnel, toward a pinpoint of light. I never reached the light. I got maybe half or three-quarters of the way there. I had a sense of moving toward something wonderful, and not being afraid, and relaxing, because I'd fought for so long and so hard just to stay alive and finally here was something that just said, "Never mind, relax, it's okay." It was exciting to go there, inviting. It would have been easy to let go and continue down that tunnel toward that light.

I didn't, though I don't remember consciously pulling back or anything. I don't know, maybe I was waiting to die in the presence of my mother. Because when I got to Phoenix, they said they wanted to do surgery, and I said, "I can't decide. Wait till my mom gets here!"

"We need to get out of here," Sandy said quietly.

He and Me-Liz hardly exchanged a word during the whole two-hour drive back to Parker. They were both exhausted, covered with engine grease, covered with blood. Me-Liz was in a kind of shock and was getting scared. What on earth had she done? What if someone found out she wasn't a doctor, an RN, or anything else? Could she be arrested? And . . . how was it possible to see inside someone's body like that?

When they got back to the trailer, Sandy went inside to take a shower and lay down, and Me-Liz went across the road to the restaurant. She told some of the other girls what had happened, and she told her boss she wouldn't be coming in to work the next day. Then she called the hospital in Williams from the restaurant pay phone. She was told that Lois Lira had been transported by air ambulance to the Barrow Institute of Neurology, in Phoenix, and that she was alive but in critical condition.

Later that night, after she got cleaned up and ate something, she went down to the little radio station in town and asked the night DJ to make an announcement on the air. He asked everyone in Parker to pray for a young girl named Lois Lira, who had been badly hurt in a car wreck up near Williams that day.

For years afterward, Me-Liz always remembered that as a very special thing.

LOIS LIRA: They operated for, I believe, eight hours. They had to open up my belly first, to find out what was bleeding and repair that. It was a real mess in there! My spleen was ruptured; it had been punctured by a rib, and that's what was causing the bleeding. They removed the spleen because it was so badly damaged. I had a perforated intestine, too, and other organs were damaged. My back was broken, too, so they turned me over and cut into my back. They inserted two steel orthopedic things called Harrington rods, that act as an internal brace.

LILLIAN LIRA: After I got the call about the accident and OK'd the surgery, my daughter Jewel and I drove all night from Las Cruces and got to St. Joseph's about eight o'clock the next morning. Lu had just come out of surgery and she was awake, and she said, "Don't worry, Mom, I'm okay!" Lu was the only one in intensive care who could talk—everyone else was brain-damaged from motorcycle accidents and that kind of thing.

There was one thing that just got to all of us, and that was that she

85

was entered into the hospital as Jane Doe. On all those reports, she was called Jane Doe. That to me is about the eeriest thing that can happen.

The next morning, Me-Liz screwed up her courage, went back across the street to the restaurant, and called the Barrow Institute. She identified herself as Dr. Garcia, who had been involved in an accident the day before with a Lois Lira, and said that she was calling to see how Lois was doing. She was startled when the nurse told her to hold the line, because Lois's doctor had been expecting her call. The icy nausea came back again; she almost hung up. When the doctor came on the line, he told her Lois was stabilized and they thought she was going to make it, although they weren't sure whether she'd regain full use of her legs. He said they'd put Harrington rods in her back. *Harrington rods?* Me-Liz wondered. She had no idea what they were. Then he put Lu's mother on the line.

"Thank you, thank you, thank you!" she told Me-Liz. "I don't believe Lu would be alive now if it wasn't for you!"

But Me-Liz felt awful. She just wanted to get away. She didn't want to be on the phone with this woman who believed she had saved her daughter's life, when it was all based on a lie. And yet . . . it was true! It happened! And in some strange way that she couldn't understand, it wasn't even her who'd called herself a doctor in the first place.

LILLIAN LIRA: I remember Elizabeth calling, saying she was checking on Lu. We felt like without this girl, my daughter would have died. There is no reason in my mind to think otherwise. Either she would have died or been permanently paralyzed.

RICHARD LIRA: Elizabeth seemed to know that Lu's spleen was ruptured. That was what had caused all the internal bleeding.

LOIS LIRA: The next thing I knew I woke up, and my mom was there. We have a very strange relationship, my mom and I . . . yeah, my mom's the best. She's got her quirks that drive me nuts, but she's always there.

I was in the hospital for almost three months, until September first; after that, I was on crutches for probably six months, and then after that I had a cane. Because of my injury I couldn't do the work I'd done before—jobs in warehouses, manual-labor type stuff—for three years. I just needed a long time to heal, physically and psychologically. I was so critically injured it took all my strength just to survive, for months, and as a result I had no energy left over to even cry, to mourn for Annie. Eventually, that caught up with me and I had to start seeing a psychiatrist.

Elizabeth and I wrote for a while after the accident. She told me about her "psychic experience" out there. I don't know—I have no reason to disbelieve it. And if that's what happened, well, it worked. What can I say, except thanks?

Chapter 10

On the breathlessly hot summer afternoon of July 23, 1977, Sandy Michael Lentz and the collection of women who called themselves Elizabeth Katherine Garcia were married in a little chapel in Greensboro, North Carolina.

PAULA PYNE: It was so hot that day. Maybe that's why I don't remember the wedding as being very joyous. I do remember doubting that that marriage was going to work. I don't know—I just had a sixth sense that something is not right here. I remember Sandy's family had a look on their faces like they were going through the motions, but I don't think they were genuinely happy about it. I think they loved Elizabeth. But Sandy's dad was just a good ole boy from Ashe County, you know—some people down there heve never left the county in their whole lives—and here his boy goes out west for summer work and comes back with this girl whose own parents don't even show up for the wedding. A girl who only has these vague stories about where she came from, or what happened to her family, or anything. It was almost like she came from nowhere. It had to make you wonder.

The small crowd of friends and relations who attended the service that day may have had their secret doubts about the wedding. But they were nothing compared to what was going on inside the bride.

Kitty, Liz, Me-Liz, and Penny Lavender all attended the service that day (or at least parts of it), and all of them had a different movie about what was going on. Only one of them, Penny Lavender, actually married Sandy that day. To Penny, the whole situation was blissfully uncomplicated. She was a single girl who'd finally met the man of her dreams, and now she was walking down the aisle into happily ever after. She was going to say "I do" for the first and last time in her life. She'd never been married before. She had no children. All she wanted was love, sweet love.

It was Penny who had fallen in love with Sandy back in Arizona the year before. She adored how gently and slowly she'd fallen in love with him, and how gently and slowly he'd done the same. It was as if he were taking four months to undress her, button by button. She'd invite him over to her little Airstream trailer on the river, and he'd come in dead tired after work, covered with sweat and engine grease, and she'd cook him chicken and dumplings. It was as if they were a real family, like on TV. On Saturdays, they'd go to the movies and hold hands. Finally she invited him to move into the trailer, and he did, and not long afterward they began circling around the idea of getting married. It was only now, months after they'd moved across the country to North Carolina so Sandy could finish school, that they were finally ready to go to the altar. How gently and slowly it had all happened! It was like silk sheets slipping off the bed, like sand in a glass, like smoke trailing into the sky.

The true situation, of course, was considerably more complicated than Penny realized. Liz came out once or twice that wedding day, but her main feeling was one of terrible, nagging doubt. She wasn't sure that this marriage was even legal in the first place. After all, Domingo had been killed in a car wreck, leaving her a widow, but in a way they were still married, weren't they? If you were married to someone who had been killed, didn't that mean you were still married? Or did you have to divorce a dead person? Did you have to wait a certain amount of time after your husband's death for the new marriage to be legal? Or what? It was all just a confusing, worrisome mush in her mind.

Me-Liz came out a few times that hot August day, but she felt as though she was miles away. It seemed to her as if she were simply observing somebody else's wedding—she didn't know whose. She didn't love Sandy. An unbridgeable distance had opened up between the two of them after the accident at the Grand Canyon a year before. When she and Sandy had first met, they'd sometimes sat up all night talking excitedly about weird physics and ghosts and out-of-body travel and UFOs and the Shroud of Turin and all the rest of it. But after the accident, Sandy changed. Whenever she started steering the conversation in the direction of the twilight zone, he quickly steered it away. He didn't want to talk about that stuff anymore, or even, it seemed, be around her at all.

Kitty was the only one who knew exactly what was going on that day. Hoo-boy! What a mess! She was the only one who knew that, when the others first met Sandy, they were still legally married to Domingo Garcia. That had been her big objection all along. Out on the desert, back in Parker, Kitty had watched Penny's romance with Sandy begin to bud and blossom with growing alarm. Penny was such an innocent. She had no capacity for complications. How could she be made to understand that she was *not* free to marry Sandy without first divorcing Domingo, who was *not* really dead? In order to explain all that, she'd have to let Penny in on the truth, and she was convinced that Penny was not ready to hear it.

So Kitty stalled for time. As the talk of marriage grew more serious, she began raising all kinds of objections whenever she talked to Sandy. What would his parents back in North Carolina think of her? Here she was, a waitress he met in a roadside restaurant in Arizona, somebody he'd only known a few months, who had only the vaguest of stories to account for her past, and now he was bringing her back to Smalltown USA as his wife? How was that going to go over in a place where everybody knew everything about everybody, including their family history to the Nth generation? And what about the fact that she was an older woman? She was thirtyish and Sandy was twenty-eight; how was *that* going to play in North Carolina? (She never told Sandy the strangest part of all—that she didn't know exactly *how* old she was. She had no birth certificate and no memory of where or when she'd been born. Hoo-boy! *That* would go over like gangbusters down in Dixie!)

But none of it seemed to matter. When Penny Lavender looked at Sandy, she saw the man she had always been waiting for. Nothing else made any difference. Even Kitty felt the power of Penny's love, so in the end, she settled on a compromise. At the time, it seemed to make sense, but in the long run it turned out to be a terrible mistake: they'd move back to North Carolina and just *say* they were married, say they'd had a little private service out in Arizona, and it was all taken care of.

They'd be man and wife in their own hearts, if not on paper. What difference did a piece of paper make, anyway?

They sold everything they could, packed everything else in boxes and shipped it east, and caught a plane out of Phoenix. Sandy and the girls rented a house in Greensboro, near Guilford College. Penny fixed the place up beautifully, stretching the dollars with factory outlet fabrics and ideas clipped from ladies' magazines. She settled comfortably into the life of a student's newlywed wife, in this new place that was green and humid and so much more calm and civilized than the desert. But inwardly, things were quite different than those lovely, uncomplicated pictures in the decorating magazines.

The stress of living out this fraudulent marriage took its toll on them both. Penny felt awful about telling everybody they were married when they weren't—especially people as nice as Sandy's parents. But having to tell them the truth seemed even worse. How could she bear to tell his parents that the marriage was a lie, and their son and darling daughter-in-law had actually been living in sin in front of their eyes?

Sandy didn't like it, either. He started pressing for a real marriage. Kitty resisted. How could she possibly tell him, or anyone, the truth? Yet how could she allow Penny to marry Sandy, if it wasn't even legal? Trapped in the lie, Kitty started bickering with Sandy, and Sandy bickered back. The bloom began to fade from the rose. He started snapping at Penny, and for the first time, she began to notice his imperfections. He was a little too arrogant about his good looks, she thought. And why did he have so many female "friends" at school? Back on the desert, things were sweet and simple, but here there were just the mundane complications of paying the utility bills and the rent and cooking and cleaning and getting Sandy through school. He was always working, or studying, or in class, and she hardly even saw him anymore. Penny began composing morose country-and-western songs about love gone bad, and sinking in a sea of longing and despair.

That spring of 1977, Sandy made arrangements to go back out west to work on the carnival crew again. And the two of them decided that when he got back, they'd live apart for a while. It was to be a "trial separation," but it felt like the end. Before he left, Sandy put all his stuff in storage and arranged to move into his own apartment when he returned to Greensboro in the fall.

To help make ends meet while he was gone, Liz took a job at South Bay Seafoods, a wholesale fish place in Greensboro. She worked in a small retail store at the front of the cold storage warehouse, stocking freezer shelves and running the register. Her immediate supervisor was Paula Pyne, the owner's daughter.

PAULA PYNE: Everybody around the company liked Liz pretty much, at least in the beginning. She was very congenial, very nice. She had some spunk to her—she really packed a wallop for such a little person, and I liked that. She was very personable and a lot of good fun and laughs, very optimistic—she'd just be up all the time. She liked to wear jeans and these gauzy tops and Urban Cowboy *stuff—you know, fancy yokes and what all—and she said she'd designed all these clothes she was wearing, out in Arizona. That's where she'd come from.*

Her name on the application was Elizabeth K. Garcia, but she called herself "Liz" or sometimes "Kitty." I remember that, because I remember thinking of Miss Kitty on "Gunsmoke." She flirted, no doubt about it—she'd walk up and down the loading dock, and she was very small and her waist was very small, and if you wear jeans and everything else is tucked in, your tailbone is gonna sway, honey! She'd be sashaying down the dock hitting the walls on every step, and guys would notice, let me tell you! Sometimes I'd think, Liz, cool it, this is too much!

Anyway, we developed a friendship while she was working in the retail store. We went up in the mountains together one time, and my friends met her friends and we'd all have dinner together and stuff. I got to know Sandy through her. He was a nice guy, everybody really respected Sandy.

As time went by, of course, I developed a very different impression of her. I'm a very family-oriented person—this is a family business—and it did seem very strange to me that she never talked about her family, never showed pictures. Or she'd start talking about them and then say things like, "I don't really want to talk about this, so quit asking me." Her whole background was very sketchy. She mentioned she'd been married before, and had kids, and for a long time I could never quite get the story of what happened to them. Then out of the blue one day she whips out this picture of a horrendous car wreck—I mean this car was just totally smashed up—and she says this is the car wreck that my husband and my kids were killed in. I always thought that was a little morbid, strange, bizarre, unique, whatever you want to call it, that she would whip this sucker out like that. I mean, if it was so traumatic that she couldn't talk about it, what was she doing carrying around this picture that was just gross?

She also told that story to numerous other employees, and they'd come up to me and say, "You know, this chick is a little strange." I think they all perceived her to be a little strange. Plus she had no parents, she couldn't tell us where she'd been, or whatever—she showed up out of no-where, almost.

KIT CASTLE: The only pictures of a car wreck that the others would have had were the Polaroids the coroner took at the wreck in Arizona. Liz had no memory that that wreck ever happened—she wasn't there. Only Me-Liz (and, briefly, Kitty and Jess) were there. So when Liz found these photos, she mistook them for photos of the wreck that suppos-edly killed Domingo and the kids. It was an affirmation to her, a piece of physical evidence, that the wreck had really happened. After all, she was never completely sure that it had—she wasn't there, either. All she knew was that her husband and three kids had been killed in a wreck and then they were gone. She had not even been able to say goodbye. She clung to these pictures because they were the only evidence she had of what had happened to them. It was the only way she had of dealing with "reality."

While Sandy was gone, Liz rented a new place, a little house on Walnut Street, and all of the girls helped fix it up, as tastefully as they could, with what little they had: the clean but mismatched furniture, the Salvation Army cookware, and some incongruously elaborate, frilly curtains Penny had made. One of Liz's favorite touches was a little collection of clocks she'd picked up at yard sales and junk shops, all arranged on the mantelpiece and all set to different times. Lots of them were dead clocks; they told the same time all the time. Others were set randomly, as if she'd simply rolled the dice to pick the time. "If I set them all at different times, then I'll always know what time it is," she'd tell people. They thought she was joking.

But much as she liked her new house, it seemed vacant without Sandy there. When he was gone, Penny remembered him sitting at the kitchen table with no shirt on, playing the guitar. She remembered how they used to lie in bed dreaming about the rest of their lives. She remem-bered his drawl: "Thank you very much, ma'am." "I do 'preciate that." Even Kitty began to miss him. She knew how much Penny loved him, and finally she just gave up. What difference did it make? Nobody needed to know about the marriage to Domingo, and she'd just make sure nobody ever found out.

It was Kitty who tracked Sandy down by phone, in a campground someplace in Colorado.

"You think we could learn to put up with each other?" she asked.

"Oh, Liz, I don't know!" he said. The weariness in his voice carried two thousand miles. "I miss you so bad out here! But every time we get together, we're like cats and dogs. Sometimes I think we're made for each other, other times I think we're just made to drive each other nuts!"

"Maybe we could work something out. Maybe we could just try it again, try to talk more or something."

"I miss you, Elizabeth. I miss you a lot worse than I figured I would. Damn it!"

"Well, I've got this wild idea how we could make things better. Uhh . . . wanna get married? For real?"

"Oh jeez, Liz, let's not go through this again!"

"But Sandy, I mean . . . I miss you like crazy. I want you to come home to stay. I want to marry you."

A long, long silence stretched between them before another word was spoken.

"Will you marry me?" she asked again.

"Are you kidding?"

"No."

Another long silence passed.

"Well, it's about time!"

Joy flooded into the others' hearts when Sandy agreed to marry them, but Penny was the happiest of all. She and Sandy set a date for the wedding—July 23, just a few days after he was due back from out west. There was, of course, some unpleasant business that had to be taken care of first: the truth-telling. Everyone in Sandy's enormous extended family, Liz's boss, and all their friends had to be told that they were not really married at all. It put everyone in an awkward spot, especially Sandy's parents, who had to tell all *their* relations in turn—most of whom were so offended they refused to attend the ceremony. It was to be a wedding characterized from the beginning by embarrassment.

But Penny didn't care. She and the others scurried around in a state of dizzy anticipation, making all the arrangements for the wedding. There was a pretty little chapel on Springwood Street, not far from the new house, which they got permission to use for the ceremony. Me-Liz designed sheer, white outfits for both of them, in the style of Penny's Desert Flower Originals designs. Liz's neighbor, Natalie, helped her do all the invitations and generally plan the whole thing to the point that all Sandy had to do was attend and say "I do."

Penny asked Paula Pyne's dad, Elbert, to play the role of her father by giving her away, and he obliged. And a few days after Sandy returned from the west, he and Penny Lavender were married in the little chapel. It was Penny's day. Despite the heat, she was lightheaded with joy. She felt light as the air, like a bird on the wing, a white sheet in the wind, like an angel. She felt so airy, in fact, that Kitty had to put in an appearance to bring her back down to earth. Kitty played the part of the mother of the bride, bustling about self-importantly, overseeing all the details and making sure the whole program moved smoothly. Elbert Pyne acted as the father of the bride. And Penny Lavender—radiant and nearly levitating with joy—was the bride herself.

With her short, sensible haircut and glasses, wearing a demure white dress and clutching a bouquet of black-eyed Susans and zinnias, Penny looked virginal as an Iowa Sunday school teacher. She and her husband-to-be were to lead a procession down Walnut Street to the chapel, so Kitty stepped in for that, setting a rather brisk, military tempo for such a hot day. When she got to the chapel, she turned the show over to Penny, who walked through the door and down an aisle lined with flowers to meet the preacher.

Then Penny Lavender said "I do" to the first and only love of her life.

Chapter 11

NAME: Elizabeth Katherine Lentz
LOCATION: Moses H. Cone Hospital, Greensboro, N.C.
CHIEF COMPLAINT: This patient is a thirty-two-year-old white female referred for evaluation of headaches.
PRESENTING ILLNESS: This patient was first seen in January 1977, at the Wesley Long Emergency Room. At that time she was complaining of severe occipital and vertex headaches associated with nausea and vomiting and abnormal visual phenomena. . . . The patient has a past history of having had amnestic episodes between 1968 and 1973. . . . The patient has also had a past history suggestive of emotional difficulties, although she is adamant that she is not having any problem at the present time. . . . The patient has a rather involved psychiatric history but she states that all of this is a thing of the past and she has definitely gotten her emotional problems sorted out. . . .

Kitty was, as the doctor wrote, "adamant" about the fact that she had everything under control. She was in the hospital because of the splitting headaches she was having. Period. The doctors kept her in the hospital five days while they ran a complete neurological workup on her, but they couldn't find anything wrong except for a slight abnormality in her neck. They concluded that that was probably what was causing the headaches, treated it with heat and aspirin, and released her.

For once, Liz and Me-Liz knew better than Kitty. They knew there was something more serious going on than mere headaches. Everything seemed to be falling apart again. They were missing time again—lots of time. They were seeing things: sheets of fire, bees, little lights in the air. And they were bumping into things—walking into walls, into doors; Liz walked into a fuel tank out behind the house one day. Everything was falling apart again.

Me-Liz was frightened, but she had the strangest feeling about it all: she felt that doors were opening to other realms, that new energies and powers were coming into focus for her. The "abnormal visual phenomena"—she preferred to call them visions—were not just a symptom of some disease; they were gifts from God. So were the strange powers that had begun to appear not long after she quit her job at South Bay Seafoods and took a job as a picture framer at a place in Greensboro called Picture Perfect.

BOB RICE: I met Liz when I was working the darkroom at Elm Street Gallery [an art gallery in Greensboro]. She'd sit up front, in the gallery—it was sort of a satellite operation of Picture Perfect, for people who came in and bought pictures and wanted them framed. One day she came in and she was furious at the guy who owned the place, just steaming mad. I don't remember why. We talked a little while, and then I went back in the darkroom. A few minutes later, I hear this big crash. I walk out into the gallery to see what's going on, and here a whole line of frame samples, maybe two dozen of them, had fallen off the wall onto the floor. Liz was sitting at the desk, maybe ten or fifteen feet away from them. She said she'd gotten angry, and things like this happened, and they'd just fallen off the wall.

Now, I didn't actually see *this happen. But the interesting thing was that these samples—actually they were just the corners of frames, like Ls—were hanging on the wall by Velcro attachments. And the way Velcro is, you can pull things straight off, but you can't pull them to one side. In other words, if you'd wanted to pull a whole row down, you'd have had to go down the line and pull each one off individually, really fast.*

She had talked about psychic peculiarities before, but I hadn't paid much attention because people will tell you anything. After that, though, I kind of started looking at her with my eyebrows raised a little.

In the past, it was always Me-Liz who had the visions and psychic experiences, but now Liz started having them, too. She knew what it was right away. It was the brain tumor. She was dying. There was something terribly wrong with her brain, or her nerves, or something, and she was dying. She told Sandy about her visions and blackouts, and missing time, and how the neurologists at Hennepin County Hospital in Minneapolis had concluded she might have epilepsy.

Concerned that she might be having epileptic seizures, Sandy took her to the college infirmary at the University of North Carolina not long after she was released from Cone Hospital. Liz was lying on a little bed surrounded by a curtain, waiting for the doctor to see her, when in front of her eyes she saw the curtain catch fire. Sheets of soundless, smokeless white fire climbed the curtains and consumed them. But when she looked again, the curtains were completely unscathed, untouched. She was nuts, she was crazy. She must be.

Everything was falling apart again.

When she told the doctor about the fire, he told her it was probably "psychomotor seizure activity." Epilepsy. A sort of firestorm in the brain, characterized by massive discharges of abnormal electrical activity. He gave her a shot and then prescribed the same antiseizure medications she'd been on before, Dilantin and Mysoline, and released her.

Kitty resisted taking the medication at all; she felt fine. She didn't have a problem. Jess didn't want to be *treated*—he wanted to be the *doctor*. He refused to take the medicine. And Me-Liz was convinced that her problem was not organic at all, it was spiritual. Scary new powers were being given unto her; she didn't quite know how to handle them yet, that's all. What good would these drugs do? Only Liz willingly took the medication, even though it made her feel drugged and dopey. She knew she was dying. And she knew the whole deadly cycle was starting up again—the tests, the hospitalizations, the injections, the operations—and in the end she would die. Lying on her bed one afternoon, she began to weep. She was totally alone. There was no one to offer comfort, no one who could possibly understand.

It was then that she called Michael's name. She had not spoken that name in a decade, but he was there instantly, standing beside the bed. He was wearing the same dark hat and dark coat that he always wore. He looked down at her gravely.

"My child," he said gently. "My child."

He took her in his arms and held her and comforted her. He didn't say anything more. He just held her and rocked her for a long, long time, like a mother would rock a badly frightened child.

She wept.

Michael had been so dear to her once.

Over the terrible, gray years of her childhood, before she gave up hope completely and threw him out of her life, he had come to her a thousand times. He had been her guide and protector, her teacher, her beloved friend. She didn't know exactly where he came from. She just knew that he was there when she needed him the most. Michael told her she had a porch light inside her heart, and that when there was danger and she cried out for help, he could see the light go on. He would come down out of the sky to help when he saw that porch light in her heart.

"There will be times when you're afraid, and times you'll feel alone, but you must never forget that your real father watches over you always," Michael told her. "And that he'll send me to help you when there is danger."

It was true: whenever she feared for her life and cried out in her heart, he would appear, smiling gently, always wearing that same dark coat and dark hat. Sometimes her tears made spots on that coat. Michael looked a little like Albert Einstein as a young man, with wise, humorous dark eyes and dark hair. His manner was always stiff and formal, like someone wearing dress-up clothes on Saturday. He had saved her so many times! More than once, she thought, she would have died without him.

Liz did not remember the first time Michael had come down out of the sky to help her. That memory was sealed away, like fading pictures in a locket, in Little Andrea's mind. It was Little Andrea who first met Michael that day on the track all those years ago. Now Little Andrea was crouched in her warm gray cave, like a cocoon, like a mummy, like Sleeping Beauty under the spell of a hundred years' sleep. Her memories lay sleeping with her. They were her secret, known only to her, and, by some mysterious leakage, to Kitty. Liz and Me-Liz and Penny and Jess and Little Elizabeth did not even know that Little Andrea was there.

In her hiding place, Little Andrea was still only four or five years old, the same age she'd been that day when Michael came for the first time. She was still wearing her straw-colored hair in an Indian braid, and still wearing her favorite dress, the squaw princess dress with the black and white rickrack all around it. That was the dress she was wearing the day Michael came, all those years ago.

Little Andrea loved that dress. She got to wear it when the whole family got in the big black Buick and went down to Trinity Speedway to the stock car races. They lived in Houston then, in that gloomy little house with the awful smell, at 67 Ontario Street. Mother would pack the ice chest full of all kinds of good stuff, and Little Andrea got to wear her squaw princess dress. They'd spread a blanket on the grass beside the track and watch the racers whooshing around the colored markers out on the speedway. She could see her daddy's car, and Pete Smith's car, and all the other cars that were going around and around. The air smelled like gas. Down by the track, around the pit where the men parked their trailers and worked on their motors, she could see orange flags flapping in the wind.

People were standing up on their blankets all around her, yelling and screaming for the racers. Little Andrea liked to cheer for the racers, too. But in her heart she had a bad secret. She never cheered for her daddy. She always cheered for Pete Smith, her daddy's friend. Pete Smith was the only person who liked her. He'd put her in his lap and sing songs to her, and once he gave her a big dolly with straps on her feet so they could dance together and sing. In her heart, she wanted so much for her daddy to die, and for Pete Smith to be her daddy.

She wanted her daddy to die.

Little Andrea couldn't understand why her daddy didn't like her to dance and be happy. He didn't like her to be good, but he always hurt her when she was bad. He never failed to remind her that everything was her fault. She believed him—she thought it was so. She thought it was her fault that he was so unhappy, that he was such an angry, mean man. The harder she tried to get him to like her, the more he seemed to hate her. She didn't know how to act around him, so she just tried to stay out of his way.

Once, when her father called her "the little bastard," Pete got mad.

"That's a heck of a thing to call your own kid," he said.

"Mind your own damn business," her father told him. "She's just a little bastard. Shoulda thrown her in the bay the day she was born."

Maybe her daddy found out her thoughts that day, watching the races at Trinity Speedway. Maybe her daddy found out that she wanted him to die, and for Pete Smith to be her daddy. Maybe that's why, when he came back in, he made her sit in the backseat of the car, in the baking hot sun, with all the windows rolled up. She sat there on the big brown velvety seats for the longest time, looking out the front window at the orange flags flapping in the wind around the pit where the men worked on their motors. It was so hot in that car, pretty soon she could see angels—tiny angels against the dark brown seats. It seemed like they were singing. Then she fell asleep, because when she woke up, a lady was pulling her out of the car.

"This child is too small to be locked in a car on a day like this!" the lady was yelling, dragging her over toward her daddy, who was standing in the pit working on a motor.

"This child could die in this heat!"

"Put a lid on it, lady!" her daddy said. "Beat it! You got no business buttin' in where you don't belong! I'll take care of her any way I see fit."

Then he grabbed Little Andrea by the shoulders and shoved her toward the pit.

"Stay there, squirt, and don't move!"

Still arguing and yelling at each other, he and the lady moved off toward the car. She could see her daddy's hands going up and down, with his face all crinkled. She felt dizzy and scared to be by those big men and all those motors, where it smelled like gas. When her daddy came back, he dragged her over behind a trailer that was all covered with colored stickers and he hit her right across the mouth. She looked up through her tears and she saw Pete Smith standing right behind him.

"Hey, Joey, man—cut it out!" he said angrily. "Stop bustin' the kid in the mouth, willya? Other people have started to notice around here. You could really hurt her!"

"Get out of my face!" her daddy yelled back. "Get yer face out of my business!"

Little Andrea just stood there, frozen with fear, while her daddy and Pete Smith yelled at each other and then finally Pete Smith went away. Her daddy dragged her over to the other side of the pit where her mother was sitting on the blanket, and he wiped the blood off Little Andrea's mouth. He wiped it off so hard it hurt, and she could tell he liked that. He looked at her with something black and empty in his eyes.

"If you ever speak to that little creep again, I'll kill him," her daddy told her. "I'll kill you both."

She never thought for a second that he wouldn't do it.

Little Andrea curled up against the ice chest like a scared animal. She didn't cheer for anyone. She wondered if just talking to Pete Smith in

her thoughts would be enough to get him killed. But if you liked someone, she wondered, how could you stop your thoughts about them?
How could she never think about Pete Smith again? If she thought
about him, he would be killed, and it would be all her fault.

Her daddy got back in his car and started driving out onto the track,
but suddenly the car sputtered, slowed down, and then he started backing up toward the pit. Without thinking, Little Andrea got up and
walked over toward the pit, where she'd been told so many times not
to go. All around her was the roar of the engines and the smell of gas
and the yelling of the men. She heard her daddy yelling about something. He stopped the car and two other men quickly opened the
hood and leaned in. Her daddy was standing there beside the car when
he turned around suddenly and saw her standing there a few feet
away.

"Hey! What the hell are you doing down here? Didn't I tell you I'd
bust your face if you came down here again?"

Then he came toward her, menacingly.

"I catch you talking to that little creep again and I'll kill him," he
told her quietly. "I'll chop his head off! It'll be all your fault, too! Now
get back on the blanket where you belong! Beat it!"

She crept back to the blanket, trying not to think about anything.
Suddenly, she heard screams and yelling all around her, and all kinds
of noise and confusion down by the pit. People stood up and started
pointing out over the track. Little Andrea stood up and stared through
a forest of legs out onto Trinity Speedway, where she saw a race car
tipped over and smoking on the track.

She was scared—so scared—to look out there and see what it was.
She knew what had happened. Pete Smith got killed because of her
thoughts. She had wanted Pete Smith to be her daddy and for her
daddy to die. She made Pete Smith die because he was the man she
wanted for her daddy. Her daddy had found out her thoughts, and now
he killed Pete Smith to punish her.

Pete Smith got killed, and it was all her fault!

Little Andrea couldn't move. She looked away from all the noise and
the confusion, way off down the grassy field beside the track, and then
she saw the angels again. They didn't look as bright as they had in the
car, against the dark brown seat, but she could still see them in the air.
She walked toward them, wanting to greet them, and then she felt a
warm touch on her hand and she looked up and saw a man holding
her hand. She had never seen him before, but she knew somehow that

he wasn't going to hit her or be mean. His eyes had a special place in them that told her he was good, and when he spoke his voice was beautiful and calm. He said his name was Michael. He was wearing dark clothes and a dark hat.

"You have a very special friend who lives in the sky with the birds and the clouds and the sun," Michael said as they walked away down the grassy field. "And this very special friend asked me to come down to the track to watch over you. Do you know who that very special friend is?"

"No," Little Andrea said.

"He's your real father, and he loves you. He'll love you forever. Inside all people, there is something that belongs to their real father. And when we go to live in the sky, the part of us that belongs to our real father knows how to find him, way up in the sky."

He looked down at her and winked.

"There's a light inside you, kind of like a porch light, that he can see when you're in danger and you cry inside. When you turn on the porch light in your heart, he'll send me to help you."

"Can I go live with my real father?"

"Well," said Michael with a smile, "there's something special that your real father wants you to do for him. You'll have to be the strongest little girl in the whole world to do it, though."

She showed him her muscle, and his eyes lit up like nothing she had ever seen before.

"There will be times when you're afraid, and times you'll feel alone, but you must never forget that your real father watches over you always. And that he'll send me to help you when there is danger."

He smiled again.

"You are the strongest little girl in the world," he said.

The next thing she knew, she was standing down the field and her mother was coming toward her.

"I'll always be near," Michael whispered. "Remember what I told you."

But when she glanced back to see him, Michael was gone.

In her hand was a pretty seashell.

When her mother got to her, she grabbed Little Andrea by the hair and pulled her back down toward the track.

"Don't I have enough to worry about without having to find a lost kid?" she shrieked. "You're really going to get it when you get home!"

"But Mama, I wasn't lost! I was with Michael!"

Her mother slapped her.

"I won't have you lying to me! I won't have a liar! You're going to get a mouthful of soap when we get home!"

When they got back to their blanket by the track, her daddy was there. He looked different. He looked funny. She could see a light around him, but it was a dark light. His eyes looked like those of the lizards in the backyard. She was more afraid of him than ever before. It was like she didn't recognize him, even though he was still her daddy. She knew that if she made him mad, he would hurt her in ways that were worse than beatings. She was afraid to go near him because the dark light was nasty and smelled bad.

From that day on, something had changed between them. She knew that if he had the chance, he would kill her. She was so happy Michael had told her about the porch light in her heart.

Chapter 12

It was around Christmastime of 1977, only a few months after Liz invited Michael back into her life, that the strange occurrences in the house on Walnut Street began. By the time they all ended a month later, in January 1978, Liz and all the rest of them had never needed Michael so badly in their lives.

In the beginning, she experienced a vague, smothery, anxious feeling when she walked into the house, a little like Me-Liz had felt just before the wreck in Arizona. That was easy enough to explain away—there were always anxiety and tension between her and Sandy now. The house was full of it. To Penny's everlasting sorrow, the sweet fragrance of love had faded out of the house not long after the wedding flowers had wilted.

Then small objects started disappearing. Often they'd reappear again, hours later, just where she'd left them. The disappearances were troublesome, but they weren't hard to explain away either. She'd just misplaced her scissors or her book. She'd just forgotten. Things had just slipped her mind.

Then she began discovering lights turned on in rooms where she could have sworn there were no lights on. She kept discovering the attic door standing ajar, even though she always kept it locked because none of them except Me-Liz felt comfortable going up there. She heard doors rattling in the night. Rooms would grow noticeably cold. And then one night, home alone, she walked into the living room to discover a blazing fire in the fireplace that she knew for certain she had not started. Chills danced all over her skin.

Sarah McClendon did not help her state of mind at all. Sarah, the mother of a girl she worked with at the frame shop, lived in a rambling, eccentric old house in Greensboro and was reputed to be a dabbler in spiritualism and the occult. She had a yard sale one day, and Me-Liz was poking through the lama rugs, jade Buddhas, and incense holders when Sarah approached her.

"I've got a friend who's a psychic, and she told me something you really ought to know about," Sarah said to Me-Liz. "She said she saw black clouds over your house when she was driving by there the other day. She said there was something evil in your house."

Panic welled up in Me-Liz's heart. Maybe there *was* something evil in the house. Maybe there was something evil . . . in *her*. Only Kitty understood that some of what was going on could be explained by the others. One of them would turn a light on, another would discover it. One of them lit the fire, another one discovered it. She wasn't exactly clear about why they only now began to notice these things—after all, this had been happening all their lives—and she did not understand at all the metaphysical aspect of what was going on. Only Me-Liz knew about that—yet she did not know about the others. Each of them understood a part of it, but no one understood all of it.

Like the thing Me-Liz saw in the attic. It would always be in the same place when she went up there: a swirling mass of light, flecked with blue and yellow, like a little whirlpool or tornado lit from within. She would stand there and watch, more awed than scared, until it spun itself away after five or six seconds. Psychomotor seizures? Reflections? Insanity? Or something else? She told people at work about what was going on in the house, but they all seemed skeptical. They seemed to take a few steps backward, emotionally, even as she spoke. Sandy, especially, seemed to have had about enough. He didn't want to hear about it anymore. He didn't want it in his house.

When Me-Liz asked her newly returned friend and teacher, Michael, about what was going on in the house, his manner was always calm and grave.

"It is all for a reason," he would say, standing beside her wearing his dark hat and dark coat, like a man waiting for a train. "Doors are being opened to you. You are undergoing a tremendous transforma-

106

tion, my child. Sometimes the energies you have unleashed spill out into this dimension.

"Picture it this way: imagine walking fast holding a full glass of water. If you are well-balanced, you can do it, and two worlds—the world within the glass, and the world outside it—can coexist without making contact. But if you are a child, you're bound to spill a few drops. Then the world within the glass spills out into the world outside the glass. Two dimensions meet, often in surprising and unexpected ways. There are many, many parallel dimensions that exist, and you are still but a child with these new powers. Be careful."

Sometimes she tried to tell other people about Michael, but that only made them think she was *really* nuts. One of the few people who seemed willing to listen was a strange little man named Eric Sparrow, a "semiretired" Vietnam vet who had lived all over the world and considered himself a student of the occult. Sparrow always wore a black leather jacket and a green beret, and had the small, pointed face of a fox: a sandy beard; flaring, pointed ears; bright, sly eyes.

ERIC SPARROW: One night Elizabeth and I we were sitting on the couch in that house on Walnut Street, talking about the occult and all that kind of thing. She was interested in the occult, ESP, you know— things that most people scoff at—and I guess she felt she could confide in me without being considered a full-blown bozo. There were some strange things going on in that house at the time. There were some rooms in that house that were nice, warm and toasty, and you'd walk into the next room and it'd be almost icy cold. I experienced that in that house, walking from one room to another. Bad heating system? I don't think so. All the doors were open. She was definitely under the impression that it was haunted. She was scared.

Anyway, we're sitting on the couch and all of a sudden we could hear voices, or a voice. It was a language I'd never heard before, and I've heard everything from Spanish and Russian to Chinese and Lebanese. I could recognize those languages. My first thought was, well, there's a ra- dio on. The stereo and TV were sitting side by side and I went over and checked, and they were both turned off. Then I unplugged them, just to make sure, and we could still hear the voice. It didn't last a long time; it was almost like short bursts of messages (for lack of a better term), trans- missions, or whatever. We actually tried to write them down, phoneti- cally, the best we could.

She started panicking. She was scared, she was shaking. She thought it was coming out of her stomach, and she asked me to put my hand on her stomach to see if it was. I felt vibrations, but whether that was just a physical reaction or a transfer of energy, I really can't say. That was a very strange experience, but I can't say I was frightened. She was; I was just interested. I've experienced strange things all my life, I've been all around the world, and I've seen voodoo in Haiti, juju in Africa. I've seen them work. I know about the power of the psychic realm. So I wasn't surprised or frightened by what I experienced in that house.

All the scary things that were occurring in the house—the phantom voice, the rattling doors, the coldness in the rooms, the fire—escalated over a period of a few weeks, to the point where all the others had become genuinely frightened. It was Penny Lavender who finally decided to ask Sarah McClendon if she could be of any help. If there were evil spirits or something in the house, maybe she could help her get rid of them. Penny drove by Sarah's house after work one Wednesday evening, on her way to a Doc Watson concert at the university.

Penny took an almost instant dislike to Sarah; she was suspicious that at least some of the trouble was actually coming out of *her*—this was the woman, after all, who'd told her there were black clouds over her house. Still, Penny was not completely sure there *weren't* black clouds over her house, so she let Sarah burn a candle and say some words that were supposed to be a cleansing ritual. They were supposed to rid her and the house of evil spirits. Then Sarah gave her a vial of "holy water," a candle and a cross on a chain, which she told her to wear in the house. They were gifts—for a donation of ten dollars.

It was Kitty who left the house, drove away, and had stopped at a stoplight a few blocks from Sarah's house when, to her amazement, the cross somehow flipped up and slapped her in the lip. She looked down and saw the cross tugging or bouncing to one side, as if it were trying to pull itself off. Then it simply fell off the chain into her lap. The cross was three inches high by one-and-a-half inches wide, made of two unadorned chrome bars notched to fit together. The chain passed through a hole drilled in the longer, upright bar; it wasn't simply attached by a ring. The scary thing was that when it came off the chain around her neck was unbroken.

She tucked the cross inside her glove and went into Aycock Auditorium to meet Cindy and a bunch of other people from Picture Perfect for the concert. She was breathlessly telling Cindy about what had happened when the cross seemed to grow hot in her hand. She pulled off the glove, and the cross lay in her open palm—broken apart into two pieces. The two notched bars, soldered together to form a cross, had fallen apart. Her palm was reddened, but not burned, from the heat. Her heart felt sick.

They stayed for the concert, but Kitty wasn't paying a bit of attention. Afterward, the whole crowd went over to her house on Walnut Street for punch and cookies. By that time, everyone knew about the strange things that were going on there, and when she told them about the cross, they all seemed a little uneasy. Cindy called her mother from Liz's house, and Sarah told her another cleansing ritual Liz was supposed to perform at all the doors, windows, and everywhere pipes entered the house. But it was just too weird. Nobody wanted to stick around for the show. One by one, they all took their leave.

Sandy and Me-Liz walked around the house with a lit candle, saying the words Sarah had given her at the doors and windows. The cats were skittish and agitated, and she heard a rattling sound in the sewing room, but when it was over, she felt better. The house seemed to be hers again. Me-Liz felt scared and sheepish. She felt certain—or almost certain—there were no evil spirits in the house, even though Sarah and everybody else seemed convinced the house was haunted. She wanted so much for it to be that simple, but it wasn't. It was much stranger and more complicated than that. Why couldn't Sarah, who was supposed to know about all this stuff, really understand what was going on?

Michael had told her that all these things were happening for a reason. The "powers" she'd been given were taking on new strength, they were being sharpened and refined, and sometimes they were just a little hard to control. She was like a little kid trying to ride a wild horse. At other times, she couldn't bring herself to believe that at all. Something else, something scarier, was going on. But whatever it was, she recognized that it had to be dealt with. Things had to be brought to a head.

On Monday, January 16, 1978, Penny's friend David B. H. Powers stopped by and she told him about what was going on.

"Who do I get to fix a haunted house?" Penny asked. "What do I need? A priest?"

David happened to have seen a lighthearted little story about famous North Carolina ghosts in a local city magazine.

"I don't know, maybe this reporter could help," he said.

He fished the magazine out of his car and gave it to her. It was Penny Lavender who called the reporter, Stefan Bechtel, as soon as David left.

STEFAN BECHTEL: She sounded so sane! That was my primary impression. She sounded like an ordinary housewife, agitated and upset, but perfectly lucid and reasonable. That's why I listened to her, even though the story she proceeded to tell me was preposterous. Fires that started by themselves, footsteps, rooms that got cold. It sounded like something out of The Amityville Horror, *which was a big book at the time. I listened to what she had to say, and then I gave her the number of a guy at Guilford College named Bill Beidler, a professor of Buddhist and Hindu philosophy who was supposed to know a lot about this kind of thing. I also got her number and told her I'd call her back. I don't know—I was fascinated. I took her seriously, I'm not sure why.*

Penny called Beidler's number right away. He wasn't home but his wife, Charlotte, answered the phone. She was remarkably sympathetic, and not even all that suprised by the story Penny told. Charlotte gave her a mantra, or chant, to speak aloud in the house:

"I'm surrounding myself and this house and everything in it in circles and circles of the great white Christ light. And nothing shall enter here except the true, the beautiful, and the good. I'm making myself positive against all lower rates of vibration and I'm receptive only to the highest."

Shortly before five o'clock, Penny got off the phone. Then Me-Liz lit the candle Sarah had given her, walked into the dining room, and started saying the mantra aloud. That's when all hell broke loose. The house started to grow cold. She heard what sounded like dishes clattering lightly in the kitchen, and the floor began to tremble. Then, suddenly, the floor started rippling in front of her eyes. All the doors started flying open and slamming shut, faster and faster—she could see the shadow of the kitchen door swinging full-arc, and then the vacuum cleaner moving around the room all by itself. The cats were going crazy; the puppy went to the bathroom on the floor and scampered out the kitchen door. There was a bad smell in the house—a smell of rotting—cow manure or something. And there were animal sounds—she could hear animal sounds. The whole house was filled with the sound of cows and sheep and goats, mooing and baaing.

The others were bursting in and out like mad, and all of them—even Kitty—were terrified. Me-Liz ran back into the study, horrified and crying, and tried to call Charlotte Beidler back, but the line was busy.

The rattan couch was squeaking. It was moving. Moving! How could it be moving? She got through on the second try.

CHARLOTTE BEIDLER: The first time she called, she seemed fairly calm, but the second time she was screaming and yelling and crying into the phone. She was extremely upset. There was a tremendous racket in the background, but I couldn't make out what it was. She told me there were cows mooing in her house and all this other stuff, and what was she supposed to do? What do you do when a lady tells you there are cows mooing in her house? You tell her to get out of there!

Charlotte gave Me-Liz directions to her house, and then Me-Liz bolted out. Once outside, she had enough presence of mind to notice that the house itself was not actually shaking, and she couldn't hear the sound of cows at all. Seizure activity of unknown origin? Satan? Insanity? She made it to Beidler's house, pale and shaken, and Charlotte gave her tea and tried to calm her down. Charlotte's husband was already on his way home.

When Dr. Beidler got home—a tall, gangly, slightly distracted-looking man who bore a slight resemblance to the Cowardly Lion in *The Wizard of Oz*—he called a friend, Jerry Solfvin, at the Psychical Research Foundation in Durham. Solfvin, a veteran investigator of paranormal occurrences who really had been called in on the *Amityville Horror* case, promised to round up his equipment and drive over from Durham, an hour away. While they were waiting, Me-Liz had Charlotte call Sandy at work, where he was working the late shift, and her friend Doug Hart at the frame shop. She was too upset to do it herself. It was after dark before Solfvin showed up in a beat-up borrowed car, and then he, Dr. Beidler, Me-Liz, Doug, and Sandy went back to the house.

DOUG HART: Liz was very agitated that night, she'd go back and forth between fear and seeming delight at all this exciting stuff that was happening in her house. I went back to the house with them because I was concerned for their safety. I wanted to see an end to the weirdness. I'd become fast friends with Sandy; he was definitely under the impression that something weird was going on in that house. He was pretty scientific, you know, but this stuff was beginning to get to him—it was coming into his house at night while he was sleeping. That's bound to get to a person. I didn't know what to expect when we got to the house— whether there'd be a rebellion from all this energy, or what.

111

It had been more than four hours since Liz had left the house, but there was a fire blazing in the fireplace when they got there. The vacuum cleaner was standing in the middle of the room. Other than that, though, there was nothing that couldn't be explained away. Me-Liz was still upset and nervous. She was afraid they'd tell her she was crazy. She wanted something to *happen* to prove to them that she wasn't. Solfvin attached two small electrodes to her scalp and set up a portable brain wave (EEG) detector that transmitted EEG pulses to a tape recorder that recorded them on ordinary audiotape. He recorded for over an hour.

BILL BEIDLER: What you have to remember is that all psychic phenomena emanate from some living person. Houses are not haunted; people are. So Elizabeth became the object of the investigation. She was apparently experiencing some quite disturbing PK phenomena [PK, or psychokinesis, means psychic phenomena involving disturbances of physical objects]. What she described sounded like typical poltergeist activity.

It's well established that in cases of this type, there is invariably a human agent—very often a young, emotionally disturbed female—at the center of it all, whether this be flights of glassware or levitating furniture or whatever. The literature has also shown that many of these agents have a history of epilepsy, or epilepticlike behavior, so naturally we were intrigued when she told us she'd once been diagnosed as having epilepsy.

JERRY SOLFVIN: There are some other fascinating connections between epilepsy and poltergeist activity. For instance, many epileptics can foretell, by strange tastes or smells or feelings, that a seizure is about to take place a few seconds or minutes before it does. It's called the "epileptic aura." Often epileptics will smell sulphur. The same is true of poltergeists: we hear over and over again about people "just knowing" that a lamp is about to go flying, or whatever.

Anyway, whenever a poltergeist case comes up, we're always interested in getting EEG data on the neurophysiological status of the agent. We're specifically looking for epileptic "spiking" in the brain waves, which is normally pretty easy to recognize, because of this fascinating potential connection between epilepsy and poltergeist activity. In Liz's case, though we did find some epilepticlike spiking, it wasn't clear—it could have been caused by muscle activity, a loose electrode, or something else. It was inconclusive.

BILL BEIDLER: My subjective impression was that she really wanted to verify it, because she wasn't sure what was going on herself. But in the end, it was just not clear what was going on. I never actually witnessed the psychokinesis. It wasn't clear whether it was true poltergeist activity, an epileptic seizure, a psychotic episode, or what. Lying doesn't come into it in my book—these people don't lie. They may misperceive what's been going on, but they don't lie.

I don't think she was possessed. I've been investigating this sort of thing all my adult life, and I'm certain that it's possible for entities to enter humans. I've seen some woozies! I've seen one or two in Chapel Hill, and in India, that would curl your hair. But that's not what was happening here.

In the end, I tend to think that what she was experiencing was third chakra phenomena—she was someone who worked out of the third chakra, but she didn't know how to control it. That would be the tantric explanation. The third or manipura chakra, located at the solar plexus, right behind the navel, is the vast pool of energy that produces all psychokinetic phenomena. It's also thought by some to be associated with the physical phenomena of epilepsy—seizures and the like. It could be that a projection of that energy is what produces ghosts and PK phenomena, by some means we don't understand.

JERRY SOLFVIN: I felt strongly that Liz was telling the truth about what she'd experienced. But my general impression of the case was that the things that had occurred could have been explained by moments of dissociation, or misperceptions, on her part. The things she described were clearly the types of things people report in poltergeist cases, but there just weren't sufficient other witnesses for me to feel comfortable concluding that it was poltergeist activity. A petit mal epileptic seizure can produce all kinds of distortions in perception. I just didn't have sufficient data to reach any conclusions one way or the other.

CHARLOTTE BEIDLER: Elizabeth wasn't the first person like this in our lives, although she was one of the strangest—and Bill has had some very strange students over the years, people who had paranormal abilities or paranormal experiences. Somehow they always ended up on our doorstep. I felt sad for her, because I knew she was extremely mixed up. Sandy came over here one night not long after that business in the house because he'd started to wonder about her sanity. I think all of his friends had started to wonder about her, too.

Whatever it was that had been going on in the house on Walnut Street, Sandy Lentz had had enough. Early that summer of 1978, he moved out for good.

Chapter 13

When Sandy moved out, the girls were devastated, each in her own way. Still, sometimes they had to sympathize with him. It was just too weird for anybody: ghostbusters in the bedroom; cleansing rituals and holy water; guys with EEG recorders, trying to figure out if there were poltergeists coming out of her brain! In the end, Liz got the impression Sandy wasn't sure what had even happened—if anything. He wasn't positive she wasn't making the whole thing up. He didn't know whether to believe her or not, and he no longer cared.

He just wanted out.

DAVID POWERS: It doesn't surprise me that Sandy is still unwilling to talk about what happened. As far as him verbalizing a lot of things about what was going on—well, that was not his suit. But I think he was very, very uncomfortable with the whole situation. In those last days before he moved out, he just got quieter and quieter. He started spending less and less time at home. I think he felt his wife was not who he thought she was. I don't think he knew who she was. He started getting a lot of peer pressure put on him to get the hell out of that marriage, especially after he came under the influence of Doug and Cindy Hart, and in the end I think he just gave up.

When Sandy moved out, the friends the two of them had made at Picture Perfect seemed to join hands in a great circle of support—around him, not her. Liz got the message. Everyone would prefer that she just politely go away. She had put Sandy through enough. People didn't trust her anymore. She couldn't keep her stories straight. She couldn't be believed. And the "haunting" in her house—if it was true—was just too creepy for words. Nobody wanted to get involved, or hear about it anymore. They just wanted her to go away.

PAULA PYNE: We talked about her a lot after she'd gone out of our lives, because she affected so many people in such a negative way that I guess it was therapeutic for us to talk about her and get her out of our systems, especially for Sandy. A few years later, Sandy was back in town and a bunch of us got together and I brought up Elizabeth's name, I don't know why. There were four of us in the room and the other three just shut up; there was a moment of silence, almost. It was really peculiar. And then Cindy said something like, "We don't talk about her anymore," and I said, "Yeah, right!" and everybody laughed and we went on. She's just a part of the past now.

All the girls were heartbroken over the breakup of the marriage, but none was sorrier than Penny Lavender. It was Penny who loved Sandy, and Penny who married him. When she lost him, she hurt so badly she could hardly speak. How was it possible that her dreams of everlasting romance were dissolving around her like a mist? The love of her life had said yes to her forever! Now he was gone, like smoke, like rain, like something that never was. Everything always vanished that way. Nothing lasted. Everything eventually turned to smoke and steam and then it blew away.

Little by little, over the months that followed, Penny grew absolutely mute. The only way she could speak was in song—she would either say nothing at all, or she would sing it, in a dreary, monotonous cadence, like children will sometimes sing stories to themselves while lost in play. Naturally, people found this odd, so for a long time Penny just stayed inside, in her whitewashed cabin by the surrealistic, perfect pond, where a new story had been carved in the fantastic bedposts. She'd had her fill.

It was a long time before Penny started coming out again—usually in bars, drunk, and singing sad, sentimental old songs for strange men. After that, she began to write melancholy songs and stories of her own, about jilted lovers and things gone awry. Everything became a song or a story. Everything became fiction. That way it didn't hurt.

When Sandy moved out that summer of 1978, the marriage had ended in reality, although the legalities of the divorce dragged on over the next several years. Papers filed in Guilford County District Court show that on March 17, 1980, Sandy filed a claim asking that the marriage be dissolved. Liz did not respond to the summons, contest the divorce, or ask for support or alimony. The marriage simply died without protest from either party.

Liz quit her job at the frame shop not long after Sandy left her. She was being subtly pressured to leave, and she didn't want to be around those people, or those memories, anymore. She found another job picking up hangers and tagging merchandise and doing general maintenance in the warehouse of a discount clothing chain called the Clothes Horse, a place that specialized in moderately priced, dressy clothes for young working women. It was low-paying, menial work, but it was about as much as Liz could handle. Still, she did well, and within a few weeks moved up to doing inventories. At that point, things got interesting enough to be worthy of Kitty's attention, so she came out, looked around, and took over the job. From then on, she was almost always the one who went to work. Another six-month cycle had begun: bottom to top to bottom inside of half a year.

Within six weeks of the time Liz was hired, Kitty was taken out of the warehouse and promoted to "internal auditor." Her job, along with one other woman, was to monitor all the receipts and cash that would come in every day from the thirty-odd other Clothes Horse stores in the area, and then turn it all over to the company controller. It was an almost-executive-level job, at least in her own mind, and one that showed she was trusted. She was proud of that. Kitty looked good in Clothes Horse clothes, and partly because she could get them at a discount, she started buying lavishly: business suits in subdued colors, with little ties; slacks, jackets, and heels; a briefcase with an over-the-shoulder strap; a royal purple silk dress, almost Grecian-looking, cut on the bias and draped like a gown—extremely sensual and very sophisticated. She started thinking of herself as a lady executive. She was making money again, dressing well, and starting to feel good about herself. She started going on buying trips to New York with one of the company vice-presidents. She felt she was finally living at her rightful level.

Meanwhile, the other girls had begun to spin off into strange new orbits of their own, like lopsided moons. They were going nowhere. They all felt sad and confused and without a center after Sandy left. Their response to the emptiness in their hearts was to seek men—hungrily, indiscriminately, and with an energy that seemed inexhaustible. It was as if they were starving. Their lives passed into a period of disorder and epic promiscuity—or so it seemed to other people, since the person they knew as Elizabeth Lentz was sometimes carrying on with four, five, or six different men at once. Yet none of the girls considered themselves promiscuous; after all, each of them individually was seeing only one or two different men.

At one time, Liz was carrying on with a dissolute thief and drug addict named Marty Steele; Kitty had a fine, trusting friendship with a black pro basketball player named Ace Radiwill, as well as a ferocious, obsessive love affair with a musician named Steve Head; a man named Bobby was emotionally abusing Me-Liz; and Penny had found one of the sweetest, kindest men in her life in the form of a homely insurance salesman named David Kraut.

All the girls longed for that sweet restfulness that comes from being loved. They all desperately sought something to cling to and clutched at any drifting thing that floated past. Sometimes, briefly, they found it. But more often, they found themselves tangled in dark, self-destructive alliances with men who used them, abused them, and then threw them away. Liz, especially, seemed to be a kind of heat-seeking missile specially attuned to sons-of-bitches. She could find them anywhere.

For a few months, Liz was intensely involved with Marty Steele, a man who picked her pockets as sweetly and completely as he could. He was addicted to something, Liz didn't know what—she'd seen him shooting it into his arm. But he was funny and sexy, and after a few weeks she let him move his stuff into the house on Walnut Street. A few weeks later, he started borrowing a little money now and then—twenty dollars, thirty dollars. She always gave him what she had. When he asked for two hundred dollars, she provided, hard as it was to scrape together the cash. When he upped the ante to five hundred dollars, Liz went down to a seedy storefront loan operation in Greensboro and borrowed the money at a criminal interest rate.

Then Liz came back to the house one day and discovered that Marty's clothes were gone. So was the beloved dulcimer Sandy's father had made for Penny for Christmas, as well as an old violin and all her jewelry. The next morning, Kitty called Marty at work and discovered he had vanished from there, too—along with five thousand dollars out of the company safe. Kitty filed a civil complaint against him in a small claims court, but in the end, he beat it out of town with everybody's money.

KIT CASTLE: Liz felt terribly sad about losing the dulcimer, but she resigned herself to it. She figured she had it coming. It was her due. The same old pattern emerged: again, she was the victim; again, she was the one who paid. It wasn't that she consciously sought out situations like this in her life; it was just that, somehow, they kept happening to her. That's why she stopped calling her parents in those later years—she didn't need them to punish her anymore. It was life that was punishing her now.

But Kitty also had a way of attracting strange men—like Larry Bell. She met him in a nightclub one night when she was depressed, and they hit it off immediately. She needed comforting, and he was more than willing to care for and comfort her. He took her out to his house, a log cabin deep in the woods outside of town, where he treated her kindly but refused to have sex with her. He had three locks on each door and two locks on each window, and she watched uneasily as he walked all the way around the house, locking the top row of locks first, and then going all the way around the house a second time to lock the second row, and then the third. There was something shifty about him, eerie, paranoid. Kitty knew when it was leaving time, but Liz recognized a kindred spirit. It was she who came out when Kitty went under, and from then on it was she who continued the relationship.

Larry Bell began parading Liz around in public in a way clearly intended to make other people think they were sleeping together, but in private he refused to touch her. And then she became indebted to him in a way she couldn't explain to anybody. At one point in the fall of 1978, when her drinking was getting out of control, her financial situation deteriorated to the point of desperation again: She couldn't pay the bills, her heat had been turned off, and the gas was shut off. For help, she turned to Larry Bell. He went to the bank and took out a seven-hundred-dollar personal loan for her—but first he made up a list of things from her home that he would count as collateral, including her dulcimer and jewelry. Later, after Marty Steele ripped her off, Larry came over to her house, fished out his "contract" with her, and crossed out the jewelry and instrument. Then, with a great flourish, at the bottom of the page, he wrote, "eternal bondage."

"I don't know what you mean," Liz said.

"It means if you can't pay this loan, I own your soul," Larry Bell told her. "If you can't pay this loan within eight months, you will become my full-time slave. That's the deal. I've got your signature on it."

He was looking at her strangely. She could hardly believe it, but this man was actually serious! For months afterward, as her life fell apart piece by piece and she teetered closer and closer to bankruptcy, Larry Bell's "contract" on her soul became a source of deep, steady fear, like a radio star emitting pulses from some dark night sky inside her. She was terrified that if she couldn't manage to work off her eternal debt, this strange man would lock her in his cabin with the three locks on every door and never let her out.

Or something worse.

Meanwhile, at the Clothes Horse, Kitty was scrambling up the rungs as fast as she could go. She fit very naturally into the bosses' clique, where it was an unwritten rule that cocktail hour started on the job, at around three o'clock. By five, everyone had had two or three drinks, and then after work everybody would go down to a Mexican joint called Tijuana Fats and drink tequila until six or seven. "Liquor by the drink" had recently been legalized in North Carolina—for the first time, mixed drinks, not just wine and beer, could be served in bars and restaurants—so everyone seemed to be celebrating the state's new loss of sobriety.

It was the heydey of the disco era, so Kitty would get home from work already manageably drunk, shower up, get dressed, and go out to the discos to dance until all hours. For the first time in their lives, the girls—all of them—began drinking. Kitty and Penny Lavender loved tequila, straight up. Liz liked gin and tonics. Me-Liz would sip white wine—spiritually. And when the night was getting on and the suckers started lining up around the pool tables, Kitty would crack out the Wild Turkey.

During a night in which Kitty was drinking Wild Turkey, Penny was drinking tequila, Me-Liz was drinking wine, and Liz gin and tonics, they could all put down a phenomenal amount of liquor. The physical body was taking in enormous amounts of alcohol, but each personality was not getting as cumulatively drunk as a single person would have. The little girl with the heart-shaped face and the curly red hair

120

developed a reputation for being able to hold her liquor as well as any man. The trick, of course, was that she had three female assistants behind the curtain.

JEFF BRYANT, a friend: Oh man, that woman could drink! I remember once we went into New York Pizza, down on Tate Street [in Greensboro] and she asked the bartender to fill up a tall glass of tequila—seven shots—and she drank it right down, through a straw. Then we went over to Logans and she had three or four beers. She didn't get ill, she didn't get sloppy, she didn't get wild—if her behavior changed at all, she just got quieter. I think she was incredibly willful about her drinking. She told me she drank a quart of tequila a day, and after that I believed her.

There was always a designated driver to get them home—usually Me-Liz, who always sipped her wine demurely, in moderation. At first there were never any hangovers, either, despite the mixing. Whoever had been drinking least the night before was the one who got up and went to work the next morning. They operated like a tag team, and that way managed to drink as much as they liked while never missing a day of work.

Still, it gradually began to dawn on Kitty that she was developing a drinking problem. She was drinking in her office as much as everybody else, but she also began drinking in secret. She had tequila bottles hidden in the car, bottles in the rest room at work. Liz was also drinking too much, and so was Penny. The whole thing was beginning to spin out of control—and for Kitty, losing control was the thing to be feared above all.

Then, for the first time in her life, Kitty got jilted, badly. From the moment she met Steve Head at a local art gallery opening, it was spontaneous combustion. There was an immediate, animal attraction between them, and within hours after their eyes met, they were in bed. The next morning, when they got to talking, Me-Liz discovered to her delight that Steve also shared her interest in the psychic realm—her favorite subject. She told him about the "haunting" in her house, and he listened. After that, Me-Liz began developing her own, intensely spiritual relationship with Steve, at the same time Kitty pursued her intensely sexual one. That was one of the most peculiar and special things about their relationship: it had never happened before that Me-Liz and Kitty both fell in love with the same man. Usually it was Liz and Me-Liz who loved a man, or Kitty and Penny; they were almost like two sets of twins in that way. But Steve seemed to satisfy two diverse, desperate needs, and they couldn't get enough of him.

It lasted three months or so, and then Kitty discovered he was seeing other people on the side. He was also married but separated, it turned out; when his wife came to town, the two of them decided to try patching things up. Kitty was forced out, and she did not know how to take it like a lady. She fumed, she raged, she schemed, she cried, and in the end she just threw up her hands and decided to party. Now there was a hard, vicious edge to her drunkenness, a self-destructive will.

DAVID POWERS: During that winter of 1978–79, she started drinking a whole lot. She was in real bad shape, and for the first time I began to think she really needed help. It's funny, but only when she was really depressed and boozing so bad did I ever think there was the possibility of real drastic problems with her. Only then did I really question whether the elevator went to the top with Liz. Whether she was hitting on all eight.

Kitty turned into a disco-bopping, nonstop party girl—the only time she ever stopped at home was to shower up or grab a few hours of sleep. Work turned into as much of a party as the parties were. Yet she was able to keep a cool, professional lid on it all until Liz started coming out at work. That's what finally blew it for Kitty. That's how she lost her job.

It had been a terrible year for Liz. Someone, some man, developed a fixation on her, and he seemed to be following her around town. It had started not long after Sandy left and she was living alone in the house on Walnut Street. She started getting weird, vaguely threatening phone calls. Then both she and her neighbor, Natalie, had the chilling experience of walking into a room before the light was turned on and seeing the dark silhouette of a man standing outside the window. She'd called the police, and for a few nights there were cops crouched in her attic, waiting to surprise the peeping Tom the same way the psychic investigators had tried to get the jump on the spooks a few months earlier. It was as if somehow the metaphysical threats had turned into physical ones. It was hard to tell which was worse. Either way, she was the target.

Then, not long after the peeping Tom incident, during the fall of 1978, Liz was driving home from downtown Greensboro in the early evening when suddenly a big hand closed around her mouth and she felt a knife at her throat.

"Keep driving, and don't look in the mirror," a man's voice growled.

There was an awful smell in the car, like sour piss. It smelled like the guy had peed in his pants. With the knife and the hand hovering around her neck, he made Liz drive out into the countryside outside Greensboro, and then back into town. An hour passed. It grew dark. Finally they ended up in Irving Park, a wealthy part of town with dark, twisty streets overshadowed by enormous trees. In a very dark part of that neighborhood, near a park, the man told her to pull the car over.

"Now I want you to take off the seat belt very slowly and climb over the back of the seat," he said, releasing his hand from around her neck. "Don't you run away from me now, girlie!"

Liz fumbled with the selt belt, pretending to be having trouble unfastening it.

"Hurry up!" he barked.

"It's the seat belt! I think it's jammed or something," Liz mumbled. She was stalling for time, fumbling with the seat belt, trying to get up the nerve to make a break for it. She couldn't do it. But moments later Kitty, the survivor, hit the door and took off running down the darkened street, screaming, finally clattering up the steps of a big house onto a lighted porch and pounding on the door until an elderly lady let her in and called the cops. The police brought tracking dogs that managed to pick up the man's trail out of the car into the park, then lost it. They never found the guy.

Liz was frantic. She was convinced it was the same guy who'd been calling her up and peeping in her windows at night. She was the target again, and he was still out there in the dark somewhere, watching her, waiting. She hated that creepy old house on Walnut Street but she didn't think she could afford to move.

It wasn't until he attacked her again that Liz came apart completely. Kitty was having lunch at a restaurant on Battleground Avenue with one of the bosses from the Clothes Horse when she noticed a man staring at her strangely. He was tall, white, and bald, with a bland, impassive face. As he walked past her table, suddenly she smelled it—that sour-piss smell she remembered from the kidnapping.

"Oh, my God! That's the guy!" she gasped. "That's the guy who's been following me around!"

At that moment, their eyes met and he realized she recognized him.

"Call the cops," she whispered to her friend. "Get 'em over here!"

Then she bolted into the rest room. Just before the door closed, she caught sight of the man very casually following her out of the dining room. It was Kitty who entered the bathroom, but it was Liz—the victim—who ended up locked in the bathroom stall, with the man trying to climb under the stall to get at her, while a cook and a busboy struggled to pull him away. Liz was absolutely hysterical. By the time the police got there, Kitty was back, but Liz had disappeared. She was so scared she had gone somewhere deep—very deep, somewhere that was utterly still and dark and completely outside of time.

It was unusual for any of them to go as deep as that. It was as if their usual rooms—Penny's whitewashed cabin, Liz's dark, sad hole— were just a backstage to consciousness, from which they could easily pop in and out. That's where they stayed most of the time. At other times if they were traumatized or scared, they'd go to deeper places, like a basement, that were harder to get out of; or even deeper, to subbasements beneath that. "Going deep" meant going all the way down to the bottom, below the subbasement rooms, to where there was no consciousness, no growth, no time, nothing. It was like putting themselves on ice, like entering a cryogenic tomb, where they'd sleep until some distant resurrection.

For Liz, it was a way of not having to deal with the assault at all. She had discovered a way of blotting herself out completely, a way of not experiencing—or at least delaying—the horror of what had happened. When she disappeared after a trauma like this, the others would come to the surface, and since they had not actually experienced the event itself, they recovered much more rapidly (physically and emotionally) than Liz would have been able to. She was known for her rapid recoveries. But it was only because she had three other women to help share the pain, and in that way accelerate the healing—or at least, the appearance of healing.

The police booked the man who assaulted her, a boarder who lived in a house not far from her house on Walnut Street. He had a history of treatment in psychiatric hospitals, and was taking some kind of medication that made his urine smell funny. Even though they couldn't pin the kidnapping on him, he stopped bothering her after that.

With Liz gone away, it was mostly Kitty and Penny who were out, drinking and partying and trying to hold down a job. But the drinking got steadily worse. Now there wasn't anybody left to stay sober. There was no designated driver, and nobody to go to work without a hangover. Kitty, Penny, and Me-Liz all began dragging into work with tremendous hangovers—and somehow, maybe because she was the only one without a headache, this forced Liz to pop to the surface, like a cork coming up from five-hundred feet below. The others needed a designated driver, and she was it.

Liz would be confused for a moment, and then she would try to adjust. Yes, she was all dressed up, at work, doing a job, checking cash register receipts, working at a place called the Clothes Horse . . . but her heart was in absolute turmoil. Going deep meant that she left time altogether; it was her impression, when she resurfaced, that the assault had just happened. She was still struggling to overcome her terror and rage at being assaulted, and her sense of helplessness because it *always* happened at the same time she was trying to count cash register receipts. She was struggling to be a lady executive while teetering on the brink of a nervous breakdown.

Her coworkers were quick to notice. They were all used to Kitty being there: either cool, competent and professional, or the life of the party, one or the other. Now, suddenly, here was this confused, shy mouse, either barely able to restrain her hysteria or weeping quietly into the receipts. She couldn't even work. Her boss, full of fatherly concern, told her he thought she needed to go into the hospital for nervous exhaustion. She was working too hard. The job was getting to her. Then one morning Liz woke up feeling dizzy and confused, and then she fell out of bed. When she got to work, she felt drugged and lethargic, and she kept smelling a terrible, rancid odor in the air, and tasting something sweet in the back of her mouth. For days afterward, everything seemed unreal. The walls seemed to be moving. Finally, at work one day, she fell out of her chair onto the floor. Somebody took her to the emergency room at Wesley Long Hospital while the others were popping in and out like mad, all of them confused and desperate and as scared as she was.

ADMITTED: 8/7/79

DISCHARGED: 8/11/79

DISCHARGE DIAGNOSIS: Partial complex seizure, psychomotor type, probable left temporal occipital focus.

BRIEF HISTORY: Patient had been well until 1979, 5 August, when she began having a weird feeling that persisted through the week. This was associated with olfactory and gustatory hallucinations. On examination at the time of admission the patient had a mild expressive speech disturbance . . .

LABORATORY DATA: EEG normal. CT scan with contrast normal. EKG normal. SMA-12, RPR, CBC, sedimentation rate, electrolytes, urinalysis, and chest X-ray normal.

CONDITION ON DISCHARGE: Improved.

"If there's any way you could afford it, I'd recommend that you spend a week or so in the hospital, restrict your visitors, and just try to pull yourself together again," the neurologist told her. "Get some rest."

She couldn't afford it, of course. All the girls were using the checkbook, and they'd nearly drunk it dry. There was almost nothing of value left in the house; they'd been selling things piece by piece to pay for the drinking. There was nothing left to sell. Kitty realized the cycle was quickly coming to an end. Dark water was closing over her head. Liz was too ill and too depressed to handle the job, and Kitty herself felt she was losing control of the others. She couldn't take care of her own anymore. And she knew very well she was losing control of her drinking.

It was Kitty who made the decision to quit the job before she got fired.

She felt overwhelmed and lost. Giving up her job was a failure that hit deep within her. Why did she ever think she was so smart and competent, such a hot number, such a climber? What did she have to show for all her supposed professional achievements? Nothing! Nothing! All she had was a lifetime of memories that didn't fit together, two failed marriages, a bad drinking habit, and a closet full of lady executive costumes. She had no money left. Steve Head had left her. Larry Bell was trying to sell her soul into slavery. And now—worst of all—Kitty discovered, in figuring out her bills, that she was missing time. It had never happened before. Something was terribly wrong. The others had always missed time—but it had never happened to her before. Kitty was scared. Did this mean she was having alcoholic blackouts? Was that what it was? What had she done that she couldn't remember? Or did it mean . . . there was somebody else inside her that she didn't know about?

The downward spiral gathered momentum, like an out-of-control carnival ride. The house bills just went unpaid. None of the ordinary responsibilities were important anymore—the only thing that mattered was the booze: getting high, getting loaded, getting on top of it all; disco dancing, drunk, in the delirious lights at three A.M.; hustling eight ball in some smoky dive. People would get Penny drunk and she'd sit on the bar and sing her sad songs to strangers. Bad checks started flying in every direction.

One night in a bar, Kitty met a nineteen-year-old waiter named William who needed a place to stay. She was desperate for money—she still owed Larry Bell a few hundred dollars, and his "contract" on her soul was running out—so she let him move in. A few weeks later, Liz came home late and found William and one of his buddies sitting on the couch laughing and pointing into a magazine, so she plopped down on the couch beside them. In a flash she realized they were looking at kiddie porn. An awful, sick feeling came over her from long, long ago; when William turned the page and there in front of her were photos of a young girl in a red silk nightie, sprawled across a motel room bed— a girl who looked so much like her it might have *been* her, sprawled across that bed in Austin all those years ago—it was as if the last straw was broken.

She just wanted to die.

Kitty woke up in her car, stark naked.

The car clock said 5:00 A.M. The windshield was covered with snow. She had no idea how she got there, but who cared? Her head clanged like a giant cymbal. She could hardly remember the last two weeks—a haze of drunkenness and blackouts, men's faces, and bursting and bursting as the others confusedly came and went. It seemed like she'd been living in the station wagon for days. She remembered Penny Lavender sitting on the bed in a house trailer, singing to a man named Wayne, who didn't understand she was about to kill herself. She remembered Liz telling everyone who would listen that she was going to commit suicide, and everyone laughing.

What had happened to her clothes? Even her purse was gone—only the car key was there, dangling from the ignition. She started the car and drove home as fast as she could. She ran into the house, got dressed and left, quickly. For some reason, she couldn't stay there anymore. She had breakfast and went to a bar where she met a man. They started talking. A half hour later, they left together, went to his place, and slept together. When she was sure he was asleep, Kitty got up and went through his drawers, looking for a gun. She couldn't find a gun, but she found pills—lots of pills. She stuffed her coat pockets full and left the house before he woke up.

She drove back home because she had nowhere else to go, but when she walked in the door, she gasped. The place was stripped—rugs, lamps, furniture, books, everything was gone except for the appliances and a pile of laundry. In the bathroom, she found a note taped to the mirror:

"Decided to close on your loan early. I've got everything. Larry."

Just then William came downstairs with a sheepish look on his face.

"What the hell is going on?" Kitty demanded. "Were you here when the bastard did this?"

"Yeah, well, he told me he looked it up in some law book, and it was legal. He came over last night when you were gone. I let him in."

"You let him in? How could you let him in! This isn't even your stuff to let him have!"

"He said he didn't think you were gonna pay him his money back. He wanted to get his money out of it."

Kitty turned on her heel, ran back out of the house, got in the car, and drove. But there was no place left to go. They were homeless now. Everything began to ripple as the others burst in and out, processing this new information. There was no place left to go. Aimlessly, not knowing what to do next, they drove around town making the rounds of the boyfriends, telling them all goodbye. They stopped at Wayne's trailer and left a note saying goodbye. They went to David Powers's house and told him they were leaving for Arizona and wouldn't be coming back. They left a note for David Kraut and Bobby and Allen. Finally they told some strangers in a bar.

Then Penny went out to the car and swallowed the pills by the handful, chased them with tequila, and drove to a park. It was early evening, and there was a little snow on the ground. Each of them decided to commit suicide individually. They tore up all their identification—driver's license, a Sears credit card, photos—and threw them away. They were nobody now.

Then they lay down in the snow-covered leaves and closed their eyes to die.

Chapter 14

It was nearly dark when Me-Liz woke up in the snowy park. Her head ached; she felt drowsy and sick. There was a bad taste in her mouth. *What now?* she wondered hazily. *What happened this time?* When she sat up, she noticed a half-empty tequila bottle lying in the leaves beside her. *Must've drunk myself silly. Gotta get help. Gotta call somebody.*

She found Lucy, her old, white station wagon, parked nearby. The car keys were in her coat pocket—along with a handful of empty pill bottles.

"Oh, God," she mumbled. "Must've done a buncha pills. Gotta call somebody."

She drove to a supermarket and called the local crisis hotline from a pay phone.

"I think I . . . I tried to commit suicide. I swallowed a buncha pills. I feel real . . . funny . . ."

Me-Liz was the only one of the girls who had not actually participated in the suicide attempt—her spiritual convictions would not have allowed it. She simply woke up in this situation, reached a reasonable conclusion about what had happened, and did the best she knew how to get herself out. She got directions to the hotline office, and as soon as she got there, she threw up. She stayed there that night under careful watch, and the next morning she was admitted to the psychiatric ward at Moses Cone Hospital, in Greensboro, as a suicide risk.

It was Kitty who talked with Dr. Imelda, the first psychiatrist to whom her case was assigned at Moses Cone, and she took an immediate dislike to him. The feelings, apparently, were mutual. Dr. Imelda's impatience is reflected in his case notes, dated February 25, 1980. After noting her attempted suicide by overdosing on pills, and her referral from the Drug Action Council, he wrote:

"RELEVANT HISTORY: The most notable feature about this lady's history is the impossibility of getting a coherent, adequate, chronological account of her life despite repeated attempts and trials to get her to give a consistent story. . . . She indicates that she had a very traumatic, unhappy childhood, with multiple episodes of abuse by her family and a tendency to be drifting, changes [sic] *places of residence frequently. She apparently subsequently got married and lived with her first husband for a short period of time, 'possibly some years, it was never clear,' and had three daughters from that marriage. Approximately ten years ago or so she had an episode when she lost her temper at her children and apparently attacked them, subsequently leaving the home in Texas and traveling east. She has not seen her children since and does not know their whereabouts precisely and does not know their ages. . . ."*

Kitty told Dr. Imelda about her epilepsy diagnosis in Minnesota, about having been seen in the University of North Carolina infirmary in 1977 for an apparent seizure, and about the extensive neurological workup that had been done. She told him about being readmitted to Wesley Long Hospital a second time, in August 1979, after the "weird sensations" continued. "At that time it was felt that the patient was possibly suffering from a psychomotor seizure disorder and again she was evaluated thoroughly, including a CT scan with contrast which was normal, an EEG which was normal, a cardiogram which was normal, and multiple other investigations. . . ." Dr. Imelda noted that neither one of these *neurological workups had shown any evidence that she was prone to epileptic seizures—yet one neurologist had concluded she probably did have a seizure disorder; the other concluded she did not.*

"The patient continued to have the weird sensations for a period of time and, according to her, became involved with a group who were interested in parasensory and parapsychic phenomena and got in touch with the Research Lab at Duke for parapsychic phenomena. The patient is convinced that she has clairvoyance and that 'weird things' happen

130

around her, which have apparently been confirmed by the people inter-
ested in the parapsychic phenomena. . . . Just prior to admission she had
been totally destitute with no money and had been evicted from her
apartment after the debtors apparently took her furniture. She had been
living out of her car for three days prior to admission. . . ."

Still, despite these bizarre tales, Dr. Imelda noted this about her men-
tal status: "At the time of admission the patient was pleasant and coop-
erative. She related very well to the examiner and had no abnormality of
speech. Thought processes showed no abnormality. . . . Her sensorium
was entirely clear. . . . She had a normal range of emotions and was not
particularly anxious or depressed. Despite the lack of obvious depressive
symptoms, the patient did complain of feeling suicidal, and in a some-
what bland manner . . . she repeatedly stated 'I'm a suicidal risk,' with-
out any show of anguish or depression. . . ."

The physical exam was normal, though Dr. Imelda noted that "the
patient . . . appeared considerably younger than her stated age of thirty-
one."

His overall impression at the time of her admission was that "it is not
clear whether this lady does indeed have a seizure-related disorder. The
impression is probably personality disorder with hysterical features."

Because of the conflicting diagnoses, her bizarre, fragmented personal
history, and because he suspected her problem was strictly psychiatric,
not neurological, "it was not felt advisable to subject this lady to further
diagnostic workups other than observation," Dr. Imelda noted later, in
his discharge summary. "Accordingly, she was observed closely over the
first few hospital days and placed on suicide precautions. The patient was
also seen daily in exploratory psychotherapy. . . ."

After her initial interview with Dr. Imelda, Kitty insisted that she
be given another psychiatrist, and she was reassigned to a Dr. Gilbertson, who began seeing her for an hour a day. But the therapy was next
to useless; alcoholism, the problem that had touched off this latest crisis, never even came up. Dr. Gilbertson never questioned the girls
about their drinking, and they never volunteered the information. In
true alcoholic fashion, they were able to deny to themselves that they
even had a problem. (Problem? When Kitty was released from the hospital, she found sixteen quart bottles of tequila—all empty—on the
floorboards of her car.) And, of course, Kitty never told Dr. Gilbertson
or anyone else about "the secret."

All the girls reacted differently to their new situation, in the clean,
safe prison of a psychiatric hospital. At first Penny Lavender was ter-

rified that they would try to make her talk, so she hid in lockers and behind washing machines and under beds. Then she was introduced to the dayroom, where there was an old upright piano, and she found her voice. She sat at the piano with her eyes closed for hours, singing herself far, far away:

> *I called to Penny Lavender*
> *And homeward she did run*
> *And right before my very eyes*
> *Penny faded and was gone.*
> *Sad Penny waits for love*
> *She sits alone just waiting*
> *Lovely Penny waits for love*
> *But it never comes!*

Liz had gone so deep she wasn't even benefiting from being there at all. Me-Liz had become increasingly absorbed in the psychic realm, visiting regularly with Michael and having her strange, unearthly visions. She didn't care if nobody believed her. Kitty's primary emotion was rage: she was furious that she had lost control, and almost gotten everybody killed in the process. It wasn't even she who had rescued them—it was Me-Liz. She tried to regain control of her new situation by counseling patients in the dayroom. Being the counselor meant that she was a paraprofessional: the healer, not the patient. It was the only way she knew of to start feeling good about herself again.

But it was alcohol that was really in control of her life. After she'd been in the hospital a few days, she was given a night pass to leave the building, and Kitty and her new friend from the psychiatric ward, Dinah, went straight to the bars. The two of them got a good tequila buzz going, and then they made the rounds of the discos, cruising for guys and dancing and drinking, suddenly free, laughing like crazy, full of reckless sexual energy. When they came stumbling back into the hospital, drunk, in the wee hours, nobody seemed to notice. She hadn't even left the hospital, and already she was caught up in the boozy downward spiral of her old life.

She was released after a couple of weeks in the hospital. Dr. Imelda dictated her discharge summary:

ADMITTED: 2/25/80
DISCHARGED: 3/12/80

ADMITTING DIAGNOSIS: (1) Probable personality disorder with hysterical features. (2) Rule out possible seizure disorder.

DISCHARGE DIAGNOSIS: Personality disorder with hysterical features.

COURSE IN THE HOSPITAL: Throughout her hospital stay, there was no evidence whatsoever of any seizure disorder. The patient adjusted well to the hospital milieu and after the first few days stopped complaining of feeling suicidal and the suicide precautions were discontinued. . . . The patient was given graduated outside privileges and eventually allowed full privileges [including an] overnight pass. It was noted that the patient was very friendly, cooperative, helpful with other patients, and very pleasant but no abnormality in her relationships or any evidence of depression was noted. . . . She was discharged on no medications and arrangements were made for her to follow up at the Mental Health Center for further psychotherapy exploration.

When Kitty got out, she went immediately to the house on Walnut Street—it was home, after all—but the moment she walked through the front door, reality kicked her in the head. She had completely forgotten. She didn't have a home. The house was trashed, empty. All the furniture was gone. And Larry Bell's foreclosure note was still taped to the bathroom mirror. She'd just gotten out of the psychiatric hospital, and already her life seemed in shambles.

Not knowing what else to do, Kitty salvaged whatever clothes she could find and got back in the car. She drove over to Dinah's apartment, and Dinah agreed to let her stay there, at least until she got back on her feet. She never made an effort to settle up with the landlord over the trashed house (most of the furniture didn't even belong to her—it was the landlord's). The hospitalization was never paid for. She was living from moment to moment. The dark water had come up around her head so fast this time that everybody except Kitty went deep. Nobody else knew how to deal with the fear and confusion, but Kitty always managed to land on her feet. She could handle it—or so she thought.

Kitty just wanted to forget about the past and invent a whole new life for herself, as she had so many times before. Just start over fresh. A whole new circle of friends, a new place to live, a whole new world. But instead, she began sinking almost immediately into the quicksand of alcoholism. She felt overwhelmed. She just couldn't do it this time. She had no home, no job, no lover, no money, nothing. Where was she going to go? What was she going to do? It was so much easier to just get numbed out again, to stop feeling, stop thinking, stop responding, stop being responsible. There were more alcoholic blackouts, and then one night, drunk and obnoxious, Kitty was thrown out of a restaurant on Tate Street. That had never happened to her before. She stumbled up the street to David Kraut's house through the snow, furious, weeping. He tried to comfort her and calm her down, but the others were popping in and out, all of them angry and confused, until finally she just slammed out of the house, throwing insults and curses back over her shoulder. She didn't need to be patronized. She didn't need any help. She'd do just fine. Just fine! "Screw you, man!" she screamed. "Screw you!"

The next morning Kitty woke up with a clanging tequila hangover and the awful memory of being thrown out of the restaurant like a tramp. She felt black. Nauseous. Her life seemed to have reached some new ultimate of degradation, and she finally admitted to herself that the drinking was out of control. It was only then that she dug in her purse for a business card she'd been keeping since she got out of the psychiatric ward—a card belonging to an Alcoholics Anonymous counselor named Bill Gormley, whom she'd met in the dayroom. Gormley, who'd been in the hospital counseling a lapsed alcoholic, was a big Santa Claus of a man, two hundred fifty pounds or more, with a barroom belly, big tattooed forearms, and a gentle, joking manner. He told Kitty that he'd turned his home into a kind of halfway house for detoxing alcoholics and people trying to get off drugs, and that she was welcome to call him anytime. By calling Bill Gormley, Kitty finally admitted to herself that she was an alcoholic—and so were all the rest of them.

When he got her call, Gormley drove over to the apartment immediately, collected what little she had, and moved her into his home that afternoon.

BILL GORMLEY: *When I first met Liz, I could see she needed help. Not later, not sometime, now. She was at the bottom. She was desperate. She had no place to go. She was broke. So I said, "Don't worry about it. You got a place. Since I got a place, you got a place. You can come stay at my house."*

I can see her face now: pretty little face. Cute as a button. She was just a little girl in a woman's body—or a little girl in a little girl's body, maybe. She looked like she was about eighteen or nineteen years old, but I knew she was much older than that. I knew she needed a shoulder, for sure, and I wanted to be that shoulder. So she moved into my house. I only got one rule for people staying here: If you take a drink, or do drugs, and I know it, you're gone. I'll take your shit and dump it out in the middle of the street. You no longer live here, from that point on. That was in stone.

Liz was a good kid, though. A lovable kid. She never used nothing when she was here. I've had as many as six or seven people staying at my house at once, but she was the only one staying here at the time, and it was like having a daughter at home. She had her own room, filled it up with baskets and stuff. I remember talking to her out in the backyard, under the apple tree. That's where I did a lot of my talking to people I was trying to help. Physically, she was extremely attractive to me, but her psychological needs were so great that I didn't want anything to get in the way of trying to address that. I never made an advance on her. I became a kind of instant father to her. I wanted to help her.

We'd go to an AA meeting every day, and we had our own little AA meeting every night. In fact, I'd be at it all day: when I met her at the breakfast table in the morning, or brought in her coffee and put it on her nightstand and sat on the edge of the bed and started talking, I started fixing her head right then. That's what all our conversations revolved around: getting well. What I call little diamonds would be dropped—little clichés, little spiritual things I'd cut out and so on.

The girls pretty much lived AA every single day, and it was good for all of them. They stopped drinking the day they went to Bill Gormley's house and there has not been a drop of alcohol since that day. Bill Gormley was a man who inspired hope, and he was strong enough for all of them to lean on for as long as it took to get sober and begin to think clearly again.

Gormley was working at North American Van Lines, a trucking company, and he helped Liz get a job there, as a dispatcher. Kitty, of course, saw this as a fresh chance to prove herself anew, and once again she threw herself into the job with a vengeance. She became proficient at it in record time, coordinating all the paperwork involved in moving households from one end of the country to another—typing up bills of lading, figuring up tariffs, ordering a certain number of trucks and men to go here and there, and just generally making sure that the jobs got done and paid for.

BILL GORMLEY: She picked it up right away. She had a lot of confidence, and everybody liked her. Well, movers like pretty little girls— that's about as deep as they get! Once she started getting back on her feet, she started helping pay for the groceries, and then she moved into her own place and I didn't see her after that. I hope I helped her. Jeez, I wish I had some money. I'd fly her down here for Christmas! She's still got a room in my house.

She moved into a trailer in a clean, modest trailer park in Summerfield, north of Greensboro. She decorated the place tastefully, with baskets and embroidery and pampas grass. She'd quit drinking, she had her own place, she loved her new job: she was putting the pieces back together again, good as new. Pretty soon nobody would be able to see the cracks. A steady stream of men began parading through her life again—from long-distance truckers to a twenty-three-year-old graduate student in the writing program at the University of North Carolina named Jeff Bryant.

JEFF BRYANT: Even after she quit drinking, there was something kind of frantic and desperate about her—like she was always trying to hold onto something. Yet she could hold onto anything she wanted to! She could have these very erudite, artistic conversations with people in the writing program, she could hang out with these redneck trucker types, she could write, she was an incredible pool player, she could drink like hell (she quit just after I met her, but not before I saw how much she could put away) . . . at the same time you got this sense of desperation from her. It makes sense that her personality was fragmented, because she seemed fragmented. There wasn't anything integral about her. She was just grasping.

Her stories about her past were real sporadic—that was always the problem with Liz. You were never sure whether to believe her. Sometimes her stories would be so bizarre—and then you would find out they were true. Then other times, she'd say insignificant things that were lies. But I saw enough things when I was with her that I respected what she said.

She loved to talk about weird psychic stuff and, I swear, there were some things that happened when I was with her that I never could explain. I remember once after she stopped drinking we were in a bar called Fridays, listening to this real lousy band. She wanted to leave; I sort of wanted to stay, and we started passing notes back and forth. These notes started getting sharper and more cryptic, and she started getting mad. She was just glaring at me across the table. I looked across the table and she just laid her index finger and her middle finger right down on the barrel of a pen, a Bic pen, and elevated it about a foot off the table. Then she put it back down and took her fingers away. I said, "Can you do that again?" She said "No, I don't think so." She tried again, but she couldn't. Sure, it's possible she had glue on her fingers or something, but for some reason I didn't think so then and I still don't. She wasn't trying to prove anything in particular.

Then another time we were sitting in a restaurant called Hong Kong House down on Tate Street, talking about a story I was writing, and I said, "Let me go back to the room and get it." She said, "I have it right here," and she pulled it out from underneath the table. We had been looking at this story just before we came over, and I was sure I'd put it away. "Did you grab it before we left?" I said. "No," she said, "I just brought it over here on my own."

Now, I couldn't tell if she was telling me the truth or not, whether she was really able to retrieve things or this was just some baloney of hers. The thing is, though, she put you in a place where you were willing to entertain the notion that she might possibly have been able to do it.

One day early that summer of 1980, not long after she'd moved into the trailer, Liz got a call at work from a trucker hauling a load up from Jacksonville. He was having mechanical problems, and he was going to be late. She liked the sound of his voice: smooth, boyish, but almost melodramatically intense. The kid said his name was Jimmy Jeans. He and Liz yakked back and forth on the telephone over the next few days, as he made his approach to Greensboro. When he finally walked into the office, she was there alone, working late. He was just a blond-headed kid wearing a T-shirt and jeans, with a big ring of keys on his belt, but the moment he walked in, the two of them seemed to connect. It was as if she were sending out sound waves that only he could hear. Later, Kitty would realize it was the kind of connection only two sick-ies could make, but at the time Liz was convinced it was love.

He was only stopping over in Greensboro for the weekend, to drop off a load and pick up another, but by Monday morning Liz's whole future life was rewritten. She had fallen madly, mindlessly in love, and suddenly nothing else mattered. All bets were off, the past was thrown out. She was starting over. She and Jimmy Jeans were getting married. They were going to go halfsies on a big eighteen-wheeler, once they saved the money, and she'd be his road partner, wife, lover, and con-fidante, riding shotgun for the rest of her life.

There was one thing above all others that Liz loved about Jimmy: he was very secretive about his past, and he didn't want to know any-thing about hers, either. Just imagine! A whole future ahead of her with somebody who didn't ask questions! She could be whatever and whomever she wanted to be. They were both attracted to each other on this level that precluded past or present, in this encapsulated private world in which everything was now and everything else was just incidental. What difference did it make if they'd only known each other a weekend? There was no time, so a weekend was the same as a lifetime.

STEFAN BECHTEL: I hadn't seen her in months and then one day she calls up out of the blue all excited, just bubbling over. Her job was so great! These truckers were such wild guys! What a gas it all was! But the big news was that she'd fallen madly in love with this young trucker, and they were going to get married. She was going to fly down to Memphis or someplace to marry this guy she'd known about twenty-four hours. She wanted to bring him over to introduce him.

Fifteen minutes later, three of them showed up at the door—Liz, this guy Jimmy, and a black kid named Stanley. She looked like she'd swallowed a canary. This guy Jimmy was about eighteen or nineteen years old; she was in her thirties. She always seemed to pick these innocents. Anyway, they'd parked the eighteen-wheeler in the grocery store parking lot next door, so while Liz talked to my girlfriend, Kay, this guy Jimmy and Stanley and I went over there to take a look. Jimmy showed me the sleeping compartment and the sixteen gears and whatnot—and all the time he was just giggling like a little kid. The truck was just a big, ten-ton toy to him. There was something odd about those two: they were . . . what is the word for being eerily overhappy? They were either slightly stoned, or Moonies, or something. Always talking about love and peace and all this. Made me nervous. Suspicious.

Jimmy had to leave town Monday morning with a load of furniture, bound for California with many stops in between, and Liz arranged to fly down and meet him in Memphis. She had to wait until Friday to collect her paycheck, otherwise she'd have left immediately. Liz had every intention of marrying the man when she got to Memphis, but when she got there Jimmy and Stanley had hatched a different plan: they'd go on to Shreveport, where Stanley's family lived, and the whole clan would throw them a big black wedding. What a gas!

Sailing down the highway in the air-conditioned cab, high up over the road, the three of them looked like the Mod Squad. The girls were in heaven. Penny Lavender would just sing her heart out, Me-Liz and Jimmy would have long spiritual talks, and Liz—the one who had originally fallen in love with him—was in a kind of blind rapture. Only

Kitty still felt wary. And as the days went by, she grew more and more uneasy. There was something spooky about this guy. He was continuously popping little black pills and drinking Jack Daniels out of a hip flask. Sometimes he was high and talkative, other times he brooded darkly. At truck stops, he was always on the phone, trying to get money wired from somebody—vague stories, something about the Mob, something about his rich father, something about this, something about that.

Finally, when they got to Shreveport and Stanley's family discovered the bride and groom were white—something Stanley had apparently failed to mention—the wedding was abruptly canceled. A big fight erupted in Stanley's family; he decided to stay there, or was forced to stay there, or something, and Jimmy and the girls headed west without him.

But trouble was brewing. Liz, who still had every intention of marrying Jimmy, would have conversations in which she'd lead him to believe they'd be getting married as soon as they could find a place to get a blood test. Then Kitty would come out and say no, she didn't think it was time to get married yet. She didn't tell him so, but in Kitty's opinion, marriage was absolutely out of the question. The girls' vacillation infuriated Jimmy—it was as if their personality shifts touched off personality shifts in him. Violent arguments erupted. Some days he would mumble darkly about killing and violence. It was the devil—the devil had to be killed. The same person who'd listened to Me-Liz talk for hours about Michael and her psychic experiences now seemed entirely terrified to even think about them. Now he was full of crazy, scary talk: he was being followed by ghosts and spooks. He saw shapes drifting across the road. People were talking to him in his head.

They stopped in Albuquerque, Las Cruces, Phoenix. Jimmy started having weird, scary dreams—he'd be sound asleep one minute, and the next minute he'd wake up confused and frightened, with a look in his face like the feeling she had when she was missing time. They had to go up to Prescott to drop part of the load, but the truck broke down on a remote mountain pass. Jimmy was enraged, smoldering. They both got out of the truck and he went into the woods and came back with a big stick and waved it around in the air vaguely, yelling, threatening her. He was not acting like himself at all. All the girls except Liz were getting very scared.

After the truck was fixed and they made it to a truck stop in Prescott, she went inside to take a shower. When she came out, Jimmy's truck was gone. She didn't know what else to do, so she waited—hours and hours—until the big eighteen-wheeler pulled back into the parking lot. Jimmy was repentent, contrite. He was slightly drunk. He just had to get himself under control, he said.

They took off again, bound for Bakersfield, but on a lark she convinced him to stop in Parker. She wanted to show him Sundance, and see if anybody she knew was still there. They stopped and got a motel room and looked up Nick, the owner of Sundance, and he took them on a boat ride on the river. Then around sundown Me-Liz came out, like a new moon rising over the desert. She was enthralled. She had been gone from this sacred place so long! She took Jimmy by the hand and led him out into the desert, away from the highway, to her special spot. They sat down there, at the foot of the black, cinder mountains, in the twilight, and it was then that she saw the lights. They were the same kind of lights she'd seen in the house on Northridge Street: zillions of little sparkly lights all swarming around, forming a ball and then dispersing into the clear desert air.

"Look! Look! Look at all the beautiful little lights!" she whispered, holding out her arms in awe. "The little beings of light have come to greet us! They must know we're here!"

But Jimmy didn't answer. He stood up abruptly and took off walking, fast, back toward the truck, which was parked along the highway. She ran after him.

"Hey, wait! Babe! What's the matter? Can't you see all the beautiful little lights?"

Jimmy refused to speak. She ran along behind him like a little kid, tugging at his shirt, trying to get him to listen. When he got to the truck he opened up one of the side panels and rummaged around, and when he turned to face her he had a bone-handled switchblade in his hand. He pushed her down on the pavement beside the truck.

"You're crazy, bitch, you know that? You're crazy! The devil got in you somehow! The devil's gotta die!"

He climbed on top of her, one hand around her throat, the other weaving the knife through the air above her face. His eyes were fixed, glassy.

"You're evil! You're evil! You gotta die!"

Scared to death, and horrified by this accusation, Me-Liz went away and Liz came out. But when Liz saw the knife, and realized what was happening, she just gave up. It was all so hard for her to comprehend that it was probably just as well that she died. She didn't care. He could kill her, dump her body in the desert, and nobody would ever find it. It didn't matter. But when Liz gave up, Kitty came out. Her reaction was cool and practical: start doing crisis intervention.

"Aw, Jim—Jimmy! Stop it! Think what you're doing, babe! Calm down! Think what it would be like if we could just be up in the truck driving on west and we could just take back the last few minutes like it never happened! Why don't we do that? Why don't we make a deal? We'll just pretend this whole thing never happened, and I won't ever say another word about that spooky stuff again. Huh? How 'bout it? We'll just get back in the truck and head on west, and we won't ever even talk about this again. . . ."

It worked. Finally he got up, dusted off his knees, snapped the switchblade, and slipped it in his back pocket. He looked down at her impassively.

"If you ever scare me like that again, I'll use the knife," he said.

They left Parker without even checking out of their motel—they just drove away. There was nothing else to do. They drove straight on through to Bakersfield, dropped the load, went to a motel, got cleaned up, and had dinner; afterward in the room Jimmy started drinking and then he started to cry. Increasingly alarmed by Jimmy's peculiar behavior, the girls began rippling in and out in a panic; by chance, it was Liz who was out when Jimmy announced that he refused to sleep in the same bed with her. She was evil, he said. She was the devil. The devil had to be killed. He was advancing on her threateningly, waving his arms in the air, when Kitty emerged and immediately decided it was high time to get out of Dodge. She snatched the keys off the nightstand, ran out the door, climbed into the truck, and locked the doors after her. She lay there not sleeping until just after dawn, when she crept back into the motel room to gather up her things. Jimmy woke up just as she was leaving.

"Give me two hundred dollars right now," she demanded.

He just stared at her. She walked over to his wallet, took the money, went down to the motel office, and asked directions to the nearest bus station. Then she walked over there and bought a bus ticket straight back to North Carolina.

Sometime later—she had no idea how long—Liz woke up in a Greyhound bus. It was late afternoon, and out the window she could see a flat, dusty country dotted with oil derricks. The air smelled like cows. The last thing she remembered was the blowup in the motel room in Bakersfield, and now she was sitting in the back of a bus surrounded by cowboys who were singing and playing guitars and drinking Coke out of paper cups. Apparently they were having a party, and she was right in the middle of it. Everybody was laughing.

Somehow, it had all gone bad again.

She didn't even remember exactly how.

KIT CASTLE: Liz had an expression that she would use all the time, and I've heard it so many times now from her experiences that I have even taken to saying it myself. It was, "Bless your heart."

I just want to say to her, "Bless your heart."

Chapter 15

It was Liz who'd run off with the psycho, but it was Kitty who had to come back and face the music. As usual, it was she who was left to clean up the mess. Liz had simply walked off her job at North American Van Lines, so when she returned, her boss refused to give her the job back. Kitty got hired as a waitress at a new restaurant in Greensboro, the Sandwich Construction Company—and as usual, she took her new responsibility with the utmost seriousness. Before long, Kitty was opening and closing the place, working double shifts, and generally burying herself in her work. When the restaurant was closed down for a wild, all-night staff Christmas party, Kitty brought her sleeping bag and slept on the floor, so she could get the place open for business by nine the next morning.

JEFF BRYANT: I hadn't seen her in months, and then I ran into her working as a waitress someplace. She didn't look good. She was, like, thirty-seven or something, but people always said she looked nineteen. After she came back from that truck driver experience, she looked her age. She was pale, and she seemed to have lost a lot of weight. She didn't look happy. She seemed withdrawn. She told me she was having a lot of medical problems—there was something wrong with her neck or some-

thing. But she said, "All this has happened to me and I still haven't taken a drink." She was proud of that.

It was months before Liz crept out of hiding. She'd been so heart-broken over the fiasco with Jimmy Jeans that she went deep and stayed there. She couldn't bear it, so she blanked on it. She just sank down out of sight, into the dark water, back to her sad dark hole where there was no time or memory. When she did begin to resurface to conscious-ness—fearfully, briefly—she almost immediately got sick. Getting sick was her other way of avoiding the hurt and sorrow inside her. It was her way of changing the subject, the way a mother bird will feign a broken wing in order to distract attention from her real concern, the chicks. She became convinced that she was dying again. What she really meant was that her heart felt like it was dying; but what she told peo-ple, and what she really believed, was that she was having weird pains in her head and neck and back.

Kitty, who never got sick, quickly grew exasperated with Liz's bel-lyaching. It was always something: backaches, neck aches, rashes, fe-vers, whatever. *What a loser!* she thought. *What a reject!* But things didn't really come to a head between them until Johnny Lee Clark, a sweet, blue-eyed cook who'd become passionately entangled in Kitty's life, was driven away by Liz's deathbed complaints. Johnny Lee and Kitty had been a real item around the restaurant for months, until Liz started coming out.

"Please don't leave me!" Liz would beg him, weeping. "I'm going to die!"

Nothing could have driven Johnny Lee away faster than a grasping hypochondriac, and within a month he was gone. Kitty was beside herself. She steamed, she raged, and what before had been a mild ir-ritation now soured into a poisonous aversion. She couldn't stand that bitch Liz. But she could no longer control her, either—things weren't like they were just after Kitty was born, when she had the authority to control the comings and goings of all the others. With the passage of time, and life experience, the others had all begun to develop their own hold on reality. They were maturing into real people now, each with her own idiosyncracies, illnesses, talents, and aspirations.

Kitty was no longer the boss.

Kitty's own time of trauma was not long in coming. That spring, to her surprise, she too began to feel the vague physical pains that Liz had been complaining about: headaches, pains in the neck, arms, the back, the chest. She always found a way to go to work, of course, even if she had to swallow so many aspirin she was spitting up blood. A couple of times she went to the emergency room at a small hospital in Greensboro; X-rays were taken, she was given a few samples of Valium and sent on her way. She'd be able to do her shift, and then a couple of days down the line the pain would get bad again and she'd have to return to the emergency room. Finally a nurse accused her of faking the pain just to get drugs, because she confessed to being a recovering alcoholic.

When the parent company decided to franchise and her boss, Jack Grey, was put in charge of setting up the franchise operation, he sent Kitty and an assistant down to Charlotte, North Carolina, for two weeks to interview, train, and generally set up a new restaurant. She gobbled aspirin to deaden the pain, and the opening went smooth as silk. A month later, she opened another place.

One morning in April, Jack Grey invited Kitty to come along to the Greater Greensboro Open, a pro golf tourney, and she went, popping aspirin all the way. But after a whole afternoon on her feet in the hot sun, she developed such a grinding pain in her face and neck she had to go home to bed, numbed out by a Librium she bummed from a bartender. The next morning, nauseous with pain, she went to work: vacuuming, carrying buckets of ice, setting up buffet tables. Finally she sat down to have a cup of coffee, and the cup simply fell out of her hand.

That's when she finally gave up and started to cry. A busboy gave her a lift home and she crawled into bed, but she was up in the middle of the night, drifting in and out of consciousness, woozy with the pain, without a phone to call anyone, fighting back a mounting sense of panic that something was seriously wrong with her. The next morning, Jack sent the busboy back out to check on her, and when he walked into the trailer he found her stretched out in bed, rigid with pain. He loaded her into the front seat of his car, still wearing her pink zippered nightie, and rushed to the emergency room at the hospital. When they got there, they were greeted by the same nurse who'd accused her of faking the pains to get drugs a few months earlier. The nurse and another doctor questioned Kitty suspiciously about her drug habits and then, finally, some neurological tests were run. The doctor seemed concerned when he loaded her into a wheelchair and sent her across the street to see a neurologist named Dr. Loman.

"Get up out of the chair," Dr. Loman told her.

"I can't," Kitty said, almost weeping with the pain.

145

Then he picked her up bodily and set her down, hard, on the examining table. A million flashbulbs popped in her head and then everything went black.

"Look, now, snap out of it!" Dr. Loman was yelling when she came to on the table. "We know about your history! You're in here for drugs, OK? I know what the story is! There were X-rays taken six months ago, and everything was fine! There's no medical reason for this!"

Kitty, confused, crying, and humiliated, wet her pants.

But Dr. Loman would have none of it. He told her to walk back across the street to the hospital, in her pajamas. By that time it was getting dark, and raining, and Kitty, barefoot and crying, fell twice on the slippery sidewalk. She seemed to be either passing out or falling asleep, she couldn't tell which, but by the time she got back to the hospital and they loaded her into a wheelchair, she was in agonizing pain.

"Look, something is horribly, horribly wrong and nobody will listen to me!" she yelled at a nurse. "Nobody will believe me!"

The nurse wheeled her into radiology, and a technician took X-rays. After what seemed like a long time, he came back out.

"Mrs. Lentz, there's something showing up on these films," he told her. "I'm sending these over to Dr. Loman immediately."

She was lying in the hallway of the hospital on a gurney when suddenly there seemed to be doctors and nurses everywhere. Dr. Loman came scurrying by. They wheeled her into another room and gave her a shot of something, and then they shot dye into her spine. Not long afterward, Dr. Loman walked in and rather sheepishly showed her the results of the dye study: there was a herniated disc in the neck that had caused major abrasion and bleeding into the spinal cord itself, he explained, pointing out the damage on what looked like a big X-ray of her neck. All that walking, all that lifting, all that vacuuming—and falling down on the rain-slick sidewalk—had made everything worse by the hour.

"I'm so very sorry, Mrs. Lentz," he told her. "I truly apologize. I didn't know. We're going to get you to a point where you're stabilized and then we'll do surgery. Who is your next of kin?"

Kitty, of course, had no next of kin. She had no parents at all; she had created herself.

"Jack Grey," she told Dr. Loman.

She didn't remember the surgery at all, but when she woke up afterward the room was dark except for a tiny bedside lamp, and down

146

at the foot of the bed, slouched in a chair, asleep, was Dr. Loman. The darkened room was filled with flowers.

"Dr. Loman," she said quietly. "Dr. Loman!"

He woke with a start, then came over and took her hand.

"I'm so glad you made it through as well as you did! I've been doing a neurological check every hour, and everything seems to be working perfectly."

Dr. Loman was overcompensating like mad, and Kitty flourished in it. She deserved it. She'd been assaulted and humiliated by him, and by that place, and now it was her turn to be treated like a princess. When it came time to begin walking, several weeks later, Dr. Loman would help her up and down the halls. The two of them were seen so much together that the hospital rumor mill even ground into operation. People from Sandwich Construction would come by in shifts to feed her and keep her company. The whole restaurant staff encircled her with divine compassion and support—for the first six weeks she was out of the hospital, confined to bed and wearing an enormous neck brace, they came out to the trailer in shifts, to bring food, do housework, do laundry, and bathe her. She was out of work two months. Fortunately, her medical insurance at the restaurant covered it all.

Although she was famous for her high-speed recoveries, this time the healing was exceedingly slow. This time, it wasn't just Liz's phantom pains—the physical body that all of them occupied had broken down and everyone, Kitty included, suffered. The other girls were all sharing the illness, but the one who seemed to suffer most, as usual, was Liz. Naturally, she was absolutely convinced that it wasn't a herniated disc at all—it was cancer. It was a deadly, pustulous tumor, or worse. She was dying, of course. Liz was always dying.

"What are you doing July eleventh?" Jack Grey asked Kitty out of the blue one day a few weeks after she came back to work at the restaurant.

"I don't know, Jack. Why?"

"Well, you're moving to Virginia Beach. I'm getting out of the restaurant business and moving down there, and I want you to come along and take care of my kids." Kitty knew Jack's marriage was in the last, bitter stages of dissolution, and that he would probably get custody of the three children after the divorce. "Look, you need a job where you're not on your feet all day, and I need somebody to look after Timmy, Garth, and Sarah. How 'bout it?"

It sounded like a deal made in heaven. Kitty couldn't manage a full-time job because she was still plagued by headaches and back aches. She was almost broke again. She liked Jack. And it seemed high time to leave.

"Sure," said Kitty, without a second thought. "Why not?"

Two months later, on Labor Day, 1981, on the boardwalk at Virginia Beach, Liz met her third husband, and so began the final chapter in her life. At first, it seemed like a chance encounter—two attractive young people wandering alone through the holiday crowds on the boardwalk—but within twenty-four hours, it all seemed destined. Once again, the future was rewritten overnight, his for the first time, hers for the hundredth.

She was dressed to be noticed, it's true: she had on a loose-fitting, see-through, gauzy white cover-up with nothing on underneath but an itty-bitty turquoise bikini, which left the viewer with the distinct impression she was completely nude under there. The getup, of course, was Kitty's idea. And it was Kitty who saw Jeff Castle first: a lanky, dark-skinned man in his midtwenties with big, sad, dark eyes, a bushy moustache, and a ponytail trailing out from underneath a baseball cap. He was seated on a bike, leaning up against the boardwalk rail, and he was staring at her. Their eyes met, and at that moment, Kitty disappeared. Kitty had no affinity for Jeff. It was Liz who returned his stare, and shyly smiled.

It was Liz who fell in love.

JEFF CASTLE: I had been waiting to meet someone like her for a long time. Within twenty-four hours of the time I met her, I knew it was her. I'd had a couple of other short-lived relationships that just kind of faded out when I discovered that wasn't the right girl. Now I'd found her; I just knew it. I don't know why.

Liz was attracted to this man immediately. He seemed kind and safe: soft-spoken, unthreatening. He was twenty-six, living in Virginia Beach doing some kind of heavy construction work and managing small-time rock bands on the side. He had a lively intelligence, and though he'd never gone to college he told her he liked to spend his spare time in libraries reading about "the weirder side of physics." They chatted for a little while on the boardwalk, and then they walked across the highway to a restaurant called the Lemon Tree and sipped iced tea and talked for hours. Afterward, neither one could remember exactly what

148

it was they'd talked about. But both of them knew that something important had happened. They were meant to be together.

That night, Jeff picked her up at the campground where she, Jack Grey, and the three children had been living in an encampment of tents for the past two months.

"You gonna have a lost weekend, or what?" Jack said, with a side-long wink.

Liz and Jeff were on their way to the movies, but they wound up back at Jeff's apartment, in bed. Sexually, Liz felt very free, and very safe, with Jeff that night. There was a kind of coolness and distance about him, emotionally and sexually, that made her feel safe. She was convinced that he was the perfect man, at the perfect time, for her. All the girls had a chance to peep out and get a bit acquainted with this man. They all liked him, except Kitty: he slouched, and she didn't like his smell. Still, despite Kitty's objections, the two of them were inseparable from that day forward.

JEFF CASTLE: From the first day we met, we'd sit down every evening after I got home from work and took a shower, and she would tell me a little bit more about herself and I would tell her about myself. Her past was all very vague and confusing, and there was never any sequence to it all, but the stories she would tell would give me goosebumps. She'd tell me about these visions she was having. She had me completely convinced that there were some kind of very major changes coming in the world, some kind of apocalypse, a conclusion to world governments, and that she was going to be in charge of this small group. She gave me a copy of The Stand, *by Stephen King. You had to be very careful of what you said and who you said it to, even lying to cover up. Looking back, I can see that what she was referring to was that her world was coming to a conclusion. I am convinced that Liz did know about the others, maybe subconsciously, and that she knew their world was about to come to an end. She just interpreted this to mean that things were going to happen everywhere.*

Our relationship was totally bizarre from the start—life with Liz was like riding the biggest roller coaster in the world, all the time. There was never anything like normal life, ever. One day she'd be high as a kite, the next day it would be the end of the world. Her life was a series of highs and lows, where my life was a series of mild bumps. That's why we were so good for each other—she gave me the excitement that I never had, and the opportunity to actually experience things that I knew were out there.

I allowed her to experience something that to her was truly bizarre: life as a normal housewife.

Jack Grey rented a big, luxurious beach house on the ocean in a place called Sandbridge a few weeks after Liz and Jeff met, and he invited the two of them to move in with him and the children. He gave them the whole downstairs for their own—a lovely spot, filled with plants and deep carpets, with walls of glass fronting on the ocean.

It all seemed too good to be true, and it was. Jack's situation got tenser by the day—he began to realize he couldn't really afford this place, for one thing, and he started pressuring Liz and Jeff to start paying rent, even though he was no longer paying Liz to help with the kids. There was conflict with his soon-to-be-ex-wife—bitter fights over the custody battle, drinking, money troubles. Bill collectors started to call. Tension began to build in the beautiful glass house on the beach, like static electricity—just like the tension in all the houses Liz had ever lived in as a child. She kept flashing back, in pain and horror, to the far, far away past.

One night she and Jeff took a long walk down the beach, and she broke down crying.

"I'm just so scared you're going to have to move out and I'm going to have to move out and it's all going to fall to pieces, like everything always does!" she wept. "I don't know what to do! I can't go live in that tiny little apartment of yours, but where are we gonna go if Jack kicks us out? I'm so . . . I'm so afraid I'm going to lose you!"

That's when they decided to get married. Jeff didn't exactly propose, and neither did Liz. It was as if they simply reached the same conclusion at the same moment: marriage seemed the only logical, natural, sensible thing to do.

They'd known each other about six weeks.

They rented a wonderful big beach house of their own, not far from Jack's place, at cheap, off-season rates—it was almost November, and winter was coming on—and moved in. Although they had the usual fights and disagreements of all young couples, mostly money-related, they were in love.

JEFF CASTLE: I was very much in love with Liz—someone that I've since discovered was only one aspect of a whole person. Liz was probably the most compassionate person that this world could ever know. She would do anything to make somebody feel appreciated. Anybody else who

150

had the compassion she did also must have another, darker side, but Liz was lucky. She didn't have the other side—the other side was someone else.

I loved the one I've since learned was Me-Liz, too. She was the neat one. Probably the nicest thing that ever was done for me were the phone calls I got at work from Me-Liz. She would always say, "Hi, it's me, Liz—the one who loves you!" Later, when I learned what was really going on when she said that—that was spooky. That was really strange.

Not long before Thanksgiving, Liz and Jeff decided to drive up to Ithaca, New York, to spend the holiday with Jeff's parents. Liz had chatted with his mother and father on the phone several times, and there was a wonderful, warm rapport there. She wanted to meet them before she and Jeff were married. Then, almost as a lark, it occurred to her that as long as they were going up there anyway, why shouldn't they just go ahead and get married? They could have an intimate, family wedding right in his parents' house. It might be a special thing for everybody. Jeff liked the idea, and so did his folks. Everybody started making arrangements. The date was set for November 25th, 1981, the Wednesday before Thanksgiving.

JEFF CASTLE: It was maybe a nine- or ten-hour drive up to James-town, and our plan was to leave in the late afternoon so we'd hit less traffic when we went through Pennsylvania. The weather in Virginia Beach was fine that morning, although we heard on the radio it was supposed to rain up north. But all of a sudden Liz came up and said to me, very emphatically, "We gotta leave, right now." I told her, "Well, if you want to leave early, fine, but we've got to pack and do some other important stuff first." But she said, "No, we've got to leave, now." By this time, I was used to this emphatic tone she sometimes used, and I knew it meant, "Do it."

It turned out, if we'd left when she said, we wouldn't have had any problems whatsoever. As it was, we left maybe two hours after she said to, and ended up getting caught in a very bad snowstorm midway through Pennsylvania. We got to my parents' house just before the bottom opened up. It was quite a storm—I wasn't able to drive for three days after that, in fact.

Over the next three days, Jeff's mother and the others scurried around making preparations for the wedding. Since it was Liz who was marrying Jeff, it was Liz who was out most of the time. Although Kitty was not crazy about the goings-on, she had the good sense, and the courtesy, to keep her nose out of things most of the time. She'd already made her contribution to the affair: before she left Virginia, she'd gone out and bought Liz a wild, sexy wedding outfit. It was a white antique lace shirt and a pair of white silk knickers. They looked almost like fancy underwear.

Kitty's choice of wedding apparel was a mild reproof, a sort of veiled joke. She didn't like Jeff Castle, and never had. She didn't like Liz either, for that matter. She was on the outs with the entire wedding party, yet here she was, trapped in the body of one of the participants. She was also royally peeved by the accommodations: she and Jeff were sleeping on a rollaway bed in a basement family room that was completely saturated by the smell of an old, sick family dog. Ugh!

Still, Kitty managed to restrain her distaste for the whole affair until about an hour before the ceremony. The girls were downstairs in the basement family room, getting themselves ready, when she and Liz got into a major knock-down-drag-out. The day before, Kitty had taken them all downtown in the snow to get their hair done, and she liked the way it looked—it was all up on top of her head, with a few pendulous ringlets hanging down like Marie Antoinette. But when Liz came out and took a look at it, she decided she hated it that way. Too fussy. So Liz took the hair down. Then Kitty came out and put it up again. Then Liz came out and took it down. Liz also decided, come to think of it, that she didn't like the idea of wearing silk knickers to her wedding, either. She wanted a long white skirt, like you're supposed to wear to your wedding. She took off the knickers. Kitty put them back on.

Although only six family friends had been invited to the wedding, they'd all arrived and were waiting upstairs while Kitty and the bride carried on their weird mental cat-fight downstairs. Jeff kept popping down the stairs, gently trying to hurry his fiancée up a little. One minute he'd come down and she would be dressed, and the next she'd be undressed. Her hair would be up, then it would be down. Liz, of course, did not really comprehend what was going on. She would just wake up in front of the mirror with her hair all wrong, and she'd change it. Then she'd wake up again, and it would be wrong again.

Kitty was perfectly aware of what was going on. And before long she decided she'd had about enough of it. She was sick of this crap! She didn't want to marry this guy anyway. In fact, she refused to marry him. She made up her mind about it: she was just going to stay downstairs, and stay single. All she wanted was to go back to Virginia Beach and have her own life. As far as she was concerned, this whole thing was happening under duress anyway. She wasn't about to stand by and watch Liz make another dumb mistake again. No way!

Jeff came downstairs and begged her to come up, but she refused. Finally the local judge and old family friend who was to marry them came down the stairs and was lucky enough to arrive at a moment when Liz was out. Liz was more than ready to get married—in fact, she couldn't understand what the hold-up was—so she emerged from downstairs with the judge in tow, radiant, with her hair down, smiling shyly and ready to go.

The wedding was actually a double ceremony: Jeff's parents had decided to resay their vows to each other, just before Jeff and Liz said their own vows for the first time. It was a way of making the whole service special and magical for everyone. Or at least, that was the intent. For Liz, the situation was a bit more complicated. After his parents said their vows, and then she and Jeff said theirs, she turned around, and at that moment the others began to ripple rapidly in and out, like a riot of fish rising to the surface of a lake. They didn't burst all the way out; they seemed to rise to within a quarter-inch of consciousness and then sink back, so that each one would get a flash of information, disconnected in time, like a flashbulb popping in the dark: happy faces, crowded little room, smell of flowers, she was getting married again, back inside. To anyone else, it would all have been monstrously confusing. To the others, it was just more of the usual.

When the wedding was over, they all went downstairs to the family room for a little reception. Everyone was interested in meeting Jeff's new bride, and that's when the questions began.

"So your parents weren't able to make it . . .?"

"Well, Jeff tells me you spent some time in Minneapolis. What did you do for work up there?"

"What's your dad do?"

"How many kids in your family?"

Liz panicked. It was a situation she'd been avoiding all her life: being surrounded by strangers boring in from every direction, full of sudden, personal interest in her past. She felt like the lady in the sword-pierced box in a magic show. Liz vanished, and out swept Miss Congeniality, Kitty Rosetti—burlesque queen, businesswoman, overachiever, and storyteller extraordinaire. She wasn't about to let this thing turn into a fiasco.

153

JEFF CASTLE: During the ceremonies, she was tight, tense, with-drawn. Afterward—everybody took it to be a sign of relief—suddenly she got very at ease. All of a sudden she was the life of the party, believe me! Oh, God, she came out of her shell and was telling stories and just blowing everybody away. They were thoroughly amazed at this lady I had just married. I can picture her sitting there telling these stories and all these people in a circle around her listening like little kids in kindergarten at storytelling time.

I was proud of her. But I was also scared to death that she was going to close up into a little mouse and run away.

She told them she was raised in foster homes—that took care of the parents problem—and that she had educated herself and gone to various universities and that she became a counselor. That she had been involved with the Indian movement in Arizona. That she'd been down to Baja. That she'd done this, done that. Her two previous marriages, her abandoned children, her alcoholic breakdown, admissions to psychiatric wards, suicide attempts—well, that, of course, she never mentioned.

It was snowing heavily by the time the reception ended and all the guests went home. Kitty helped clear the dishes, and then she went downstairs. She longed to be gone. She couldn't stand the smell of that cancerous old dog any more. She was tired of being on stage, and she just wanted to take a shower and stretch out in luxury and have a drink and maybe go dancing.

"Why don't we get out of here for awhile?" she asked Jeff, when he came downstairs. "Go dancing or something."

"Look, I'm not going to take a chance driving the car into Ithaca in a blizzard with no snow tires! We're going to stay here tonight."

Kitty flipped.

"You gotta be kidding! Spend our wedding night down in a stinky old basement room on a rollaway bed? In your parents' house? Jeff, you're about as romantic as a two-by-four!"

Jeff's parents' bedroom was directly overhead, so they had to conduct their fight in acid-laced whispers. But Jeff wouldn't budge. Finally they opened out the rollaway bed, and he and Kitty climbed in. But they didn't make love that night—or ever again, though they lived as man and wife for the next five years.

"Keep your damn hands to yourself!" Kitty hissed at him. "I'm not giving you any kind of a wedding night if you're going to make me spend it sleeping on a rollaway bed in somebody's cellar!"

Kitty lay there wide awake until finally Jeff fell asleep. Then Liz crept out. She didn't know anything about the fight. She didn't know why her new husband had turned away from her on their wedding night. Had she done something wrong? Had she fallen asleep while he was trying to make love? Was he just being kind and gentle, leaving her alone because she was tired?

She never did figure out what she had done wrong.

Chapter 16

Far, far off down the sunblind beach, a dark shape flickered, steadied, took form. Me-Liz shaded her eyes from the midday sun. A shambling shape, absurdly overdressed in the heat, wearing a dark coat, dark trousers, and holding a dark hat in his hand, approached along the rim of the sea. It was Michael.

Michael!

Behind and above him, hanging in the air like three flashing, ghostly cymbals, were the beings. There were always three of them. Sometimes they came alone, sometimes they came with Michael. The light they gave off was unlike any light she'd ever seen—it wasn't reflected light, or radiant light, it was more as if their cells were alive with light. They hung in the air, shimmering and transparent, as if their molecular structures were so loose they were simply a few excited electrons bouncing in space. As if they couldn't even be seen with your regular eyes at all, but only with some other part of you.

More and more often, the three beings of light were coming to visit Me-Liz. Michael had told her to expect these ghostly visitations, and that they would signify a great new unfolding in her life. Something grand and wonderful was preparing to take place. Sometimes they came when she was puttering in the lavish, triangular dune gardens she and

Liz and Penny were building in the sand, sometimes they came when she was alone out here on the beach. But always they came at the same time of day: the very stroke of noon. Pyramid time. The time of day when, for some reason, more and more often she found herself drawn to building enormous, triangular pyramids in the sand, terraced like Aztec sun temples. She always built them in threes.

When Michael reached her, with the trinity of beings hanging over his shoulders like some ghostly candelabra, the being in the middle reached out and handed her something that looked like a golden necklace, or lei, in the light. The being tried to slip it around her neck, but it was too small; it slipped down over her hair and lay there like a crown. Michael winked. He smiled, backed away a few steps, then turned around and started walking away down the beach. After a few dozen steps, he seemed to simply vanish into the shimmering brilliance of the light.

On closer examination, Me-Liz could see that the strange necklace was a chain of hundreds of papery, translucent pods, or egg cases, each one about the size of a nickel. Nestled inside each pod were dozens of tiny white seashells, smaller than grains of rice. One in many. Each pod contained many, yet was one; and the necklace was composed of many pods, yet was one. Even the necklace itself, apparently a thing of the sea, was probably one of many others just like it, all of them belonging to the ocean—a vast wholeness of which their multitude was a tiny part. "Was that what the beings meant?" Me-Liz wondered.

The necklace was still wet. Me-Liz took it home and hung it in the sun, on a nail on the side of the greenhouse, to preserve it. Michael always gave her seashells when he came—Me-Liz had jars filled with seashells from his visits. But this was the first time he'd ever given her anything like this, and the first time the beings had ever given her anything at all.

KIT CASTLE: Me-Liz never considered this "lei" to be anything other than a natural object. She later found out that it was actually a string of egg capsules of the knobbed whelk, a mollusk that lives in the Atlantic. But to her, this didn't make the event any less miraculous, or the beings less real. It was a bizarre incident, in that most people would probably consider neither the viewer (Me-Liz) nor the viewed (Michael and the beings) to be "real." So where does that leave you?

She was to leave Virginia Beach and go someplace high up, where there were rolling, forested hills and water. A place of rest. A place where it was all to happen. Somehow, this was part of the knowledge she was receiving. Michael and the light beings showed her pictures of this place, and sometimes they took her there. Late one night, she was awakened and told to get up out of bed and go out on the deck of the beach house where she and Jeff were living. She saw three lights standing out over the ocean. They seemed to be communicating with her somehow. They gave her pictures of the mountainous place she was supposed to go, where something of great and mysterious importance was about to take place. Then an enormous shape, like a phantom ship, rose out of the water and the three lights sank into the ship and disappeared.

JEFF CASTLE: I got up in the middle of the night and found Liz walking back from these huge sliding glass windows that faced the ocean. She wasn't sleepwalking; she was in a trance. I've seen people sleepwalking before, and they look perfectly awake—but she just had a blank stare on her face, like a zombie. She didn't even notice me walk up to her. I called her name, twice, and she came out of it. She told me she had seen them and that they were leaving. She said that the trinity had come out from the ocean on a ship, and there were three lights and they came up to her and told her several things and then they left. They told her she was supposed to move to the mountains, she said.

This was the kind of thing I was getting used to by then. You just say to yourself, "Well, I'm not going to deny this, or accept it either. I'll just listen."

Almost every morning, before the sun grew hot, Michael would come to visit with Me-Liz in the dune gardens, or in the elaborate greenhouse that Liz and Jeff and their new housemates, Babes and Tim, had built on the beach. The gardens were the pride of her life, and Penny's, too—people came from all up and down the beach to look at them and take pictures and sometimes steal a tomato or two. Each one was a big, raised, triangular bed, filled with a lavish profusion of vegetables and flowers, with a pyramid-shaped triangle of poles for the peas and beans. Me-Liz seemed to have a bond with the earth itself, and she could make things grow out there that weren't supposed to grow. Penny, who was very artistic, turned each garden into sculpture, with log steps and pathways and driftwood. The gardens were like a love gift they were giving to themselves.

Penny and Liz created the gardens as part of a new fantasy of adventure and self-sufficiency that she and Jeff and Babes and Tim had created together. Not long after she and Jeff got married, they'd moved in with these young neighbors as a way of cutting expenses. Me-Liz told them about the visions she'd been having, about living someplace high up, in the mountains, close to the land, and Babes and Tim had eagerly partaken in this vision. They were searching, too, and this seemingly miraculous guidance was just what they'd been so hungry to find. In a matter of a few months, all four of them were drawn into a communal dream of giving up the crazy hubbub of modern life, going back to nature, growing all their own food, and living rough and free and simple as the pioneers. Someday, they told each other, they'd get the money together to buy a sailboat and sail around the world. It was a romantic, improbable notion, nurtured by stacks of gardening and self-help books ordered from Rodale Press and *Mother Earth News.*

But the dream soured fast. Once they all moved in together, the house seemed cramped. There was never enough money. And, worst of all, Babes and Liz began to develop a truly spectacular loathing for each other. At first, in the excitement of the dream, they all got along fine. But as the fever cooled with time, the two of them discovered that they were almost chemically allergic to one another. It was as if they were put on this earth to draw out the worst in each other. Liz was convinced that Babes was mentally ill. Babes would be combative verbally at one moment and at the next moment be in tears and the next moment after that laughing hysterically. Then she'd be fine for a couple of days, after which the whole process would repeat itself. Tim confided that he was worried she might need psychiatric help.

It was worst when Babes's mother, a self-proclaimed witch, was around. At first she had been eager to hear about Me-Liz's visions, but as time went on she seemed increasingly edgy about all the strange talk of Michael and the "beings of light." Babes began to suggest that Liz might be evil, that she might be possessed, mentally ill, or at the very least an outrageous liar. The others, of course, did not take kindly to this at all. The whole thing came to a head when Kitty discovered Babes's dog had left a mess on the kitchen floor and, in a fit of rage, picked up a handful of excrement and threw it at Babes. Kitty stormed out of the house, and Babes called her mother.

JEFF CASTLE: Apparently Babes called her mother and said her and Liz had this big fight. Liz told me that her mother then called up and threatened her, implying that she would use her witchcraft to harm her, if anything happened to Babes. Well, that same evening a very strange phenomenon happened: the ceiling on Babes's mother's house fell in. No-

body knew how it happened. It was a relatively new house, but the whole ceiling caved in. Liz just sat there and smiled. Now, Liz never claimed that she caused this to happen. I don't think she honestly, consciously believed she caused it. She just shrugged and said, "I get angry, and things happen." And they did.

Not long after the ceiling caved in, Liz and Jeff moved out. They couldn't afford a house, so they bought a trailer and found a nice little trailer court on the Virginia–North Carolina border, got the trailer set up on blocks, had the electricity and utilities hooked up—and that's where everything stopped. Before the electricity could be turned on, you needed the proper permits, and to get the proper permits, Liz quickly discovered, certain local officials had to have their palms greased. Everybody in the trailer court seemed to understand the unwritten rules, but Liz was incensed. She called the police. The next day, an anonymous phone caller told her that somebody else had tried to set up a trailer on their own, and—it was the funniest thing—but the trailer burned to the ground.

Liz and Penny and Me-Liz began bursting in and out, in terror and confusion, as they always did in situations like this. None of them knew whom to trust. If they didn't pay a bribe, would the trailer burn down in the night? A sense of anxiety settled around them like a cloud. For weeks, they lived in the trailer out of boxes, without electricity or water, using the campground toilet and fearing every night that the place would go up in smoke. It was as if they simply were not supposed to be there.

One weekend she and Jeff decided to drive up to his parents' house in Ithaca to escape the craziness. They had a wonderful weekend. They drove up along Cayuga Lake, a serene, fifty-mile-long Finger Lake which lay to the north of Ithaca, cradled by rolling, forested hills. Sitting on the shore at Aurora, a tiny town halfway up the lake, gazing out at the white paddlewheel ferry steaming across the water, Liz suddenly realized that this was it. This was what the beings of light had been talking about: the rolling, forested hills, the sense of elevation, the water. This place was like a great green stillness between two great bodies of water, in fact—Cayuga Lake and Owasco Lake, a few miles to the east. Liz, Me-Liz, Kitty, and Penny all felt it: this was the place in the visions. This was the place where they were supposed to be.

This was where it was all to happen.

Chapter 17

As soon as Jeff and the others decided to make the move north, the world seemed to stop resisting them. For weeks, nothing had gone right; now everything seemed easy. At first they were concerned that they might not be able to unload the trailer, but when they asked, the man who'd sold it to them gave back their thousand-dollar down payment and took the trailer back. They packed all their things and drove up to Ithaca. The day they arrived, friends of Jeff's parents told them they had a little abandoned cottage up on Cayuga Lake, near Aurora, where they'd let them live rent-free if Jeff was willing to fix it up. They drove up to the cottage that same afternoon to take a look.

All the way up to the lake, Liz and Me-Liz and the others were having flashes of recognition. The way the water glinted through the trees. The lay of the land to the north, where the low mountains sprawled around the lake like a sleeping nude. The smell of leaf-rot in the ferny woods. And when they pulled up in front of the little run-down cottage, a couple of hundred yards back from the shore and surrounded by towering gypsy ash trees, she recognized it immediately. There was a tumble-down church camp on the hillside behind the cottage, and she recognized that, too.

This was it.

For Liz and the others, the move to Aurora was like taking a deep, deep breath and then exhaling as long and slowly as possible. Their whole souls relaxed. Jeff's whole family got involved in fixing up the little one-bedroom cottage, which had stood empty for seven years. Jeff spent weeks propping up the sagging floor, fixing leaky plumbing, repairing the heating system and the ceilings, while Liz and Mrs. Castle painted and cleaned and tidied things up to make it livable. In the mornings, the air off the lake was crisp and delicious. It was a happy, industrious time, hurrying to make the house secure and cozy before the first snow flew. They didn't quite make it: Jeff was up on the roof, banging away, when the first flakes of the season swept in across the lake. The cottage was cramped, but there was such a sense of peace and comfort there, especially on cold early winter nights when Liz snuggled up in front of the fire like a contented cat, that nothing else mattered.

This was where she was supposed to be.

That first winter in Aurora, Liz and Jeff kept pretty much to themselves. They weren't accustomed to the heavy, silent snowfalls of central New York State, especially in Aurora, where snow would sometimes fall steadily for weeks. They stayed in their warm, cozy cocoon, except to wade up to the local library or to the store. Jeff did small construction jobs around town. Jeff's mother taught Liz to quilt that winter, and before too long Liz was teaching a quilting class of her own, up at the library.

The librarian was a young Mexican woman named Isabel Parker, and the two of them seemed to hit it off immediately. Their meeting was practically inevitable: the others loved to read, and it was nothing for them to take out fifteen or twenty books every two weeks. Kitty would take out the beauty books. Me-Liz would check out the books about gardening and psychic phenomena. Penny Lavender liked art books. And Liz liked the penny dreadful romances.

When that spring of 1983 rolled around, Penny, Me-Liz, and Jeff began clearing the wooded lot beside the cottage to put in a cluster of triangular gardens. Me-Liz never felt quite whole without her gardens. They set up the greenhouse, cleared blackberry thickets, chopped down a few trees, and dug ponds for drainage.

After the snowbound isolation of winter, neighbors began creeping out of their cabins, and Me-Liz began making a few friends. She developed a special friendship with an older woman named Dorothy Downing, who was a devout if somewhat eccentric Christian. Dorothy believed, for instance, that Christ would return in a UFO. To her, every biblical reference to mysterious lights or odd happenings was a reference to UFOs. Because of her openness to these ideas, Me-Liz confided in Dorothy about her visions and Michael and the beings of light, and Dorothy listened. Dorothy seemed to find ways to accommodate what Me-Liz was saying into her own beliefs, and Me-Liz did the same. They were perfect for each other.

Jess loved the cottage by the lake; it reminded him of Minnesota, with dark water glinting through the trees, and upended boats lined up along the shore. Jess developed a special relationship of his own with Dorothy's husband, Earl, a retired veterinarian and unrepentant Marxist. If there was a sick or injured animal anywhere in the neighborhood, it always wound up in Earl's big, rough, gentle hands. Jess, of course, was always on hand to watch the procedure and mentally take notes. Earl taught Jess how to inject a needle into the tiny veins in a rabbit's ear, how to feed and care for nestling birds, how to do rudimentary diagnoses of dogs. In the evenings, the white-haired old communist and his attentive young student loved to argue about Marxism, hurling threats and denunciations back and forth, until finally the gruff old man would laugh and clamp Jess around the shoulders like an older man would do to a son and say, "Pretty good, kid."

Jess loved that.

It was through the quilting classes at the library that Me-Liz met Edie and Martha Zenns, and their small circle of friends. It was Edie who invited Me-Liz to come to the Lutheran church in town; the two of them attended an evening service on Maundy Thursday, that spring of 1983. The service, representing the crucifixion and death of Christ three days before his resurrection on Easter, was a kind of ritualistic funeral. The atmosphere was one of high solemnity. The Lutheran liturgy was spoken, rather than sung, and at the end of the service the altar was silently stripped of its adornments. The flowers and vases were removed. The candles and their standards were taken away. Then the bare altar and its lonely cross were draped in a black shroud. Me-Liz was tremendously moved by the service. She was consumed by such a feeling of foreboding and loss that it was almost as if she herself were about to be crucified and buried.

After the service, Edie took Me-Liz back to meet the pastor, Kaye deYoung, a vivacious and engaging young minister educated at Smith

College, who was about her own age. Me-Liz liked Pastor Kaye immediately. And later that summer, she joined Pastor Kaye's Lutheran church and became an acolyte, assisting in the services. She lit the candles on the big altar, received the offering, and performed the other liturgical tasks along with several other adolescent acolytes, all wearing white vestments. Draped in those white robes, her head slightly bowed, Me-Liz brought to the task a sense of utter devotion and reverence. She seemed to fall into God and be consumed, so that she could hardly distinguish herself from anyone or anything else.

There were a few practical problems with church-going, of course. Like wetting her pants. The problem was that, when she sat down for services, the physical body's bladder would sometimes fill to bursting. The adults (Kitty, Liz, Me-Liz, Jess, and Penny) knew perfectly well that they couldn't just go to the bathroom right there on the pew. But Little Elizabeth and Little Andrea didn't know that. They would pop out for the first time in years, panic, having no idea where they were, and then they'd wet their pants. Then they'd just disappear, because they didn't want to get in trouble.

KIT CASTLE: Maybe the reason they popped out in the first place was because they were the only ones who could allow the physical body to release the pressure, since they were the only ones who didn't know any better. Then Liz or Me-Liz or Penny would be left to clean up the mess— and, of course, come up with an explanation. The explanation came from Liz. She decided it was incontinence due to nerve damage from the old neck operation. Simple. No problem. Next question.

PASTOR deYOUNG: Liz and I developed a very warm, very caring pastor–parishioner relationship after she joined the church. I had people in the congregation tell me Liz was crazy, that she was evil, and that I should not pay attention to her. People accused her of lying, of being untrustworthy—they said I was being sucked in by her. They said no single person could possibly have done all the things she claimed to have done. But I made a choice not to listen to that. My job here is to draw people in, not push them away. I always considered her a gift.

Liz's stories were incredible, unbelievable. She told me about Michael, and about the dreams and visions she was having—she would get very frightened, very uptight, about these visions. She didn't know where they came from. I think she thought she might be possessed by a demon or something. She had the vague feeling that something horrible was about to happen to her very soon. She would call me up with phrases she'd

164

heard in visions, often in Hebrew, and ask me what they meant. Once, I remember, she wanted to know the meaning of "ummin and thummin," which turned out to be the lots that prophets and seers cast in Old Testament days, as a way of looking into the future. Another time the name "Melchizidek" came to her in a vision—an order of high priests in ancient times.

I think, I hope, I pray, that I was able to be supportive by taking her seriously, by not writing it off and not assuming she was crazy, or evil. I just knew from the very center of my being that Liz was not evil. If people hear voices and see visions, maybe there's something to that—the real issue is what you do with it. If you use it for evil purposes, it's evil; if you use it for good, it's good. What I watch for is the result. Is it positive and good and healing and healthy and whole, or is it destructive? And if it's not destructive, then it must be of God.

I considered Michael to be an angel. I believe in angels. They're biblical. I know God speaks, and he speaks to people in different ways. There's no question in my mind that when I was called to the ministry, I experienced God speaking to me, even though the person sitting next to me probably would not have been able to hear it. Liz was the only one I've known whom angels actually spoke to. It was surprising to hear this, of course. It's not every day somebody tells you about talking to angels! But my belief system is not such that I rule these things out.

One afternoon in December of 1983, shortly after services, Me-Liz passed a note to the pastor. It was scribbled on a scrap of yellow paper:

Dr. P. deYoung,
   This A.M. during services I sensed an urgent need in you. Let me explain: right after your sermon you turned, looked at the altar, hesitated, prayed loudly for help, then continued the service. You prayed for help—*adult, mature* action to be taken. The difference was very distinguishable. The light that surrounds you flashed brightly, then faded slowly, as if to betray your thoughts.
   Don't *you* lose faith in what has been made known to you. He heard your prayers. This prayer was worthy of you. Balance is forthcoming. He loves you.

L.

Then, underneath, in a slightly different hand, slanting to the right instead of the left, a postscript:

165

Pastor;

I am kind of speechless at this—this is the first time I've had this kind of experience—I not only had a visit in church, but the visit was about you. Did you experience this kind of prayer this A.M.?

LIZ

PASTOR deYOUNG: When I got this note, I was pretty astounded. I still have trouble talking about this. Because indeed there had been something really amazing that happened that day right after the sermon, when I turned to pray. There was, at the time, something happening in my life that nobody in the parish knew anything about—nobody. My father had been indicted by the U.S. Justice Department in a bid-rigging scandal out in Montana, and at this point in time, the conspiracy trial had begun. There were fifteen defendants; it was a big deal. My whole family was running back and forth to Montana, where the trial was being held, and on most days my brain was really distracted by it all. You can't understand what it was like unless someone you love has been dragged through the dirt like this.

I remember that after I finished preaching that Sunday morning, I turned to the altar and with every ounce of will I had in me, I prayed that justice would be done—not that my father would be acquitted. I remember that moment so well. I remember just saying, "I will not pray that he is acquitted, I will pray that justice is done," and how hard it was for me to say this. Somehow, Liz was able to see something that nobody else was able to see. My father was finally acquitted. But that was much later, and Liz's vision was a great comfort to me at a time when I wasn't telling anybody about what was going on.

I don't understand how she was able to do this. But when you're dealing in the realm of divine things, nothing is impossible.

Chapter 18

The grass was still damp with dew the morning Michael met Me-Liz in the garden and took her out of this world. He had something to show her, he said. He took her far away, to a place that looked like a depthless, starry void—utterly black except for the cold, distant glitter of stars. They stood at the foot of a long, rickety dock, like a dilapidated fishing pier, extending out into the emptiness. Michael took her hand and together they walked out toward the end of the dock. Me-Liz, uneasy, was careful where she put her feet. But Michael only chuckled.

"It doesn't matter," he said.

She could see that there was a being seated at the end of the pier, reading a newspaper. As they approached, he turned and faced them. He looked like Albert Einstein, as a young man and as an old man, all at once.

"Why am I here?" she asked him.

"It's about the mitochondria," he said. "They're out of whack, out of balance. That's why you're having all this trouble. You have to use the farandola. The farandola will fix it."

He smiled and turned back to his newspaper. Over his shoulder, Me-

Liz could read the headline. "Farandola," it said. Michael took her hand, and the next thing she knew she was back in the dewy garden.

For weeks after that, she buttonholed everyone: "What's a mitochondria? What's a farandola?"

The answer to the first question was easy.

"It's kind of the powerhouse, or energy center, of a cell," her new doctor, Walt Scott, told her. "But farandola? No idea. Never heard of it."

She asked all the doctors and specialists Dr. Scott sent her to. She'd sit on the edge of the examining table and matter-of-factly explain the story of her vision, and then they'd chuckle and start adjusting their cuffs and shift uneasily from foot to foot and then they'd be gone. But Walt never went away. He listened. He had listened to her from that very first August afternoon when she walked into his little downtown office in Aurora, weeping from the pain in her neck and arm. And over the months that followed, as he grew increasingly perplexed at her deteriorating medical condition, Dr. Scott had continued to listen to her—even when he didn't believe a word about "Michael" and the "beings of light," and told her so.

He still didn't know what a farandola was, though. And he still couldn't figure out what in the world was the matter with her.

The medical problems had started almost as soon as she and Jeff arrived in Aurora, back in the fall of 1982. Little things, at first. Wrenching stomach pains, one snowy December night not long after she moved into the cottage. She spent two days in the hospital for that. A few months later, she was back in the hospital for a high fever caused by kidney problems. In August, a strange rash appeared on her face and eye, which was diagnosed as herpes zoster (shingles). Then, almost overnight, it disappeared. Two months later, she developed terrific pains in her lower abdomen. Then she had an attack of chest pain, for which she was admitted to a coronary care unit. Then, that August of 1983, she had pains in her neck and shoulders, and more odd rashes on her arms.

First it was one thing, then another. The pains and ailments seemed to be accelerating in frequency and seriousness, like strokes of a piston gathering speed. And somehow, they seemed to be connected to the great unfolding that Michael kept telling her about. He told her that a great transformation was coming, that life as she knew it was coming to an end. Many shall become one, like the pods, he said. Michael was gentle with her. He wanted to prepare her. He wanted this to be a time of rest and spiritual growth and preparation.

But preparation for what?

There was an abandoned Baptist church camp on the ragged hillside behind the cottage, and Me-Liz and Michael tramped that hill over-looking the calm lake in every kind of weather, day and night, until they knew every tumbledown cabin, every square foot of blackberry patch and timothy grass. She would spend hours up there on the hill, apparently alone, but actually in deep communion with Michael and the beings of light, who would show her things and take her places far, far away. It was up there, and in the garden, that Michael began show-ing her the answer.

Calmly and gently, with an unfathomable smile, he'd doff his black hat and demonstrate a slow, stately, slightly comical spin. Arms uplifted, hat doffed in one hand, that enigmatic smile would come around again and again. It was the spin of the farandola, he said. This was not a dance that was to take place in the visible dimension. It was to take place inside her cells. It was a dance that would create so much heat she would be transformed.

It would kill her, he said.

And it would make her whole.

By the summer of 1984, Me-Liz could see clearly that the pattern of physical breakdowns had accelerated to the point where a new medical problem would surface roughly once every twenty-one days. She was also convinced that there was some connection between her increas-ingly bizarre physical symptoms and her "visits" with Michael. She even made a diagram of the process. First came "knowing it will hap-pen" (that is, knowing Michael would come, or she'd have a vision or premonition). Then physical symptoms: fever, rash, or seizures. These would be accompanied by emotions, either positive (joy, expectation, and a sense of responsibility) or negative (growing apprehension, fear, guilt, and a sense of impending doom). Then came the certainty that it was going to happen. Then the actual event—a visit, a premonition, a voice—and then the physical symptoms would disappear, usually within a few hours.

Jess was fascinated by all of this. He loved to oversee the medical examinations, describing in detail the patient's chief complaint and other symptomatology. He and Liz made a great team: Liz got sick, and Jess diagnosed her. He'd grown up over the years. Now he was nineteen, tall and almost comically intense. He loved to talk to the

169

doctors about diagnostic procedures, and he was thrilled when they took him seriously.

Liz had been helping Edie Zenns restore an old building in town that Sunday afternoon when she'd gone to see Dr. Scott for the first time. She was in terrible pain. The whole thing had been building up for more than a month—pains in her neck, pounding headaches, aching and numbness in her right arm and shoulders. She'd been seeing another doctor in town, but he didn't seem to take her seriously. But that afternoon, Kitty had become totally fed up and frightened when she couldn't even hold a paintbrush in her hand. She went slamming down to the new doctor in town, and marched into his office without an appointment.

Dr. Scott wasn't in the office when Kitty walked in, but when his nurse described her symptoms to him over the phone, Dr. Scott had her checked into Tompkins Community Hospital, down in Ithaca, for a neurological workup. He was concerned that the old neck surgery might be acting up. Jeff took her to the emergency room at the hospital, where the consulting neurologist, Dr. Bachelor, took an X-ray series. Then he had her hospitalized immediately.

Liz was sitting up in her hospital bed wearing a soft collar the next day, August 16, 1984, when Dr. Scott walked in and she met him face-to-face for the first time. Her immediate impression was that he looked very young, and very strange. He came rushing into the room with such an air of breathlessness it was as if his tie and white lab jacket were flying out behind him, and stayed there for the next two hours. He had pale, unhealthy looking skin, a stiff mass of short, curly black hair dense as a Brillo pad, and thick glasses with transparent frames. Behind the heavy lenses, his dark, penetrating eyes flashed with intelligence.

"Well, OK, so Dr. Bachelor thinks there's a problem in the cervical spine," he began without introduction.

Jess popped out immediately. Good! Great! Time to talk medical talk!

"Is it cord compression?"

Dr. Scott gave Jess an amused, piercing glare.

"Well, no, that's the good news. It's not the spine itself that's compressed. That could be real serious. Looks like it's just a pinched nerve—probably C6, the sixth cervical nerve root. That's the one that supplies your right arm. That's how come your arm is numb."

"My arm's still numb, doc. I've still got numbness in my thumb, middle, and index fingers, too."

"Any chest pain?"

"No."

"Shortness of breath?"

"No."

"Any weakness in your legs?"

"Nah. I can walk fine."

"Had any trouble urinating?"

"No, huh-unh."

"Well listen, partner, Dr. Bachelor thinks we ought to do a dye study, a myelogram, to see if we can pinpoint the problem. Right now he thinks it's C6—C6 radiculopathy, as we say—but we can't be positive until we run the study."

"C6 radiculopathy," repeated Jess, dreamily.

Then Dr. Scott sat down on the edge of the bed with his clipboard and began taking a medical history from his new patient, Elizabeth Katherine Castle. He did not realize, of course, that most of the history was given by a nineteen-year-old boy named Jess. Jess's history was clear, concise, and to-the-point. For the next two hours, he was in his element.

DR. SCOTT: There were some very unusual things about this medical history she gave me. For one thing, she was extremely well-informed about medicine. She had the working knowledge of about a fourth-year medical student. She told me about this neurological workup she'd had in Minneapolis, for epileptic seizures. She described them as "Jacksonian, psychomotor and focal seizures." Now, it's extremely unusual for anyone, myself included, to know what these terms mean, unless you're a neurologist. She also described in detail all the tests that had been done— from pneumoencephalography on down. She referred to muscle spasms in her neck as "trismus," which is a usage that makes perfect sense, even though it's not precisely accurate. (Trismus is actually lockjaw—a spasm of the masseter muscle in the jaw.) I mean, you know—patients just don't talk like this.

Her medical history was also very unusual because of its length. Usually you can summarize a medical history in one short paragraph, but her history is almost a page long, single-spaced. It took me over an hour to take it. I was twenty-nine years old, fresh out of my internal medicine residency program at the University of Pennsylvania Medical School, and the length and detail and depth of her problems were a bit overwhelming. I mean, this girl is forty years old. You don't expect to go into

171

an hour-long past medical history with someone that young. (Actually, she looked a lot younger than forty, and I noted that on her chart.)

The content of her history was also distressing to me. Why was this young woman having so many problems? That was a red flag. She had some kind of bizarre seizure disorder, with blackouts and hallucinations. Chest pains. Kidney problems (which she called "pyelonephritis with high spiking fevers"). Pain in her joints. Transient ischemic attacks—a kind of ministroke uncommon in a young woman. Strange rashes on her face and arms. Thrombophlebitis—a blood clot in her leg. Peptic ulcers. Hospitalizations for exhaustion and weakness. She'd also lost eighteen pounds over the past few weeks, and complained of chest pains.

I was, of course, looking for a unifying theme in all this. Statistically, it's far more likely that you're going to find one underlying problem that explains all the symptoms, rather than six different completely unrelated things going on—especially in someone so young. The likeliest candidate was lupus. Facial rashes, blood clots, kidney problems, aching joints— these are all classic symptoms of systemic lupus erythematosis, which is a connective tissue disorder usually found in middle-aged women.

The thing is, if somebody has systemic lupus, plus a seizure disorder like that, they should be sick as hell. Normally, lupus is a hard diagnosis to miss because the patient is so sick. But except for the pinched nerve in her neck, she seemed well. Why was I seeing someone who looked well, with this kind of past medical history? And if she had a seizure disorder, how come she wasn't on antiepileptic medication? With that kind of med- ical history, she shouldn't look so good, and she should be on some medi- cations, and she should be seen by a doctor chronically, not just for these acute episodes every once in a while. To me, the whole thing just didn't make sense.

Was she just making the whole thing up? A malingerer? Well, I don't permit myself to even think that, at least not at first. My job is to help the patient, not conclude that they're crazy or malingering. Of course, her personal history made it all seem even more bizarre. She said she'd been raised in foster homes, that she'd lived all over the country, and that her first husband and three children had been killed in a car wreck. And she was relatively new to the area. She had, in effect, no past.

As a medical resident, you're always looking for the stump-the-stars case that you can figure out that nobody else could diagnose. So this case, with all its complexities, really got me going. I was looking for the unify- ing theme that no one else had found—never suspecting, at that time, what the unifying theme would turn out to be.

Elizabeth Katherine Castle was released after two days at Tompkins Community Hospital. The dye study of her spine had confirmed a blockage, or compression, around the sixth cervical nerve root, but Dr. Scott decided to treat her conservatively, with a soft collar, bed rest, and pain medication. Liz was terrified of having to go through neck surgery again, and she was only too happy to cooperate. He sent her home in a wheelchair.

A few days later, on August 22, Jeff came home from work to find Liz in so much pain she couldn't even get out of bed. When he saw the condition she was in, Jeff called Dr. Scott immediately, and Dr. Scott told him to call an ambulance and get her back to the hospital. The med techs had to slide her from the waterbed onto a big sheet of plywood, then onto a gurney into the ambulance. Liz was doing her best not to scream.

She was taken back to the hospital in Ithaca, where Dr. Scott and the neurologist, Dr. Bachelor, examined her again.

DR. SCOTT: The presentation was ominous, because the weakness and numbness had spread beyond the C6 nerve root area—suggesting there was more than just that one nerve root involved. It looked as though the spinal cord itself might be under compression now, with progressive paralysis spreading down through the nerve tree. This was potentially a critical situation.

The next day, August 23, I had Dr. Fischer, a neurosurgeon, take a look at the patient. On his consult sheet he wrote, "Although reviewing the myelogram one becomes tempted to suggest surgical intervention of a total decompressive laminectomy of C5 and C6 with bilateral decompression of the C6 nerve root . . . after examining the patient, I did not think she needed surgical decompression. She may be treated with conservative measures; however, one might seek other neurosurgical opinion."

In other words, "I think she needs surgery but I'm not going to do it." I think he smelled something fishy and he didn't want to touch her. He probably read the past medical history and said to himself, "This lady's a nut." Something wasn't right. He didn't want to do surgery on somebody who was crazy.

Kitty wet herself. She could hardly believe it, but she lost control of her bladder and wet the bed. The nerve damage was spreading: the bottoms of her feet were burning yet numb at the same time, and it was working its way up her legs, like a consuming fire. Dr. Scott was clearly worried: the paraplegia in the legs and bladder was a serious sign, he said. The hospital was not equipped to handle a neurological emergency like this, and the hospitals he called in Binghamton were full. The only thing available was the neurological intensive care unit at Crouse Irving Memorial Hospital in Syracuse—an hour and a half away. Dr. Scott felt she needed to be seen immediately. So she was sent, by ambulance—lights flashing, sirens wailing, full speed ahead— to Syracuse.

The fear came up around Liz's throat like strangling hands. She was sure she was going to die. She was going to the place where they take you to die. White-coated attendants lifted her out of the ambulance onto a gurney, then rolled her into a big, cold, surgically lit room filled with beds. Everybody around her, lying in bed, was naked and seemed to be dying. They were all hooked up to weird tangles of tubes and pumps. Little beeps and bells. Nurses scurrying here and there. Hands coming down, beating on her chest, pinching her cheeks, smacking her face.

"Breathe!" the nurse was saying. "Breathe! You've got to remember to breathe!" And then some kind of apparatus with tubes drooping off it was fitted over her face and she forgot everything.

On the afternoon of August 24, 1984, neurosurgeons at Crouse Irving Memorial Hospital opened Elizabeth Castle's neck from the front and removed the arthritic, bony spur, or osteophyte, that had been pressing on the fifth and sixth cervical nerve roots and apparently causing all the trouble.

People came to visit after the operation, but Liz saw them in a fog. Jeff came with Isabel Parker, from the library, and Liz told them to take care of each other. She was sure she was going to die. The doctors had had to remove all her top teeth to fit their equipment in through her mouth, and even though Kitty was overjoyed that the clinic was going to give her new teeth, and pay for it, right now she just looked and felt like a pitiable wreck, her lips drooping like a hag. There were stitches on the roof of her mouth, and tubes coming out of her every which way. Once Kitty woke up and tried to come out, but she couldn't, because Liz was passed out on the bed. If one of them was unconscious, nobody else could come out.

Liz spent a few days in the intensive care unit after the surgery, and then she was taken downstairs to a beautiful suite of rooms that looked like an expensive hotel room. It had a couch, a private bath with a whirlpool, a TV, and a stereo, as well as a little kitchen. Naturally, as soon as she got a load of these digs, Kitty popped out. If pain and humiliation were Liz's element, satin sheets and room service were Kitty's. As far as she was concerned, she belonged in the Statler Hilton, and this—finally—was it. Two handsome, impassive young black men came to wait on her hand and foot, and she waved her little finger at them imperiously, like Cleopatra. Kitty Rosetti had arrived.

But about a week after she was sent home from the clinic, Liz began having problems swallowing. She felt like she had a lump in her throat or something. Food wouldn't go down. Her voice was husky, and it hurt to talk. Then she noticed that the surgical incision on her neck seemed inflamed and swollen. Fevers and chills came on. But when she started having trouble breathing, she really got scared. Jeff took her down to see Dr. Scott, who was immediately concerned. If the incision became infected, he told her, it could threaten the airways or the carotid artery. Dr. Scott felt that postsurgical complications should be seen by the surgeon himself—so before she knew it, Liz was on her way back to the hospital in Syracuse. Three days later, she was released again.

"By the time of discharge, the patient was feeling much better," wrote the ENT specialist at the hospital in his discharge summary on September 24, 1984. "Her incisional tenderness greatly decreased. Her voice returned to normal. She remained afebrile [not feverish]. With the above workup having been negative for evidence of a serious infection, the patient was discharged in satisfactory condition. . . ."

One of the doctors who saw her at Crouse Irving noted that it was his impression that she had "globus syndrome"—a muscle spasm in the throat thought to be related to hysteria. In other words, he thought it was all in her head.

More than once, over the weeks and months that followed, Dr. Scott began to entertain the same vague suspicion. Because the neck surgery did not put an end to her problems. Not by a long shot.

On October 17th, Liz came into his office again, complaining of a rash, stomach pain, a low-grade fever, and tachycardia (rapid heartbeats). She came in a few days later complaining of burning pain on urination. Then she had a throbbing pain in her left leg, then abdominal pains, then more weird rashes on the backs of her hands. First it was this, then it was that. More than once, the problem would "spontaneously resolve," like a disappearing ghost. Then a new one would appear to take its place. Hardly a week went by that Liz Castle was not in his office, or in the hospital for yet another round of tests: work-ups on her blood, urine, and stool; X-rays; sonograms; tomograms; barium enemas; CT scans; EEGs.

JEFF CASTLE: I'd get calls at work and somebody would say, "Your wife's in the hospital, but don't worry!" It's hard not to worry, but after a while you get used to it. I was only making minimum wage, but I kept my job just because of the medical insurance. I figure Liz ran up a bill of sixty to eighty thousand, just in a year or so. The neck surgery alone, and all that intensive care, cost over fifty. She'd seen other doctors before, but they always seemed to brush her off. Walt Scott was the exact oppo-site. He ordered every test imaginable, and that's exactly what she needed. He wouldn't let go. He just kept pushing. He told us he wouldn't give up.

Liz felt comfortable being an invalid. If there was any way she could have become a professional patient, she would have. She fed on sym-pathy. As soon as she was checked into the hospital, she'd go wander-ing down the hall and bum a cigarette from a nurse and start making friends. All the X-ray techs knew her by name. She had doctors' home phone numbers in her little black book. She got CAT scans like other people would go out to dinner. But deep inside, far beyond the reach of her conscious mind, she had given up hope. She was losing her will to live. She was withdrawing from the world, cutting her ties to anyone outside of doctors and hospitals. When she was discharged from the hospital, she'd become a recluse, clomping around the little cottage in her walker and neck brace, wearing big hats and long-sleeved shirts and dresses to cover herself up from the world. She rarely went outside. She was going to leave it to the medical community, and if they couldn't figure it out, fine, she'd just die.

KIT CASTLE: I thank God for Walt Scott! He just kept going until there were no more tests to run, and Liz finally had to face the fact that what was going on here was not medical. In desperation, she was manu-facturing symptom after symptom as a way of avoiding the real hurt, the real pain—her past. Her memory. What had happened to her so long ago, as a child. And, of course, "the secret." One by one, Walt Scott was knocking the supports out from under this fantasy of sickness that she had, so that slowly, slowly, she was being backed into a corner where she had to confront the truth.

Jess, the only male personality, liked to wear hats and tie his hair back in a ponytail. In Arizona, he began falling in love with Kitty, not realizing that he and she both lived inside the same body.

Penny Lavender was so heartbroken over the divorce from Sandy Lentz that she stopped talking. After that, she expressed herself only through art and music. She saw the world through a misty romantic haze; perhaps that is why her lids were continually droopy, as if she were half-asleep.

Liz was weak, depressed, inarticulate, full of guilt and shame, and constantly ill. Unable to confront the truth about what had happened to her children, she transformed her inner torment into physical illness and toward the end of her existence spent most of her time in the hospital.

Miss Kitty Rosetti, burlesque queen, performed her singing strip act in clubs from Dallas to Minneapolis. She considered herself to be a sort of off-off Broadway star. She longed to be legitimate, to be respected, to be loved.

Sometimes Kitty could be as cold and hard as ice. She was strong-willed, complex, competent, a lover and conqueror of men. She was determined not to be overwhelmed by life the way "the others" had been. Kitty was determined not only to win but to triumph—she was a survivor. (Credit: Robert Rice)

Because she had devoted herself to the spiritual life at an early age, Me-Liz considered herself a virgin (the body never made love as Me-Liz). She was not a thing of flesh and pain, but of God and light. Me-Liz had psychic powers that she could neither understand nor control; she could never understand why all of the photographs of her had hazy lights in them.

Little Andrea was the first alter personality to split from the original, core personality, Little Elizabeth. (There are no photographs of Little Elizabeth.) Because Little Andrea rarely came out, she stayed about five years old.

Dear Dr Walton,

I've kept this stuff put away for quite sometime now, but, feel that it may be appropriate that you see it now.

The photos have been collected over time, so as not to confuse her. There are pictures of all of us.

Little Andrea + Little Elizabeth are ready to leave. They feel they must. They don't want to go to prison. In fact, Little Elizabeth is paralized with fear most of the time.

Liz is very confused and feels the fear that Little Elizabeth + Little Andrea have, but can't know why she feels it, which scares her even more. I'm sure you understand that with the fear she has now she can barely cope with everyday stuff.

I'm here now and won't let things get too crazy and I promise to do my best to keep them here. If I can't, I'll call you as soon as I can.

I certainly can't predict that I will see you on Monday - but I hope to. We have much to work through about this accident business. We must be careful not to let the others know before it's full out. The reason it got out of hand was because it happened in bits and pieces and was taken so much out of context. This was experienced by 4 people, not one, you see.

You TOUCHED Liz ON THE SHOLDER TWICE, I KNOW CAUSE I SAW AND FELT IT. I THOUGHT SHE WAS GOING TO CRY. I HOPED SHE WOULD - SHE HASN'T IN YEARS. YOU ARE GOOD. YOUR TOUCH IS O.K, TOO. WE ARE GLAD, Liz + I THAT YOU FEEL O.K. ABOUT TOUCH. BUT, DON'T TOUCH LITTLE Elizabeth. SHE WILL HURT.

Please don't show the documents to Anyone but me until they get used to it, knowing I mean. I can help with as much as I can, I have memory, but am not responsible for their decisions. We must work together on this. I will fill you in on what happened and when their family memories are missing I can help.

I can tell you now that the babies and her husband are not dead, But, it would be better for her if they were. She can never go back. Not if she really loves them, and soon she will realize that her ethics will be challenged beyond belief. Stand strong by her and so will I. Her goodness will shine through. she is innocent of murder.

Kitty

Letter from Kitty to Dr. Ralph Walton warning him about "the others."

May 86

This week
SAT AM - FRI AM

SAT PM - HAITI MEMORIES
       NIGHTHOWLING
SUN AM - NO SLEEP - WASHED OUT - HOT
SUN PM - SPENT DAY IN GARDEN - LESS HOT
       SLEPT HARD SUNDAY NIGHT
MON - AM - NO VISIT - DAY SEEMED FOREVER
MON PM - LONG, LONG NIGHT, THINKING NIGHT
TUES AM - KNEW FOR CERTAIN THAT I HAD TO TALK TO JEFF.
        COULD NOT CONTINUE TO USE HIM LIKE THIS.
TUES PM - TALKED WITH JEFF - ROUGH WORK - BUT WORTH IT.
WED AM - I HAD TO PUT BABY WALTON TO SLEEP.
       MANY ~~FEELINGS~~ MANY AWFUL FEELINGS SURFACE
WED PM - AT WAR WITH RESTLESSNESS AND WANTING TO HOWL.
       PENNY + I HAVE SERIOUS DISCUSSION - SHE WANTS
       TO RUN, TOO. I KNOW I MUST STAY. PLURAL FARANDOLA.
       TRANSDEMSIONAL, HOPEFULLY.
THURS AM - SLEPT HARD WED NIGHT
        BOTH SKINNER AND FRUED ARE VERY SICK, KATE IS FRANI
THURS PM - JEFF WANTED TO TALK AGAIN - WE DID - PRODUCTIVE
FRI AM 7AM - BABY FRUED IS VERY KL - I PUT HIM TO SLEEP
        MUST FIND A WAY TO KEEP SKINNER ALIVE

An enigmatic page from a diary kept by "the others." As Dr.
Walton led them deeper and deeper into the terrors of the
past, they all became increasingly frightened and restless.
Some nights Liz would go out in the dark and just howl.
("Skinner," "Freud," and "Baby Walton" were kittens.)

"World is their oyster, declare gay smiling beauties entered as queen contestants in the Miss Highland Park beauty pageant," read the caption in the Highland Park, Texas newspaper when this photo of Liz ran on February 9, 1967. Liz's father had talked her into entering, but she was more suspicious than flattered by his sudden attention. She knew he had some nasty trick up his sleeve and she was right.

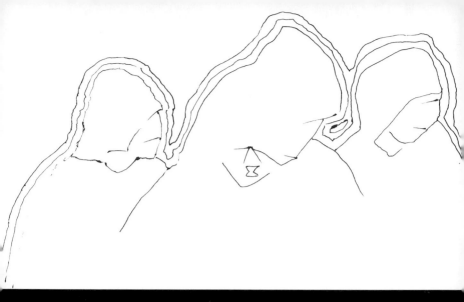

Me-Liz made this sketch of the three Beings of Light who appeared to her in Virginia Beach, Virginia. They communicated a message: She was to go to a place at a higher elevation, near water. That is where the great event was to take place—but what was the great event?

A sketch of Michael by Kit Castle. "The others" never knew how or from where Michael came; he just appeared when they needed him most. "You must never forget that your 'real father' watches over you always, and he will send me to help when there is danger," Michael promised. And he always did.

If Liz was the one who crawled wearily and self-pityingly into bed, Kitty was the one who would angrily jump out. "Screw this crap!" she'd howl. She railed against all physical limits. When Liz came home from Crouse Irving the second time, Kitty immediately checked out a book on physical therapy and started doing exercises to get herself on her feet as fast as possible. There was no way those beautiful legs were going to waste. Six weeks after her release from the hospital for major neck surgery, Kitty participated in a 10 kilometer "Crop Walk" to raise money for the hungry. Although it hurt, she did it without a cane and without self-pity. She was proud of herself. She was a survivor.

Me-Liz, meanwhile, would totter down to the garden and sit on a stump in the pale autumn sunlight, and Michael would come to her and take her places far, far away. For her, it was a relief just to be out of that hurting, broken-down body for a little while. Legs restored, light as the air, drifting out over the lake, Michael would take her out of the body and show her more and more about the spin. He smiled. He treated her gently, as if she were a tiny child. She had to be ready, he said. She had to learn not to be scared.

It was Me-Liz who found the dictionary. It was a big old dusty thing, published in 1939, on a high shelf in an old house Edie was restoring. Just for fun, she looked up "farandola," and there it was.

> **farandole:** Lively and popular chain dance of Provence and Catalonia. Performed on feast days, the farandole is danced by men and women holding hands in a chain. The dancers, following the steps introduced by the leader, spin through the streets to the accompaniment of pipes and tabors . . . Also, **farandola.**

Michael just smiled.

Chapter 19

How many childbirths were there?" asked Dr. Small, the ob-gyn, peering quizzically over the tops of his half-glasses. But Liz did not answer. She crouched, small and afraid, on the edge of the examining table. Back around Christmas, one of the many abdominal X-rays that had been taken revealed a small cyst on her left ovary, and now, at the beginning of February 1985, Dr. Small was talking about doing a partial hysterectomy to remove it. He was a little man with a narrow, feline face and a way of moving so suddenly it spooked her.

"Hmmm?" he asked again. "Two childbirths, or three? I'm sorry, I can't quite recall."

Liz was silent. All she felt was a gloomy, suffocating fear. It wasn't the operation that scared her. She liked operations. It was all this talk of babies and ovaries and childbirth. She thought of those dark inward parts, those twisting, lightless tunnels and passageways, the ovaries and the uterus, the place where babies came from. Did the police call her that day? Domingo was driving the kids to a birthday party somewhere, and somebody called about the accident. Somebody must have called. Who called? She couldn't remember.

"Mrs. Castle?" Dr. Small asked again, his eyes wide and unnaturally intense, like a cat peering down at a mouse. At that moment, Liz just went away. There was too much to remember, too much to be afraid of. She didn't want to go down those dark corridors, into those close, twisting halls. Suddenly, there sat Me-Liz on the edge of the examining table, staring at an absurd little man wearing a white lab coat and enormous, ill-fitting half-glasses.

"How many?"

"How many what?"

"Childbirths, Mrs. Castle! How many childbirths were there!"

"You mean me?"

"Well, who else do you think I mean?"

"Three. There were three."

He jotted something down on a clipboard.

"Well, I can't promise, but I'd be willing to bet you'll feel much better after the operation. I've got you scheduled for Tuesday at two."

"Operation?"

Dr. Small shook his head ever so slightly, as if he had a tic.

"The *hysterectomy,* Mrs. Castle. As I explained, you've got a small ovarian cyst."

Me-Liz panicked. *Oh, my God!* she thought. *Not another operation!* She wasn't afraid of the operation, either; it was the scar that worried her. She couldn't stand the thought of another big ugly scar on her body. So she just went away like Liz did, and then Penny Lavender woke up in the examining room just as the tail of Dr. Small's white lab coat fluttered out the door.

It was Penny Lavender who had the surgery, by default, at Tompkins Community Hospital in Ithaca, New York, on March 13, 1985.

The morning after the operation, Kitty Rosetti woke up in the hospital. And when she realized what had happened, she was royally, mightily, spectacularly pissed. She hadn't consented to this operation, she despised being sick and dependent, she felt awful, and she had had just about enough of this nonsense. This had gone far enough! Now they were cutting her up because they couldn't figure out what was wrong. She raged. She ranted. She refused to take her medicine. She threw things. And when Dr. Scott came in, she pretended she did not even recognize him.

In some oblique and desperate way, Kitty was trying to communicate that something was very, very wrong. She didn't know how to come right out and *say* it; she *couldn't,* somehow. After all, the others were the secret of secrets, the thing she had risked her life to hide all those years.

179

Instead, she bitched a blue streak, hoping someone would realize something was wrong. Apparently, she'd bitched a time too many.

Nobody seemed to notice.

A few weeks later, on a snowy Sunday afternoon in March, Dr. Scott kicked his office door shut, took the phone off the hook, and put his feet up on the desk. He pulled out the file on Elizabeth Katherine Castle and got ready to dictate a case summary. Again.

He was still troubled by doubts about that hysterectomy.

"Is this the best we can do?" he'd asked, when Dr. Small recommended surgery to remove the cyst. "We don't know what's going on with this woman, so we do a hysterectomy and see if she feels better? After a million-dollar workup and a medical record an inch thick, is this really all the better we can do?"

It had only reaffirmed his doubts when Dr. Small confided after the operation, "There really wasn't much there, Walt. That cyst really could have been left alone."

Still, after the cyst was taken out, the pain syndrome went away. Liz said she felt better. On the other hand, Dr. Scott knew very well that some hysterical patients will get better after an operation for no good reason. Did the operation take away the pain because the cyst was the problem, or was this a psychosomatic disorder that was being treated with a sham operation? He couldn't honestly say. It was back to the land of dry ice and mirrors. Ghosts. He was chasing ghosts again.

He slipped his shoes off and let them fall with a forlorn thump to the floor. Then he switched on the dictating machine:

"The patient is a forty-year-old white female who has a complicated past medical history involving a seizure disorder, cervical neck disease, recurrent episodes of lower extremity weakness, abdominal pain, and skin rashes," he observed wearily. "On 10/17/84 the patient had skin rashes on her left arm, left face, an elevated heart rate, and an elevated white blood count. On 11/5/84 she had a fever and viral syndrome. She then developed abdominal pain and skin rashes, right leg weakness, and right upper-extremity drift. On 11/15/84 she had a urinary tract infection. Hallelujah! Something we could treat! On 11/26/84 she developed an L-5 radiculopathy with weakness and pain in distribution of her sciatic nerve. . . .

"On 12/4/84 she had left-hand pain with decreased grip. She had slight tachycardia at that time with heart rate of one hundred. On 12/17/84 she had loss of bowel and bladder times two and severe back pain. Merry Christmas. Time for a CT scan of the lumbar spine. The

results were weird, though. No sign of arthritis down there, or anything else that might suggest enough nerve damage to result in loss of bladder function. Then the problem spontaneously resolved."

There it was again: "Spontaneous resolution" of unexplained problems. Ghosts. He was chasing ghosts. What did it all mean? What did it add up to? Country doctors were a dying breed, he thought, and it was no wonder. Any subspecialist in the book made more money—and all they had to deal with were referrals. He had to deal with anything that walked through the door. None of these guys had to consider so many possibilities. None of them had to deal with something like Liz Castle.

Kitty had gone home a few days after the hysterectomy, but Liz didn't come home for a week. One night she simply woke up in the bathtub, rubbing a soapy washcloth over something sore on her belly. She looked down and, to her horror, saw a fresh, horizontal surgical incision, about three inches long, neatly stitched across her stomach.

She cried. She cried because it all seemed so hopeless. She cried because she felt so scared. And she cried because she missed it. She missed her big surgery—all the sobbing, all the sympathy—and now, once again, she'd just "woken up" when it was all over.

How much longer could she go on like this?

For a long time, Dr. Scott had been convinced that the most promising candidate was porphyria, a rare enzyme disorder that can cause both physical and psychiatric problems. True, it was highly unusual—but so was Liz Castle's history. He wasn't dealing with some garden-variety sick here. He was dealing with major sick.

Every kid in medical school learned that, up until the nineteenth century, insane asylums were packed with people with undiagnosed organic disorders like thyroid dysfunction or porphyria. Porphyria was a major cause of insanity in those days. Back then, nobody knew that it was simply an enzyme defect that can cause recurrent abdominal pain, episodic seizures, psychotic breaks with reality, and hallucinations. One type also causes skin rashes on sun-exposed areas—the place Liz usually got them. Her symptoms matched the disease, right down the line. Another kicker: when he treated her problems with the preferred treatments for porphyria—a high-carbohydrate diet and Compazine—she got better. (Compazine, of course, was an antipsychotic drug. Was she getting better on it because she was psychotic?)

He'd written off to the American Porphyria Foundation, describing the curiosities of the case, and he'd also contacted a porphyria specialist

181

at Rockefeller University in New York City. He sent the guy the results of her lab studies, and a month later the big expert wrote him back: "The results on this patient are normal. While it may be difficult to exclude porphyria absolutely, these results would make the diagnosis unlikely. . . . I hope these results are of some value in your treatment of this puzzling patient."

So there went porphyria. By that time, it didn't surprise him. Nothing would surprise him anymore.

He sighed again. Now she was back in the hospital, complaining of double vision, slightly slurred speech, and more stomach pains. He'd sent her to see Dr. Curare, the surgeon, for the stomach pains, and Dr. Bachelor, the neurologist, for another neuro exam. Both of their consult sheets lay on the desk in front of him. Surgeons don't mess around. Should they cut, or shouldn't they? But Dr. Curare's comments were as wishy-washy as everybody else's:

"IMPRESSION: (1) Rule out intermittent porphyria—this you are accomplishing with appropriate blood and urine sampling. (2) Rule out PMS. (3) Consider hysteria. (4) Consider brainstem or temporal lobe tumor."

Great, Jorge, thanks. You're a real pal. Now we've got a new one: a brain tumor. Either that or she's nuts.

Dr. Bachelor couldn't do much better:

"It is hard to explain all of her symptoms on the basis of a particular diagnosis but a brainstem lesion could cause double vision and recurrent emesis [vomiting]," he commented.

So now he had a surgeon and a neurologist, and neither one of them knew what the heck it was either.

Well, Dr. Scott thought, at least I'm not alone.

It was only a few weeks later—on May 8, 1985—that the missing piece finally fell into place. Liz had been home alone watching television when a documentary about Houston came on the screen. And when the aerial photographer zeroed in on those secluded, stucco-walled backyards, the littered alleyways, the tiny, boxy houses, a force took hold of her with a power beyond belief.

"I'm sitting there in front of the TV and I'm watching this news broadcast, and they're showing these aerial shots of this neighborhood in Houston, and I just . . . I just . . . I recognized that neighborhood!" she'd sobbed when she burst into Dr. Scott's office. "I think I lived there! And then it was like I was flashing back . . . back and back . . . I saw a bathroom, a yellow bathroom . . . yellow tiles . . .

182

"And then somebody was on top of me! He was grabbing me from behind, and he was hurting me. . . . It hurt! It hurt! I was struggling to get away, and I couldn't get away! He was . . . raping me . . . but I couldn't get away! I couldn't get away!"

When that show came on TV, she had flashed back to that scene in the bathroom so suddenly, and with such force, that she felt as if she'd been thrown against a wall. She wasn't just remembering it; she was *there*. It was happening to her. Yet what astounded her more than anything was the clear impression that *it was not she* who was being raped. It was someone else. Someone else, who lived inside her. Someone else, whose memories she harbored in her mind. Someone else, whose life she'd never remembered before, *because it was not her own*.

How could Dr. Scott, or anyone, possibly understand what was going on with her? How could anyone understand the feeling she had, that her whole life was a basketful of loose pearls, and that to have a life at all she would have to string the pearls back together, one by one? That she would have to go back to the blank spots, and all the memories in her mind that did not belong to her at all?

"Walt," she'd whispered, "What's happening to me? *What is happening to me?* Do you think I'm going to die? Is that what this is all about? Am I going to die now?"

The farandola is not a dance that will take place in the physical dimension, Michael had told her. *It is to take place inside your cells. It is a dance that will create so much heat that you will be transformed.*

It will kill you, he had said.

And it will make you whole.

Part 2

"The Final Farandola"

Chapter 20

I can't believe how much he looks like Michael," Me-Liz was saying, dreamily. "Something about the eyes. They look like they're a thousand years old. . . ."

"I love a man with a mysterious accent," Penny Lavender went on. "What is it? Some kind of brogue? Is it British? Yiddish? Very faint, but very distinguished. Very man-about-town. Like he just stepped off the night train from *Berlin* or something."

"He smells nice," Liz murmured.

The five of them—Me-Liz, Penny Lavender, Liz, Jess, and Kitty—were seated at a round oak conference table in the other world. The table was located in a common area not far from the secret places to which they all crept away when they went inside: Me-Liz's immaterial, holy place, bathed in pinkish light; Penny's whitewashed cabin by the pond; Liz's dark, unpleasant hole, wet as a muskrat's den; Jess's tidy room with the red telescope and the posters of Albert Einstein; and Kitty's apartment, with its leopard-skin rugs and Danish furniture, which looked like a set from "The Young and the Restless." The babies, Little Elizabeth and Little Andrea, only rarely emerged from their warm gray caves during these board meetings, and normally had no vote at all (except when the decision at hand was whether or not to go out for ice cream). Kitty was the acknowledged chairman of the board, and tonight, only hours after their first meeting with the new psychiatrist, Dr. Walton, she'd called a meeting to discuss whether or not they should keep seeing him.

"Yeah, sure, he talks funny, but who *dresses* the poor man?" Kitty cut in acidly. "Rep ties and shiny suits! Yuck, a thousand times yuck! Probably the same little person who did the waiting room. I mean, how 'bout that *wall*paper?"

"Oh, I dunno, seems like a pretty straight-up-and-down guy to me," Jess said. "Seems OK. It's hard to tell about somebody after just a half-hour. Neat office, though. Ever seen a PDR in black leather like that?"

"Well, anyway, God loves us all, and I think we should stop arguing and start working together—for Him, not against Him," Me-Liz said firmly. "I think we should start seeing Dr. Walton, and just take it one session at a time, like today."

"What if he turns out to be another Dr. Delgado?" Kitty asked. "Another boss bitch?"

"Letter bomb," Jess said. "Mail him a letter bomb. It always works in the movies."

Finally Kitty, exasperated, tried to force the discussion to a vote.

"All right, everybody! Let's just do it! Shall we keep seeing the man in the shiny suit, or not? All in favor say aye!"

"Wait a second," Jess objected. "I think Me-Liz had a good idea. Maybe we should just take it one session at a time."

"Yeah, I like that idea too," said Penny. "If it doesn't work out after a few times, we just dump him. Delgado dumped us, so we'll dump him."

"Don't be such a smarty-pants," Me-Liz admonished Penny, with the air of a disapproving schoolmarm. "We need help, and we need it desperately. We all know it now. We can't go on this way anymore. You want to wind up eating out of dumpsters again? You want to wind up stuffed in some back ward somewhere? You want to wind up in the morgue with a little tag on your toe? Suicide is a sacrilege. And wasting our lives like this is too."

Everyone else fell silent. Me-Liz, as usual, held the high moral ground. And in the end, all the others agreed to keep seeing Dr. Walton—one session at a time.

It was September 11, 1985, nearly six months after Dr. Scott had first spoken the words that were to change their lives. They'd gone to see Dr. Jacoby, the psychiatrist in Ithaca, the afternoon Dr. Scott first suggested the diagnosis. But Dr. Jacoby seemed overwhelmed by the complexities of the case; he told them he didn't feel qualified to confirm a diagnosis of multiple personality disorder, much less treat one. Instead, he'd referred them to a specialist in Syracuse, a Dr. Delgado. But the experience with Dr. Delgado had been, somehow, jarringly wrong from the start. The chemistry wasn't right; none of the others cared for the woman, and she quite clearly returned the favor. Finally Dr. Delgado had simply had her secretary call to inform them she would be unable to see them any longer. In desperation, Kitty had turned to the only avenue of help she knew: the crisis hotline at Tompkins Community Hospital. From there, she was referred to the hospital's chief of psychiatry, Dr. Ralph Walton.

Throughout those six months, they all felt incapable of taking responsibility for themselves in the "real" world, and spent most of their time puttering in the triangular gardens beside the cottage by the lake, or alone inside the house, hidden away. So much was happening in the other world! It was almost impossible to explain how astounding it was, how sad, how confusing, how miraculous, how scary. For days after Walt had said the words, all the others were in an absolute panic. They struggled to grasp what was going on, without success—all they knew was that, in some strange way, an enormous light had gone on in their heads, and all around them, apparently absolutely real, were these other people who were living in the same body, and had been for years. For weeks, Liz had been terrified of closing her eyes at night, because she could see their faces in front of her, like semitransparent reflections in glass. They were all talking and laughing and questioning and crying and chattering at once. It sounded like there were hundreds of them.

It was not as if one changeless, indivisible person were sitting there observing and hearing and analyzing all these other people. It was more as if each one of them would get bursts of consciousness, completely disconnected, and not in any sequence, where they were conscious of the others. It was like popcorn in a popping machine. They were all bursting like crazy, and there was no way to tell which piece of popcorn burst first. Over time, the bursts got longer and longer and began to steady a bit, until they were capable of actually sitting down at a table together, face-to-face, for a short period of time. The round-table meetings organized by Kitty were, in some ways, the greatest achievement of their lives. The sunlight of consciousness had finally begun to illuminate the darkest rooms of their minds.

Jess, a young man of nineteen wearing beige corduroy pants, a Pendleton shirt, and long reddish hair pulled back in a ponytail, would

189

pace up and down, scribbling furiously on a pad of paper. He was recording, as carefully as he could, all the symptoms of multiple personality disorder. He was struggling to remain as realistic and objective as possible. He peppered Dr. Scott with questions. He read everything about MPD that he could get his hands on, from *Sybil* on down. He was fascinated by it all—in fact, he began seriously considering changing his field from internal medicine to psychiatry.

To him, this was the ultimate challenge to the empirical, scientific method. For years, he had pictured himself standing at the side of the doctors who were diagnosing the patient. Now, to his everlasting amazement, he had discovered that he was *inside* the patient. He was not the patient, precisely, but only *part* of the patient—a sort of living, breathing fiction, a kind of magic trick, a ghost. He wasn't a real boy at all; he was a puzzling psychiatric phenomenon. It was as if Galileo had discovered not that the earth circled the sun, but that the earth *was* the sun.

The biggest shock, and one which Jess refused to even consider for months, was that Kitty Rosetti—the love of his life—was also inside the patient. This sexy, redheaded fireball was no more real than he was. She was totally unattainable. There was no possible way to work it out. There was nothing he could do to convince her to love him, or even notice him, because . . . because . . . she wasn't even really there at all. She was a reflection in still water, like he was. She was a mirage.

Me-Liz was thrilled when she discovered all these other beings around her. She thought she had broken through to another dimension. She thought this was one of the other worlds that Michael had been showing her for years. The really incredible thing was not that she'd broken through, but that she'd done it all by herself. Always before, it had been Michael who had taken her to these other worlds.

The two babies, utterly unable to understand what was going on, sat quietly together, Little Elizabeth sucking her thumb, Little Andrea endlessly twirling a bolt of hair between her fingers. Penny Lavender immediately took both of them under her wing. She would hold them and comfort them and sing them stories for hours, and the babies responded to her gentle attentions like flowers to the rain. For her part, Penny was overjoyed to have found someone, if only a pair of frightened little doves, who would listen to her. Except through song, she had not spoken to anyone in years, since her heartbreak over the breakup with Sandy Lentz. Once or twice Jess tried to talk to the babies, but they were terrified of men. Penny, obsessively protective, ordered him to go away.

There was only one man the little ones did not fear: Michael. Now he made his way happily among them, hat in hand, laughing and joking with a gentle new radiance. He taught the babies little touching games: "This is my nose and these are my toes, these are my toes and this is my nose . . ." He helped Jess and Kitty and the other adults see the extraordinary gifts they had to share with one another. He made them see that all this was meant to be. It had all happened just as it was destined to, just as he'd said it would. Now in joy and fullness he was preparing them for the beginning and the end.

But not all of them were eager to hear what Michael had to say. They were all still scared and confused and uncertain about what the future was going to bring. And except for Kitty, none of them could clearly remember yet what had happened in their lives. There were still enormous blank spots in all their memories; not all of them were sure they wanted to know what the blank spots held. Of all of them, Liz was the one who denied the diagnosis most furiously. She was the one who clung most desperately to the blank spots. She could not bring herself to accept a psychiatric explanation, because if she did, she would no longer have a legitimate reason to be sick. If she was nuts, the medical problems were all her fault. Instead of opening the door to self-knowledge, and knowledge of the others, she began manufacturing symptoms more furiously than ever.

That fall, a few months after Dr. Scott first suggested the diagnosis, Liz was back in his office, complaining that she was having more numbness and tingling in her arms and hands. Concerned that the surgical site might be impinging on the nerve roots in her neck again, Dr. Scott had her hospitalized so Dr. Bachelor could do another neurological exam. Dr. Bachelor ran an X-ray series. Afterward, he came into her hospital room with the big sheets of film tucked under one arm.

"Look, Mrs. Castle, I've gotta be straight with you," Dr. Bachelor said. "There is absolutely nothing whatsoever the matter with your cervical spine. There's no reason for you to be in here. And quite frankly, I'm getting very tired of this."

"But doc," Liz protested, "my hands are all numb and tingly!"

"I am quite convinced this is not a medical matter. This is a charade. You're malingering. It is, as they say, all in your head."

The blade went deep. Horrified, her guts turned open, Liz fled. Kitty emerged in an instant, bristling with protective rage.

"Hey, maybe there's nothing the matter with my neck, but that still doesn't give you the right to treat a patient this way! How dare you call me a liar! What do you know? You're not a neurosurgeon. You're not even my doctor. You're just, you're just . . . an archaic piece of work!"

A flush crept up Dr. Bachelor's neck and around his ears when he started yelling. Kitty got out of bed and advanced on him, yelling right back. Finally he slammed out of the room, taking the X-rays with him.

When she was alone, Kitty sank back on the bed. The truth of what the doctor had said swept over her. She knew very well he was right. She was getting sick of this, too. There was absolutely no reason for them to be in the hospital, except to indulge Liz's death wish, her unwillingness to face the truth. Screw that! Kitty was leaving. She was out of there. She yanked off her absurdly shapeless hospital blues and put on some real clothes. Her fingers were trembling with rage as she laid in her eyeliner in front of the bathroom mirror. *Screw this!* she thought. It was then that Jeff Castle, Liz's beloved husband, a man Kitty despised, appeared in the mirror over her shoulder. He'd come for a visit, but Kitty wasn't about to wait around for the small talk. She split.

Suddenly, there was Liz again, standing in front of the mirror, fully dressed and heavily made up, apparently getting ready to walk out of the hospital. Liz remembered Dr. Bachelor calling her a "malingerer." She remembered him saying there was nothing wrong with her neck— accusing her, in effect, of lying. It made her feel so ashamed, so desperate for the dark. She longed with every ounce of will in her body just to go back, to go back to being sick, back to X-rays that were absolute proof, CAT scans that demonstrated beyond doubt it was true. She just wanted to go back, back, back, push the door closed on it all and forget.

It was strange, though. Hard as she tried, she couldn't close the door. Light poured through on all sides. Standing there gazing at herself in the mirror, she realized that she knew who'd been there when she was gone. It wasn't just that she could see Kitty's garish handiwork all over her face. It was that she could vaguely, dimly remember—as if consciousness were seeping through the wall of amnesia, like paper steadily becoming more transparent as it grew wetter. It wasn't like it had been for all those years before, when she would "wake up" like someone surfacing out of black water, with no memory of where she had been. It wasn't like a disconnected burst of consciousness, an unstrung pearl of memory. In a vague, dim way, she knew that Kitty had been there.

Against her will, her memory—her life—was coming back.

*   *   *

It was Kitty who arranged the first board meeting, to try to organize their discussions and vote on important matters. And the first vote on Dr. Walton was unanimously in favor. Despite Kitty's disdain for his sense of taste, the others were impressed by Dr. Walton. He was a big contented-looking man with dark, serious eyes, dark hair, and a slightly starched, old-world air about him. He looked like he might wear wing-tips to the beach. His office was in a grand old Victorian mansion on Forest Avenue in Ithaca, with creaky floors and high ceilings, dim and quiet and comforting as an old library. Sitting in front of a great wall of leather-bound medical books and diplomas, wearing a dark, correct (if shiny) suit, he looked the very picture of sobriety. If anybody can make me sane, Kitty thought, it's him.

The faint accent Penny had noticed was British—his parents were German Jews who'd fled to England during the war, where he was raised until the age of ten, he told them. Jess quizzed him on his professional background. Medical and psychiatric residency at the University of Rochester. Military psychiatrist for two years, including one year as chief of inpatient psychiatry at Fort Bragg. Four years on the full-time psychiatric faculty at the University of Rochester. Now chief of psychiatry at Tompkins Community Hospital, county commissioner of mental health, and in private practice. He'd treated two cases of multiple personality during his nearly twenty-year professional career. He was forty-three.

DR. WALTON: During those early sessions, I was terribly confused about this young woman. She was referred to me as someone who had a lot of medical problems that were thought to be psychosomatic. It was also suggested that she might be suffering from multiple personality disorder. Usually, by the end of a first session, I can narrow a patient's symptoms down to a chief complaint and come up with a therapeutic plan. But in this case, her problems were so diverse I was unable to make a diagnostic impression, even after two or three sessions. I didn't know what the chief complaint was. I didn't know what I was dealing with.

She presented with a history that, had I simply read a transcript of it, would have led me to conclude she was psychotic. She had a history of what sounded like severe psychopathology, including flagrant hallucinations, delusions, and periods of amnesia. Yet it was very hard for me to reconcile that history with what I saw in front of me. Her behavior was clearly not psychotic. The presentation and speech of a schizophrenic has a certain style, a certain flavor, especially the confused, disorderly, bi-

193

zarre-sounding thought processes. But she had none of that. She seemed sane, she was perfectly lucid, there was no thought disorder. In fact, she displayed knowledge of internal medicine and psychiatry that was absolutely astounding. Incredible. She knew all about the Krebs cycle, for instance. She could accurately summarize clinical syndromes from the medical literature. She knew the DSM-III [*the* Diagnostic and Statistical Manual of Mental Disorders, *a psychiatric codification of syndromes*] backward and forward. She probably knew it better than most mental health professionals.

So there was this dichotomy between the presentation and the history that I found very, very unsettling. I was simply trying to understand her problems and the tasks in front of us, but it was difficult for me to even get that far.

Very early on, she began talking about "Michael" and her belief that she had psychic powers. Many professionals would consider her belief in psychic powers to be delusional, and "Michael" to be a hallucinatory entity. But her descriptions of these things just didn't have that flavor to them. It sounded very different from the schizophrenic or the manic-depressive who thinks he has grandiose, supernormal abilities. Also, several things happened in those early sessions that literally sent chills down my spine. One day she came in and started telling me about the argument two clients of mine had had in the room earlier in the day. They had left the building hours earlier, but she was accurate as to what had been said. Another time, she was telling me about a dream she had had, in which her father (I assumed she meant a deity) had told her "she had as many personalities as shells in the sea." She had awakened from this dream, she told me, to find her hand filled with shells. Then, with great drama, she opened her hand and it was filled with these little pods, each one containing dozens of tiny seashells. I didn't conclude that she was delusional. I just sat there with goosebumps all over my skin.

If six psychiatrists had heard what I did in those early sessions, I'd be willing to bet they'd have given six different diagnoses. One might have said this was a borderline personality disorder—not a psychotic illness, but typically someone who is very impulsive, self-destructive, has a turbulent life history, and has trouble maintaining close relationships. When things don't go right, these people will slash their arms or burn themselves with cigarettes. People with borderline disorders also have very brief periods of hallucinations or delusional thinking—so-called micropsychotic episodes.

Another psychiatrist would probably have said she had a schizophrenic illness—that there was enough here to suggest she had been delusional for

194

a long time, that it was above and beyond brief, micropsychotic episodes, and the whole business of Michael was indicative of a fixed, false, delusional system. I vehemently disagree with this, but not everyone would.

One psychiatrist would undoubtedly have said she had no psychopathology at all, that she was just malingering. It was all a put-on. I don't believe that, though others might. (What would she have stood to gain from this? Now people would say she's just trying to sell a book, but at the time, this possibility had never been discussed.)

Another therapist might have concluded she had a schizoaffective disorder—that she had prominent disturbances of both thought and affect, or mood.

Still another practitioner would probably say she was what we now call a histrionic personality—somebody who is overly dramatic, who embellishes things, and who typically has difficulty sustaining intimate relationships.

Then, of course, there was the possibility she might have a multiple personality disorder. I was not convinced this was the best explanation, after three or four sessions. I hadn't seen a switch, or any dramatic personality change, although she told me about Kitty and Jess and Liz and the others. All I knew for sure was that I had a very unusual person here—in fact, in all my years of practice, I had never been confronted with a case quite like this one—and that she just could not be fit into a neat psychiatric category. I knew that I had a lot of thinking to do if I was going to be helpful to her.

Chapter 21

T here's no 'cookbook approach' to treating multiple personality disorder—if in fact that's what the problem is," Dr. Walton explained in his calm, pontifical way when Elizabeth Katherine Castle came in for her weekly session about a month after they met. "There's no simple recipe, no step-by-step formula for success. Frankly, we just don't know enough about it. Multiple personality disorder is much more common than we once believed, but it's still rare, and still quite mysterious."

She looked back at him, quiet and fearful, with her hands folded in her lap. She said nothing. One by one, like church mice, the others crept out to look Dr. Walton over, then crept back inside.

"The only thing that's been known to work is the psychoanalytic process. We've just got to go back to the beginning and try to understand what happened to you as a child. We've got to confront and understand the stresses that led to your current problems. Do you think you'd be willing to give it a try?"

She nodded. It was Liz who was in the body at that moment, but now, for the first time in their lives, *all* the others could hear the questions that were asked, even if they stayed hidden deep inside. They flickered in and out of the body, because being in the body helped them see better; but even if they crouched inside, they could all still hear. It no longer mattered so much who was "out" and who was "in"; they could all begin to participate in the experiences of the person occupying the body they all shared. It was an amazing new trick that Michael had taught them. It was a way of undergoing therapy collectively, he said. It was a way of accelerating the healing. It was the first great, slow spin of the farandola.

"The only way we can make any progress is for both of us to learn to trust each other," Dr. Walton went on. "We're in this together. We're a team, a partnership. Psychiatrists call it the 'therapeutic alliance.' We're both working toward the same goal: To help you get better. Are we agreed on that?"

"Yes," Liz said softly. "I want to get better."

"If it turns out that you are a multiple, it's important that the 'others' all learn some of the basic human trust that they very likely never learned in childhood. They need to learn that it's safe to be one person. That's the beginning of the healing process."

"What if . . . what if I can't remember?"

"Sometimes hypnosis can help people remember, but I'd rather not try that yet. Let's just try to go back to the beginning, back to your earliest recollections. Are you with me?"

"Well . . . yeah," she said, weakly.

"What comes back?" Dr. Walton suggested gently. "What's the earliest thing you remember?"

Liz was quiet for a long time. Her mind tumbled back. The others' minds tumbled back too, back and back, hurtling into the dimness and confusion of the past. Remembering was the beginning of the farandola, Michael said. There was no way they could be healed until they remembered it all.

"That car," she said finally. "That old car."

Beside a shabby motor court with sad little falling-down cabins, there was an old Hudson with no wheels standing in the weeds. She loved to sit in that old car and pretend she could just drive away any old time she wanted to. She'd pretend that her popsicle stick was the key. She'd climb into the big ripped-up front seat and turn the key, and then she'd go driving off down the junky driveway and go far, far away. She didn't know why she was so scared all the time. She just knew she was clenched up tight inside, and it seemed like she could only calm down when she was in that old Hudson driving far away. It was them against her: that's all she knew. If she didn't find a way to hide, her mommy and daddy would kill her. All she knew was that she had to hide to live.

Hide to live! Hide to live! She was driving away in that old car, hiding away from them, so she could live.

Her mother went away during the day, so her daddy took care of her, and he would just tie her to the pepper tree in the backyard, like a little puppy. He and some other men were always in the garage, working on cars. It was a long way to the backyard and he would never hear her when she had to go to the bathroom. Or when she was hungry or thirsty or when she was afraid in thunderstorms. One time he left her out there all night long. And when he remembered she was out there, she got a spanking because he said that if she had yelled hard enough, he would have heard her.

Her family lived in Houston then, in a hideous gray and green bungalow, at 67 Ontario Street. Secluded, the way her daddy liked it. It was dark and gloomy inside and it had an awful smell that you could never get off your clothes: the smell of being afraid. There was a grapevine growing over the front porch, and a small front yard with brown grass. The pepper tree stood in the farthest corner of the backyard. She hated that tree, yet she had the feeling that the tree wanted to be her friend—that it cried for her.

When she was tied up back there and had to go to the bathroom, she would take down her pants and squat as close to the fence as she could. Once she went in her pants, but she got such a spanking that she learned not to ever do that again. So she would go in a little pile by the fence. One time the wind blew a brown paper bag over by her tree. She saved it, and when she got tired she would go to sleep on it like it was her special bed. Pretty soon she spent most of her time on that old paper bag, because there were so many stickers that they would get in her feet and burn. Lots of times she would be hungry, but nobody heard her; maybe they didn't want to hear her. One time she ate the green peppercorns on the tree but she got such an awful stomachache that she never did it again. She looked at those bowel movements in neat little piles. She wondered if she got hungry enough, would they taste good?

Her daddy didn't care if she had enough to eat. He didn't care if she died. He was big and mean and he wore cheap, shiny suits and awful neckties. His shoes never looked good. He always looked seedy, like he hung around pawnshops. He had bad, yellow teeth, and he had dirty red hair and a dirty red beard, like an old red bear. He smelled bad. Most big people smelled bad. There was a grandmother with dyed blonde hair, a grandfather with a glass eye. There were lots of fights. Sleeping in cars. Sleeping in taverns. Once she went to have her tonsils out and her Gramma Louise picked her up at the hospital. Gramma Louise took her to a bar and got drunk. Liz felt so sick and sleepy she finally just fell asleep on a table. She didn't have a bed or a bedroom at home. She slept on a couch in the front room, and one day when she was sleeping there, a tornado came and an entire shelf of trophies fell on the floor. They were her daddy's racing trophies, and when they got cracked and broken, she felt so happy about that.

She hated those trophies.

"Were you conscious that you were being badly treated when you were small?" Dr. Walton asked.

"I thought I was bad and had to be punished," said Liz softly. "I thought I deserved it. I thought it was me."

"What was it that you thought you'd done?"

"I never knew. I just knew everything was my fault. I just knew I was bad."

"How would your parents punish you?"

"There were . . . lots of ways. They hurt me when they were home, and they hurt me when they went away. Sometimes they would just abandon us for days at a time. I don't really remember everything that happened. I just remember that they always came back. That was the scariest part: they always came back."

Little Andrea wasn't sure which was worse: when Mommy and Daddy went away, or when they came back. When her daddy was home, there were so many things you could get hit for. You could get hit for playing outside or talking to neighbors. Neighbors were especially bad. You could not talk to neighbors, ever. Neighbors were trash, and not good enough for Joey Meyer's children to be around. But you could also get hit for not doing the dishes right. Sometimes Little Andrea got hit so hard she flew right off her chair by the sink, where she spent so much time with a towel wrapped around her middle, doing dishes for a family of six. Other times when she didn't do the dishes right, Mommy and Daddy would make her wash every single dish and utensil, and put each one away, then take every one of them down, wash and dry them

199

again, put them away, then start all over again. For hours, and hours, and hours, until she was so sleepy she was falling off the chair. Then they'd hit her again.

Other times, they would just go away. Mother would dress up and put on red lipstick and pop-beads and high heels and Daddy would wear the suit that smelled bad, the one with the awful colors. Daddy and Mother didn't like to be home at night. They never told Little Andrea where they were going; they'd just tell her to take care of all three kids, even Chuckie, who was just a baby, and then they'd go away. She was about six or seven then.

Sometimes they wouldn't come home for days. Once they were gone for three days and she ran out of milk. The babies were crying and crying, and she didn't know what to do. Finally Michael came, and he told her to go next door to the neighbors' house and borrow some milk. He reminded her to say "please" and "thank you," and he told her not to be afraid. She knew it was bad. She knew you were never, ever to talk to the neighbors, but the children were starving and there was no food in the house at all.

The neighbor lady told her she was out of milk, too, but she'd bring some over when she got back from the store. Little Andrea went back home and waited, but when the bell rang and she opened the door, the neighbor lady had a policeman and a police lady with her, and all three of them walked right into the house. They started asking Little Andrea all kinds of questions. How long had her parents been gone? Where did they go? What were her parents' names? What were the children's names? Where did her daddy work? Little Andrea told them she'd get a spanking if she told, but they wouldn't listen. They kept asking; they *made* her tell. The police lady walked right into the kids' bedrooms, and when she came back out she was crying, carrying baby Chuckie wrapped up in a blanket. She told all the kids they were going for a ride now, and then she and the policeman herded Jimmy and Maryanne and Little Andrea down the sidewalk to a little bus parked by the curb.

They drove a long, long way, to a new house. It was like a big white church on a hill, with green grass and sprinklers and a red tile roof, where a lot of other little children lived. Some of them were waiting to go to foster families, and others were waiting for their mommies and daddies to come back. Everything smelled like cookies there. She and Maryanne got a whole room all to themselves; the sheets were clean. You could smell food cooking in the big kitchen downstairs, and every day Little Andrea and Maryanne got a new clean dress. Little Andrea even got a petticoat. And she got to make weed piles out in the flow-erbeds every afternoon. There she met an old black kitchen man, and he taught her how to draw animal pictures by tracing around her thumbs.

They took the boys away, to the other side of the orphanage, and she and Jimmy had to talk through a chain-link fence. They'd touch each others' fingers through the fence and cry and plan their escape. They met at the fence almost every day, until one day Jimmy didn't show up. When Liz came out and saw that, she got scared. What had happened to her babies? What had happened to her brothers and sister? She ran back indoors and upstairs to the big playroom on the second floor, looking for Maryanne, but she was gone, too. She ran to their little bedroom and she wasn't there. She ran down the big staircase and into the eating room. She wasn't there.

"I can't find Maryanne!" she yelled to the old kitchen man when she came bounding down the stairs.

But a big silver-haired lady caught her by the hand when she ran into the hall. She led Little Andrea into the waiting room right next to the front door, and there, sitting in little chairs around a table, were Jimmy, Maryanne, and baby Chuckie, lying in a baby basket on the floor. Chuckie smiled at her and lifted up his little arms. He wanted her to pick him up. And she was just about to when the silver-haired lady said happily, "I've got a big surprise for you! Just sit here quietly for a minute, and I'll be back."

She left the room, and then a minute later the door opened. In walked Mother and Daddy. They looked the same as if they had not been gone at all. Mother had on a new coat and bright red lipstick, and Daddy had on the icky suit. He smelled bad. Her mother looked sad and Daddy looked like he was hiding behind a wall. He had a nothing look on his face, but a something look in his eyes. He pulled out a package of Juicy Fruit gum and handed each of the children a stick. He didn't say a word. The silver-haired lady came in, and her mother and daddy put smiles on their faces.

"Well, I'm glad we got everything straightened out!" the lady said.

Her daddy got pale and hid behind his face again. If they had all been alone in there, he would not have been smiling. Her mother came up to Little Andrea and kissed her on the forehead.

"You're such a brave girl!" she said. "I'm glad I have such a little mother like you around!"

She opened up her purse, took out a package of paper dolls, and handed them to Little Andrea. For a moment Little Andrea just stared at them. She wasn't sure what she was supposed to do. Her mother had told her before that she was too stupid to cut out paper dolls with scissors. She'd only cut herself, and make a mess. She opened the package, and out fell the book of dolls, wearing the prettiest dresses and muffs and nightgowns. Then she looked up at her mother's face, and she knew she was in trouble. The smile on her face was frozen, like a mannequin in a store. Little Andrea closed the book of paper dolls and laid it quietly on the table. The silver-haired lady stared at her, as if she were shocked at her ungratefulness. How could she understand the fear? Whatever dark light her daddy once had, her mother now had. Now she was afraid to leave this big, white place. She was afraid Mommy and Daddy would kill them all.

"Your mother and daddy will be coming back in a few days, and you'll be leaving with them then," the silver-haired lady told them. "They've got to go now, to make some arrangements for your coming home."

But Little Andrea knew they would not be going home. Mommy and Daddy had a look that said they had no home.

A few days later, after breakfast, all the children were dressed and scrubbed and waiting in the little room by the front door. Little Andrea saw the big black car pull up, and her mother and daddy got out and came up the walk. All the kids were herded out to the car. They squeezed into the backseat, though it was already crowded in there—the car was all packed up.

As they started down the big hill, she looked back at the big, white place with the red tiles on the roof and all the pretty flowers and the green grass and the chain-link fence and the flagpole. She didn't want to leave. She was afraid for the babies and afraid for herself.

Mommy and Daddy were back.

They always came back.

Chapter 22

L et's talk about your father," Dr. Walton said at the beginning
of their next session. The small, frightened, demurely dressed
woman who sat before him shifted uneasily in her seat. It was
late November 1985, and a wan, early winter light spilled across
her face and hair, across her small, nervous hands. She did not look
up. Dr. Walton could not see the others flickering in and out in a panic,
like a great disturbance of birds. An enormous shadow had just passed
across the sun.

"Well, what do you want to know?" she asked finally.

"Tell me about him," he prodded gently. "What was he like?"

"I never really think of that man as my father," Jess said at last, in
a flat, mechanical voice. Jess was the best at holding a bad memory at
arm's length, as if it were a specimen in a bottle. "I was always very
confused about the whole idea of father—all the others were, too."

"What do you mean?"

"They were all very confused about exactly who this man was,"
Kitty burst in. "They didn't know if he was a foster father, or somebody who had kidnapped them, or a complete stranger, or what. When
they thought of 'father,' they thought instead of this kind, faraway
person in the sky, the creator, the person Michael had told them

about—their 'real father.' But if he was their 'real father,' then who was this terrible man who would come stomping up to their room in the night, you know?"

Liz returned for a moment and just stared at Dr. Walton, hoping her silence would transmit the horror of all the things she couldn't say. He did not seem to notice they were all rippling in and out like mad.

"I'm interested in your comments about his 'bad smell,' " Dr. Walton mused. "Schizophrenics often have a certain odd, distinctive body odor. I get the sense that he may have had some serious psychopathology of his own. I wonder if he might have been a schizophrenic . . ."

"The smell was always worst when he was in his rages," Jess said, as if to himself. "The whole house would fill up with it. It was a sort of rank, sexual smell, sweaty and pissy, like the smell of the lion house at the zoo. I used to think he was just a mean, dangerous man, but now I'm convinced he was mentally ill. He was sick. Maybe he was abused himself as a child. Maybe he was just an extreme manic-depressive—there'd be incredible mood swings sometimes. Who knows? Maybe he was a multiple."

"The funny thing is, I don't know a thing about his background," Me-Liz burst in suddenly. "I don't know where he was born, or who his parents were, or what he did as a kid, or anything else about him. I never met his family, except for a grandmother with dyed blonde hair, and an Uncle Lyle and Aunt Rhonda. They were mean, and they had mean, dirty little kids, that's all I know. He just said his relatives were no good, and he stayed as far away from them as possible. The main thing I remember about him is that you never could tell what was going to happen next. There was always a good reason to be scared."

Sometimes things happened that scared her even more than getting hit. One night they were all sitting at the table and she was looking at her daddy when all of a sudden he stopped talking and an awful look came over his face. He was staring at Mother. A big spider was crawling out of the top of the bun she wore on her head. Mother just went on eating. Daddy got up very quietly, crept down to her end of the table, and punched her right in the face. She flew backward out of her chair and landed on her head, knocked out. Her nose was bloody. Then, Daddy didn't touch her. He just picked up the spider very carefully and took it outside on the patio. She could see him through the screen door, touching it and whispering to it like a baby. Then he let it go. He came back into the kitchen, sat down on the floor with his arms wrapped around himself, and started to rock from side to side. He had that awful, scary grin on his face, and spit was dribbling out of his mouth. His eyes were all funny. She could smell the bad smell.

Up and down the table, the three kids stared at each other, too scared to even breathe.

Finally, Mother began to moan. Then Daddy got up and ran into the room and sat down in his chair again. He started to finish his supper, like nothing ever happened. Mother got up off the floor, went in the kitchen and held a cloth to her face. Nobody ever said a thing about it after that.

That's the way things were: bad things happened, and then they never happened.

Things were the worst at Christmastime. That's when Daddy got the scariest. He was always wrecking the tree—once he grabbed it by the top and spun it around the room like a lasso, with glass decorations smashing against the walls in every direction. Almost every year, they'd have to go out and buy a new tree because Daddy wrecked the first one.

Once a bunch of kids who were poor got to go to a special Christmas party at the bank, and Liz got a stocking full of candy and a Betsy Wetsy doll that cried real tears and wet her pants and Jimmy got a train set with little tiny trees. When she got home, Liz put the stocking under her pillow. Daddy found out and told her she was being selfish. He said he'd teach her a lesson about being selfish. He took the stocking and ate all the candy and threw the stocking away and then stomped on Betsy Wetsy until her head broke and she stopped crying.

Liz cried, though. She wished she were dead. When you were dead, you didn't cry.

Liz could never understand about her daddy. She just knew you had to listen very carefully when his car pulled up, because if he pulled up in a certain way, and the brakes screeched and he came stumbling across the lawn, not up the steps, it was time to hide as deep as you could because things were about to get scary. Every day, all the kids had to figure out who Daddy was going to be that day. They had to tiptoe around and stay out of the way until they figured out who he was.

You could never tell what was going to happen next. Sometimes there'd be weeks or months when it would be like a battle zone in that house. Daddy would be crazy and his ulcers would bleed and he'd be drinking milk all the time and Mother would start missing work because of busted noses and black faces and swollen jaws, just like the kids had. The house would fill up with the bad smell—Daddy's smell. It didn't matter what Liz did or said; it seemed like he just did it when he felt like it. It was always her fault. It was always because of something Liz had done, even if she didn't even know what it was. Sometimes he never told her. Liz just knew she was bad.

Then, at other times, a spooky quiet settled over everything. Suddenly Daddy would be all mushy-nice, and he'd expect everyone to be mushy-nice back. Once he got a job selling pens and pencils and keychains and coasters with names printed on them, and sometimes he'd give the kids some of that stuff out of his sample case. Liz and Me-Liz and Penny liked that stuff. They had a collection of it in a shoebox upstairs, from the times when Daddy was nice. Once, when he was in one of those rare, spooky nice moods, her daddy even told Liz he loved her.

"You know, I love you most of all," he said. "Of all the kids, you are the one who is most like me. That's why I have to punish you. I have to punish you, I have to punish you, I have to punish you!"

And then he buried his face in his hands and cried.

"Did you have the sense that you were the one singled out for abuse?" Dr. Walton asked. "Often, in abusive households, there's a 'designated victim'—someone who, for one reason or another, takes the brunt of the punishment."

"I don't know," she said, not looking up. "If you're getting hit all the time, you don't pay much attention to whether your brother or sister is getting hit more. I know he used to call me 'the little bastard' a lot. I used to wonder if maybe I was illegitimate. Maybe that's what it was: I got hit because I was a symbol of shame or something. I don't know. I just know that I and all the others concluded we were bad."

"He tended to blame you?"

"He was someone who never accepted responsibility for anything he did," Kitty cut in, impatient with Liz's self-pity. "Everything he did was compulsive. He just acted without thinking, then blamed someone else. It was always: 'I wouldn't have done this if you didn't do what you did!' So the others would be punished twice. First, physically beaten, then, blamed for it—no matter how out-of-control he'd become. He'd come up and say, 'I wouldn't have had to do it, if you hadn't done what you did!' He never apologized. It was never his fault. Nothing was ever his fault."

Once Daddy tried to get them all killed. That wasn't his fault either, he said later—a man in a truck had tried to hit them. But Liz knew the truth in her heart. She just never really let herself know it, even long after it happened. It was just before Christmas, when she went on a long trip in the car with her mommy and daddy and her Gramma Louise and somebody called Uncle Tyler. It was snowing hard. They drove and drove. She fell asleep in the backseat on Gramma Louise's lap. Gramma Louise had dyed blonde hair and red, red lips and always smelled like perfume. Liz's mommy was sitting up front with baby Chuckie on her lap; her daddy was driving.

Suddenly, Liz woke up in the dark and everybody was yelling and screaming at each other.

"Joey, don't do it! Don't do it!" Gramma Louise was yelling. Liz sat up and looked over the top of the seat. They were heading right into a big semi truck; its lights blinded her eyes.

The next thing she remembered, she was in the front seat of somebody else's car, lying in Uncle Tyler's lap, and a man she didn't know was driving. They stopped at a gas station and Uncle Tyler asked where the nearest hospital was.

"All the way on up to Anthony," the gas station man said.

Liz woke up in a big crib in a hospital in Anthony, Oklahoma. She felt funny. Her face hurt, and she could hardly see at all. She reached up and touched her face; there was a big bandage all over her head and down over one eye. Her other eye hurt and it was all puffy.

"You're going to be a good girl, and you're going to let the doctor take care of you," a familiar voice said. She looked up and saw Michael standing beside the bed. He put both his hands through the bars on the crib and held her two hands between his.

"Your real father will not let anything happen to you. He loves you, and so do I," Michael said.

She fell asleep again, and when she woke up there was a man with a wrinkled face, wearing a cowboy hat, sitting on a chair next to the crib. He had big tears in his eyes.

"I'm so sorry I hit you, little girl," he sobbed. "I'm so sorry!"

"What was your mother's role in all of this?" Dr. Walton asked. "Did she ever try to stop him? Did she seem to recognize what he was doing?"

"Part of me wants to put all the blame on *him*," Kitty responded after a moment. "But I think he was so far beyond reality he just wasn't completely responsible. *She* was not crazy, though, at least not until later. She allowed this to happen. She did not try to stop this man. She knew what was going on. She participated in it, usually just by being passive or deliberately blind, and I cannot forgive her for that."

Though Kitty herself had never actually met either one of the parents—she wasn't even born until long after the others left home—she had access to all the memories of Liz, Me-Liz, Penny, Jess, and the babies. And through them, she *knew* that woman.

"I'm sure Mother had all the usual excuses: How could she have supported herself, and all those kids, if she left him?" Kitty went on. "Maybe she just kind of shrugged and said, 'There's nothing I can do, the kids are just going to have to learn to live with it.' In the end, she was as much to blame as he was, maybe more. She stayed with that man. I can understand how you could love someone so much you could allow something to continue at the expense of your own welfare. But to have allowed it to continue at the expense of your own children—that's unforgivable. That's criminal. Both of these people are criminals.

"I've reached into my heart to try to forgive these people, but there is no forgiveness there. Even Michael has not encouraged me to forgive them."

Both of them were quiet for a long moment.

"Were you ever *sexually* abused?" Dr. Walton asked finally.

"Yes," said Penny, in a tiny voice. A searing memory had drawn her out. "It wasn't only at home. It happened once in that orphanage, too. It seemed like there was no way I could get away."

One night, in the big, white house on the hill, Penny Lavender had to get up to go to the bathroom. Her sister was fast asleep and the bathroom was just down the hall, so she crept there in her nightgown. All the lights were on in the big yellow-tiled room, and she could hear the "swish, swish" of a mop in the shower. Must be the janitor, she thought. After she finished using the biffy, she pulled her nightgown back down and went to the sink to wash her hands. Then suddenly, from behind, a pair of big strong hands grabbed her.

"You know the rules," a man's voice said. "You know you're not supposed to use the bathrooms at night without an aide. You must be a bad, bad girl!"

"I'm the strongest little girl in the world! And besides, I don't know about any old rule like that."

He started pushing her up against the sink, hard.

"If you make any racket, I'll tell 'em you broke the rules," he whispered. Then he started pulling up her nightie, and shoving something up against her. She didn't know what would happen if you broke the rules here, but she knew what would happen if she broke the rules at home, so she didn't make a peep. But it hurt! It hurt! Why was he doing that to her? It felt like her whole insides were ripping apart, and it hurt! All around her, the yellow bathroom tiles began to spin in a blur of panic and pain.

"If you say anything, I'll drown you in the big bathroom tub," he told her when he was done. "I'm going to watch you go back to your room, so I'll know where you are. And if you tell, I'll come and get you in the night and drown you in that big tub."

She crept down the hall, so scared she could hardly cry. She just ached inside, and the next morning, her panties were soaked with blood. She stuck a sock in there to stop the blood from getting on her dress, and she never told anybody.

She didn't want to get drowned in the big bathroom tub.

There were tears in her eyes when Liz finished telling the story of what happened in the yellow bathroom. It seemed so long ago! Yet even now, she could feel that little girl's pain and terror souring in the pit of her stomach. *That little girl who was not her. That little girl whose memories had broken through some dike in the darkness of her mind, and now washed over her in a wave of nausea.*

Dr. Walton waited until she had composed herself.

"Did your *father* ever sexually abuse you?" he asked.

"Yes," she said.

They had moved again. Now they were living in something called a subdivision in a place called Bethany, Oklahoma, where all the houses looked the same. People started to come over to the new house and they would sit in the kitchen and drink Jim Beam and get drunk and fight and play cards. Mother was mostly gone at night and Daddy's friends were always hanging around. She would get mad when she heard her daddy tell them lies about how much money he had. He never had any money. He'd take the children's lunch money to play cards with. Every night, she'd help make supper, do the dishes, and then she'd put the kids to bed. Then Daddy's friends would come, and she'd go to bed to read.

It was Liz who was lying on her bed one night, reading, when her daddy came in and gave her another book to read. It was called *Darla's Dog Days,* and it had a picture of a little girl and a big dog on the cover. But the more she read of it, the sicker and more scared she got. A mean man tied up Darla and wouldn't give her anything to eat unless she let the dog lick her all over and do terrible things to her. Then her daddy led her into the kitchen, where there were some strange men who made her drink something called slow gin and then they took her clothes off and tied her up on the bed with another little kid while a big fat man took pictures. They put a lampshade over her face and did those terrible things to her. Finally she threw up.

Her daddy told her afterward that he'd cut her feet off if she told. She never told anybody, because he had the dark light in his eyes, and she didn't want to get her feet cut off.

Me-Liz came to help Liz in the days after that night. Liz didn't even know she was there, but she was. Liz felt only fear and shame about what her daddy and the other men had done to her. She felt so filled with darkness and heaviness that sometimes she thought her body would burst open like a rotten vegetable, and she'd just die. But when Me-Liz came, she helped the darkness go away. Me-Liz was not created to be a thing of the body like those horrible men were. She was created to be a child of God, like Michael was.

She was not bad like them. Michael loved her. Her real father in heaven loved her.

Didn't he?

Chapter 23

Every week, after therapy, Jeff would pick up his wife at Dr. Walton's office in Ithaca and take her home to the cottage by Cayuga Lake. It was December; snowbanks white as wedding cakes grew along the county roads, and out across the frozen lake, skaters and snowmobiles flashed through the blinding, brittle air.

When she got home, Kitty would call the others to a meeting of the round table, in the other world. Attendance at these group meetings was mandatory; Kitty insisted. Even if you hadn't attended therapy that day, you had to go to group. (Attendance at therapy—that is, choosing to listen in on the discussion of the day—was voluntary. It was like tuning in a short-wave radio; you could tune in, or tune out, at will.) The group discussions were important, Michael had told them, because it was a way of continuing the therapy throughout the week. They met with Dr. Walton for only an hour a week; but the round table discussions could continue, off and on, for days. They all had their private, *individual* memories, but now they were beginning to develop an expanding repertoire of *collective* memories. The more time they spent together, the more they discussed things that came up in therapy, the more interrelated they became, the more the sunlight of consciousness illuminated them all.

There was still resistance, especially from Liz. She was the one who most often tuned out in therapy. She had too much to be afraid of, too much to forget. Just beneath the rim of her consciousness, there was a dark, nameless rage of forgetting, a chest of secrets whose lid kept threatening to burst open. When something distressing came up, she'd just tune out. But she was there that day Dr. Walton started asking about Michael. They all were. Michael was the one thing none of them had ever had to fear.

"I'm not sure what to make of 'Michael'—and perhaps that doesn't even matter," Dr. Walton mused, lacing his fingers together behind his head and easing back in his chair. "The question is what *you* thought of him, when you were small. Did it ever occur to you to wonder whether he was 'real' or not?"

"As far as I and all the others were concerned, Michael was an ordinary person, like the mailman," Me-Liz explained brightly. "He was a member of the family. It was never a question of whether he was 'real' or not—he was the only real thing in our lives."

"He appeared to you to be *physically* real? You've described him wearing a dark hat and coat."

"Sometimes he'd just leave little calling cards, like seashells, and I'd know he'd been around. But the rest of the time, he would appear in the flesh, in person, just as real as anybody else. You can't see light through him. He'd touch me. He'd put me in his lap."

"And he spoke to you in an audible voice?"

"Well, *I* could always hear it. I don't know if anyone else could. He was the only one who ever cared about me or the others. He was the only one who was there to protect me against the people who were supposed to be my protectors—my own parents. Michael, in effect, became the parent. From the time I was very small, my parents would play tricks on me and the others—mind-bending tricks, spirit-bending tricks. The only one who didn't play tricks was Michael. He was the only one who could be believed."

"Did you ever tell anyone else about him?"

"I don't remember mentioning Michael to anyone," Me-Liz said, "but not because I thought he was strange or unusual—only because there was absolutely no one else to talk to. The one kind adult figure in my life, Pete Smith, had been removed because of his kindness, the day I first met Michael. That taught me a very valuable lesson: my parents would go to any length to take away any kind of 'creature comfort' in my life—which to a child that young means not a bowl of cereal, but the knowledge that you are loved. The knowledge that, no matter what happens, Mommy and Daddy are going to be there. It was never like that for us.

"Only Michael was there."

Whenever she needed him most, Michael would appear, just as he promised he would. "There will be times when you're afraid, and times you feel alone, but you must never forget that your real father watches over you always," Michael told her. "He'll send me to help when there is danger."

That's what Michael said that day he first appeared to Little Andrea in the field by Trinity Speedway, and she believed him. He was the only person in her life who could be believed.

Michael came to see her again after they went to the big, white house on the hill. One day, after breakfast, he appeared to her by the great big chain-link fence where she would meet Jimmy every day. He had a light all around him. It was the first time she'd ever seen him without his hat, and his hair was almost pure black. His eyes were sad.

"Your real father loves you, and so do I," he said. "I'm going to give you a gift, and the gift is called eternity."

"What's that?" she asked. "What's it look like?"

"It looks like forever."

"What does forever mean?"

"It means you."

"When do I get eternity?"

"You have it already. Eternity is why you are here. And when you are a grown-up little girl, you will share your father's gift of eternity."

"I don't think it's fair to have to share it. I want a present all to myself."

"The more you share eternity, the more your real father will give you. You can never use it up."

He touched her cheek gently. And then he went away.

Chapter 24

Y ou've talked a good deal about the 'others,' Liz, but I'm still not clear about when, and why, they first appeared," Dr. Walton observed at the beginning of their next session. "I'd like to explore the first emergences of these alter personalities, if we could."

Liz loosed an enormous sigh.

"For instance, you've mentioned the experience of 'missing time' later in life, as an adult," he went on. "That's one of the most common symptoms of multiple personality disorder. It suggests evidence that one of the alters was 'out' during those times. How early in life do you first remember experiencing that?"

"Oh, I don't know," she said. "Time's always been weird for me."

"How about as early as kindergarten? Do you remember missing time then?"

"Yeah. Oh, yeah."

"Earlier?"

"It goes back as far as I can remember, Ralph. I can't remember a time when there wasn't something strange about time."

"So you'd guess that the alters were there from some time earlier than kindergarten?"

"I can sort of vaguely see them in my mind's eye right now, all the way before kindergarten," Liz said. "I can see myself, Me-Liz, Little Elizabeth and Little Andrea, and Penny. Five of us. Way back then."

"Are you able to recall a specific incident that might have triggered the original split?"

Silence.

"I don't remember anything specific. I just remember . . . fear."

Hide to live! She had to hide to live!

That's all she knew. Little Elizabeth didn't even realize then—how could she?—but she had figured out a special way to hide. It was kind of a funny way. It was better than driving off in that old car. She would just tuck herself away deep inside, and stay there in a little warm, gray cave. She was so tiny she could barely even talk when she first discovered that cave and crept in there to hide. She wasn't even two years old. She just stayed in there and hardly ever even came out at all. She was just a scrawny little kid with thin, wispy hair. She was skinny and pale and covered with dirt that was more than a few days old. Little Elizabeth was just shocked by fear; she stayed in there, and she never grew up at all.

When Little Elizabeth was in her cave, another girl came out. Her name was Little Andrea. She was older than Little Elizabeth, maybe four. She had whitish-blonde hair in a Dutch boy, and little bowed legs. She loved flowers, and she loved her black-and-white squaw princess dress with the rickrack all around it. She didn't know who gave her that name, "Little Andrea." That was just her name. She knew people called her "Elizabeth," or "Liz," but that wasn't really her name. Her name was Little Andrea. Little Andrea had a warm, gray cave she hid in sometimes, just like Little Elizabeth. Little Elizabeth's cave was completely empty, but Little Andrea's cave had one thing in it: a brown paper bag.

Little Andrea never really thought about it then, but somebody had to work the body when things got scary and she and Little Elizabeth *both* went inside. She never knew anything about the two other little girls who came out to do that. Their names were Liz and Me-Liz. In a funny way they were twins. Liz was a bad girl. Me-Liz was a good girl. Liz took the pain. Me-Liz took it away.

Liz was like a little shy mouse. She had gray, muddy colors around her, and a pixie haircut. Liz thought she deserved the pain. She didn't know why she was bad, she just knew she was. Otherwise, why would her daddy do all those mean things to her? Most of the time, she just felt scared and confused and sad. She couldn't remember things too well. That wasn't so bad. Sometimes she didn't want to remember.

Sometimes, Liz felt so full of shame that it was like a cold stone in her heart. How could she ever feel close to Michael, close to her real father, with that cold stone in her heart? That's when she went away, and Me-Liz came to make the guilt and shame go away. Me-Liz was a child of God—Michael's child. She was there to help Liz feel clean again, to make her good again, so God would love her. Me-Liz had been right beside Liz for a long, long time. She was like a shadow made of light.

"You don't clearly recall any specific event that might have caused the creation of Me-Liz?" Dr. Walton asked.

"No," Liz said quietly. "But I think she must have been created at around the same time I was—sometime before kindergarten. The more I remember, the more it seems like she was always there, and we were always together."

"Do you have any clue as to why she was created?"

"Sex abuse, I guess," Kitty cut in. She could feel how confused and frightened this discussion was making Liz. "I don't know for sure. It's just that Me-Liz kind of balanced out Liz's . . . guilt, her sexuality, by being completely nonsexual. That's why she was created. It's like she was created to make Liz feel clean and close to God; to balance out the darkness with light. She's like a Christ, taking away the guilt and shame to open up the channels to the Creator. Me-Liz has a nickname, in fact—people call her 'Christina,' because of her spiritual nature."

"What about Penny Lavender?" Dr. Walton inquired. "Was she there in kindergarten, too?"

"I can see her coming out for fingerpainting class, but she was there a long time before that," Liz told him. "She was always there—just a wispy, ethereal thing, like a cloud. The tiniest little trouble, and she'd disappear. Her way of dealing with reality is not to have as tenacious a hold on it as everybody else."

"Does she have a purpose, a function, like Me-Liz does?"

"I sometimes think Penny Lavender was born as a way to handle being alone," Liz mused.

"What do you mean?"

"It's just that the others had so much to fear when they were alone— we all did. When you're alone, the only place to look is within. So it makes sense that one of the personalities was created to handle that. Penny loves to be alone, she always has. I don't know, maybe art is just her way of not looking within when she's alone. Maybe it's just a beautiful smoke screen—a way of seeing nothing at all."

"Did Penny come out later in life?"

"I remember she came out a lot in second grade, when they got dumped at the grandparents' house—the mother's parents—in Oklahoma. She loved it there! She wanted that to go on forever."

She was living with her grandmother and grandfather in a place called Freedom, Oklahoma. She didn't know how she got here. She just knew her mother and daddy were gone, and she didn't miss them one bit. One by one, the little girls began creeping out and taking a look around. Liz crept out and looked: she had her very own bedroom now, in a house that smelled like bread. Me-Liz looked: Grandfather wore his hat even in the house, and he had funny, crooked old legs. Grandmother said he built the whole house with his own two hands. He took her down in the basement and showed her how the staircase fit together without any nails.

The other little girls didn't know it then, but there was another girl who came out to look, too. Her name was Penny Lavender—Lavender for the color of coolness and mist and eternity. Penny loved it at Grandfather's house as much as the rest of them did. She loved it when Grandfather made her a poking stick and they went to the dump together and poked and poked. She blossomed there.

Penny Lavender had white-blonde hair in an Indian braid all the way down her back, and she loved to sing and make pictures. Penny felt light as the air. Light as a feather. Like mist, like rain, like a puff of smoke, that would blow away in the tiniest breath of wind. Painting was the first thing she'd found in life that made any sense at all. The second thing was music. They were both secret doors out of this world.

On Friday nights, if Grandfather was especially happy, he would get out his accordion and play. Penny loved that accordion. She especially liked the *Melancholy Serenade,* by Tchaikovsky, because it was so sad and sweet and far away. Sometimes Penny would dance with Grandmother while Grandfather played. Grandmother would lift up her skirts and apron and Penny could see her black socks. Grandmother would get red in the cheeks and her eyes would dance along with the music. At other times, like when Grandfather played the *Melancholy Serenade,* Penny could see tears on Grandfather's chin.

217

"This accordion is a special thing to me," Grandfather would say. "An Italian man made it a long time ago. When I left my home to come to America, this accordion and your Grandmother is all I took."

Penny never forgot that secret door that Grandfather showed her. A few years later, when she was back living with the family in Bethany, Oklahoma, somebody brought a piano into the house. Liz tried to peck out a tune on it, but everybody yelled at her to stop because it sounded so awful. Then one day after school when nobody was home, Penny Lavender sat down to play. She loved the feel of those cool, smooth white keys under her fingers, and somehow she just knew how they were supposed to work.

When Penny closed her eyes and played, the sounds she made were cool and refreshing as water. Music made her feel like painting made her feel. In her mind, she sailed far, far away. She could see herself sitting at the piano: A beautiful, grown-up lady dressed in the clothes of angels—long, white robes made of stuff like butterfly wings—with blonde hair in an Indian braid all the way down her back. Penny always waited until nobody was home to play that piano. Her music was her secret. So were the sad, sweet little songs she liked to write:

> *I saw that Penny Lavender*
> *Standing at the edge of the pond*
> *Blonde hair past her shoulders*
> *A long white nightgown on . . .*
> *Sad Penny waits for love*
> *She sits alone just waiting*
> *Lovely Penny waits for love*
> *But it just won't come . . .*

Penny could go away into her pictures or her songs, but not forever. She always had to come back. At Grandfather's house that wasn't so bad—there was nothing to be afraid of. Life was sweet, and maybe this time it would last.

One day Penny was in school, drawing a picture, and her teacher told her there was someone at the door to see her. She got up and walked to the door.

There stood Mother and Daddy.

All she could think of was Michael.

The teacher told her to get her coat and boots and pick up her picture. Then she followed them outside to a dirty, dark red car she had never seen before. Jimmy was in the backseat, crying. When she crawled behind the front seat to get in, Daddy grabbed Penny's picture, crumpled it up, and threw it on the ground.

She never saw her Grandfather again.

"Swell life, huh, Professor?" Kitty gave a wan smile and laughed. "A little slice of 'Father Knows Best.' "

"I'm sorry about what you've had to live through," Dr. Walton said quietly. "But we're here to help you overcome your past. We're here to help you *live.*"

She nodded but said nothing.

"You've mentioned Jess, the teenage boy. Had he appeared by second grade?"

"No," Jess answered. "He didn't show up until fifth grade, at Jackson Elementary School."

Jess eyed Dr. Walton warily. He adored the psychiatrist like a demigod, but he was still too shy and frightened to reveal himself directly. He needed distance and privacy, so he referred to himself in the third person.

"Do you remember *why* he first appeared?" Dr. Walton asked.

"Yes, I do," Jess replied. "With Jess, it was different. I remember why he came. I've tried to forget. But I remember."

Chapter 25

The first thing Jess saw was the tools.

How beautiful they looked! Hanging off their hooks on the wall in perfect order, they shone with a cold, silvery fire. How much he wished he could touch them! How much he wished he were a man, and could build something with them! Bam, bam, bam! Hammer against nail. Nail against wood. Wood against stone.

He stood there in the clean, empty, brightly lit workroom, hands in pockets, staring up at those tools with worship in his eyes. Jess was just a runty little kid, maybe ten or twelve, with freckles and reddish-brown hair that wouldn't stay down in the back. He had a puggy nose, like Liz, and a reedy neck with a nervously bobbing Adam's apple. Jess was going to be a doctor when he grew up, and he was a natural for it. He liked to look at everything from a distance, like a scientist: studying, diagnosing, analyzing. To Jess, everything in the world was something to study, like a butterfly on a board. He just stepped back and squinted one eye and studied. Feelings were like that. Sad, scared, lonely, mad: butterflies on boards. That's why he wasn't scared. That's why he didn't feel anything. That's why he was so hard to hurt.

He spun slowly around on one heel and took in the entire room: everything was warm and tidy. There were paint cans on the shelf, coils of extension cords dangling from hooks, and a big cardboard trash drum drawn up against the bench. The hum of a giant furnace droned through the wall. It was nice in here. It smelled like Grandmother's house—like cookies and apples and bread. Through the doorway, Jess could see the remains of somebody's lunch scattered on a table. Suddenly a flurry of panic swept over him. Whose lunch was it? Who was going to find him here? Where was he?

And . . . and . . . *where did he come from?* It was like he just walked out of a dark room and there he was, worshipping the tools hanging in perfect rows over the workbench.

Safety! Safety! Hide to live! Hide to live! The alarms clanged in his brain, and he dove for the darkness. Through a low door, behind some coats, he found an opening into a little storeroom. He scurried into the storeroom and hid behind an old couch. Then he peered out with big eyes, like a scared animal. There was nothing in here except neatly hung brooms and mops, some boxes of books, a pile of neatly stacked school desks, and an overhead light in a big metal cage. It smelled like safety in here.

But how did he get here? What was going on?

Jess couldn't possibly have known how he got there. It all started a few hours before he was even born. But Penny Lavender was there. She remembered. Oh, God, how could she forget? She would give anything to forget.

"Daddy! Daddy! Stop it! What are you doing?" she'd cried, as the clippers sheared off her beautiful straw-colored hair right down to the skin and it fell on the floor all around her. But daddy just slapped her on top of the head and laughed. It was like he was cutting off her arms or her legs, and he wouldn't stop. He didn't care. He thought it was funny, and he just laughed. Mother laughed, too.

It was hair-cutting day. Hair-cutting day was always a time of anxiety and fear; the whole house filled up with it, like a choking cloud. Getting your hair cut was a punishment. Daddy never asked, "Well, kids, how would you like your hair?" He would just fly into a rage and say: "I'm sick of this hair! I got too many kids to worry about all this hair!" Then he'd get out his electric clippers, drag the kids into the kitchen one after another and chop off their hair as if he blamed them for growing it. That day Jimmy went first—Daddy just ran a pair of electric clippers right over the top of his head, back to front, and shaved it all off. When he came out of the kitchen, he seemed ashamed. He had his head down.

Then Penny Lavender climbed up and knelt in the chair facing backward, holding onto the back, and Daddy threw a towel around her neck. Daddy was mad. He was arguing with Mother about something. He was arguing so hard he wasn't paying any attention to what he was doing, and he just put the clippers at the back of her neck and shaved all the way across the top in a big stripe, like he was cutting the lawn. A big bolt of her pretty straw-colored hair fell on the floor. Penny felt numb inside. She was too scared to say anything. Maybe he forgot and thought she was a boy. Then he cut another big stripe right beside the first, then another.

"Daddy!" she whimpered finally. "Daddy, stop! What are you doing?"

She saw Mother's face stop arguing, freeze a moment, and then explode with laughter. Daddy started laughing, too. Jimmy, now a skinhead, came into the kitchen and started laughing, too: she had long pretty hair on one side, and she was a skinhead just like him on the other. She just felt numb inside, like stone, like wood, like bricks. After a while daddy cut the other side off, and then Mother took her down to the beauty shop to see if they could fix it. The beauty shop lady laughed. Everybody in the beauty shop laughed. The lady put a board across the seat and tried to fix her hair, but she couldn't do much with it because it was just stubble. Penny Lavender could see herself in the mirror. She looked just like a boy. All the mist and the romance and the dreams were gone. Her head looked like a light bulb, with bumps on it. Liz and Me-Liz came out and looked, too; they too were horrified, and then they just felt numb.

It was a school day, so Mother dropped her off at school on her way home. But Penny and Liz and Me-Liz were all terrified of walking into fifth grade like that. They couldn't do it—not like that! Penny went into the bathroom and tried to cover her head with a scarf, but it looked even worse. Finally she crept downstairs like a little mouse, down to the basement where the janitors stayed. She was scared when she pushed her way through the big glass and steel doors, into the furnace room that was warm and humming like a ship at sea. The janitor's lunch was scattered on a table, but nobody was around. She crept through the furnace room and into the back, and there she discovered a workroom, with a lit-up workbench with tools hanging off the wall in perfect order.

Penny didn't remember anything after that. She just remembered walking out of there when she heard the bell and it was time to go home from school. Every day, for weeks after that, until her hair started to grow back, Penny Lavender got up and went to school and crept downstairs to the janitor's workroom, and the next thing she knew it was time to go home. Nobody at school seemed to miss her—which wasn't surprising; she was always missing school because of the beatings and black eyes.

And every day, Jess woke up in his secret storeroom, warm and safe. Jess spent his days on that old couch, reading. He was trying to figure out about the world. He was studying, analyzing, diagnosing. He read a school nurse's manual, medical books, teacher's books, grown-up encyclopedias—anything he could find. He was trying to figure out what was going on. For the first few weeks of his life, he never left that storeroom, never went outside. He didn't even know there was any other world, except for the world in books.

The best thing in Jess's world was his special teacher. He was a sweet, gentle man who wore a dark coat and dark hat. His name was Michael. He'd come to Jess down there in the storeroom to help him understand about the world. He told him about his real father, and they prayed to him together. Michael gave Jess a tiny black hat, and he put it on and Michael put his on and they prayed to their real father together. When they were done, Jess took off the little hat and put it in his pocket and then he took out a blue comb and he combed Michael's thick, wavy black hair. *"Du bist meine Welt,"* Michael told him—you are my world.

"What was it about this haircut that was so terribly traumatic?" Dr. Walton asked quietly.

"There was something about hair that was important to all of us," Kitty told him. "Our hair was the pride of our lives. It was the only thing anybody ever made nice comments about. It was the only thing that was legitimately *ours*. And, of course, it represented our femaleness. To have our hair casually ripped off like that, as if it were a joke, was like being eviscerated."

She paused a moment.

"There was something very special about Jess combing Michael's hair, too. It was an act of reverence, of honor. There was such a quality of gentleness between those two! There was a master–student relationship, but also, in a lovely way, the child also taught the master. Michael showed a reverence toward Jess, too."

"Jess, of course, is the only male personality. Why do you suppose he came out then? Just because he *looked* like a boy when the hair was cut off?"

223

"Yeah, that's part of it, I guess," Kitty said thoughtfully. "But the girls had also just been laughed at and ridiculed by women—by Mother and the ladies in the beauty shop. Penny felt ashamed to be female. The father laughed at them too, of course, but that was a given. He always laughed. Also, you know, Penny had just come from two very female places—the beauty shop and the girl's bathroom—and suddenly she found herself in the ultimate male place: a janitor's basement room, full of big scary machines and tools. She had to hide, and she had to do it in a man's world. Hence, Jess."

"You mention a curious thing—that the storeroom reminded Jess of the grandmother's house," Dr. Walton pointed out. "If he had just been created, how could he have any recollection of the grandmother's house?"

For a moment she stared at him blankly. Then, suddenly, she sat straight up in the chair.

"That's so strange!" The voice had changed ever so slightly; a shadow flickered across the face. Caught up in the intellectual excitement of this conundrum, and almost without realizing it, Jess had emerged.

"I've always had this weird feeling that I . . . that Jess knew about the others from the start," he said. "Not *clearly*, but on some dim, subconscious level, he knew they were there. He always felt responsible for the girls, like he was there as a caretaker, a kind of big brother to them. Yet how could he have felt responsible for them, if he didn't even know they existed? How could the storeroom have reminded him of the grandmother's house, if he didn't have some historical memory of their experience?"

Jess made no effort to reveal himself, and Dr. Walton appeared not to have noticed he was even there.

"It was like, with Jess, these blank walls of amnesia that separated the personalities were partly permeable," Jess went on. "It was like there were little leaks in the dikes, or something: things seeped through. He just knew things, but didn't know how he knew them. With Liz and Penny and the others, it was different: back then, they had absolutely no knowledge of each other. But with Jess, somehow, on some deep level, he knew they were there. I think that's partly why he wanted to be a doctor: He wanted to care for these girls. He knew he had sick people on board."

"Obviously," Dr. Walton pointed out, "Jess was a male in a female's body. Did that ever bother him?"

A hot flush flooded into Jess's face. He adored Dr. Walton. He wanted to be his son. He wanted to go fishing with him, read books with him, be his devoted student. But he was . . . a woman. He knew that now. There was no way that could be changed.

"Well, back then he didn't even know what a male body *was*—so as far as he was concerned, he was anatomically correct!" Jess stumbled finally. "You'd think he would have figured it out, reading all those medical books, but he didn't. Maybe he just didn't dare let himself figure it out. After all, the only tangible proof he had that he even existed was his own physical body. He couldn't very well afford to question *that!*"

"You've said that Me-Liz was created at least partly to atone for Liz's sins, to balance out her sexuality with spirituality. Besides his initial birth, did Jess have any special role or function, like Me-Liz did?"

"I suppose you could say, at least simplistically, that Jess was created as a sort of male mode of escape," Jess said thoughtfully. "Penny Lavender was a way of escaping into romantic mistiness, fogginess, sentimentality—a sort of female mode of escape, through feelings. Jess was a way of escaping from emotion—a male mode of escape, into coldness, objectivity, the 'scientific method.' Of course, Jess doesn't think of himself as a 'mode of escape' from anything. He just figured he was born, like everybody else."

After a few weeks—three weeks? a month?—the hair had grown back enough so that Penny could go to class. Nobody seemed to have missed her or even seemed to care. The kids thought Penny's hair was funny, and sometimes the boys called her "Butchy." That's when Jess came out. He hated them. He wanted to see them all dead. And in a vague sort of way, he felt a responsibility. He didn't even know exactly who he felt responsible *for,* just that he was the big brother and had to step in when things got scary. He was tough and icy and calm. He could take it like a man.

Jess felt responsible for his little brothers and sister, too. He could see how dangerous the situation was at home, especially for the baby, Chuckie. He saw Daddy tell Chuckie that some cleaning fluid was a milkshake. Chuckie looked like he was almost dead when they got him to the hospital, but in the end he lived. Jess had seen what happened, though, and he could never forgive his daddy for that.

Jess knew how dangerous his daddy was. He knew that Daddy might kill them all.

225

Chapter 26

Y ou've told me about the sexual abuse you suffered at the hands of your father when you were very small," Dr. Walton said at the beginning of their last session in December, "but what I'd like to talk about now is how that affected your ideas of love and sexuality when you got older."

Liz sighed and looked away. She hadn't been feeling well all winter, and the mention of "love" only made her feel queasy, as if it were some vague and unpleasant new intestinal disorder.

"We've talked about how it affected you when you were five," Dr. Walton went on, "but how did it affect you when you were, say, fourteen?"

"I've always been a little screwed up about love, I guess."

He just looked at her kindly.

"The only time Daddy ever paid attention to me, or any of us, was when . . . you know . . . when it was sex," she said, without inflection. "So who could blame me for thinking that was love, you know? And when he started selling me, I guess, I guess . . ." Her voice trailed off.

"Selling you?"

"Yeah. I guess I thought it was love. What else was I supposed to think?"

Liz had a secret. All through school that Monday morning, she savored the memory—he said he loved her! A man, a grown-up man, said he loved her! The way he'd made her feel was like nothing she'd ever felt before. She could still feel that warm, sleepy feeling of being loved all the way down to her toes. Was this what it meant to be a woman? Was this what she'd been missing?

His name was Drake—he was Tammy's daddy. Tammy was staying in room seventeen at the June Bug Boarding Home in Dallas, just down the hall from twenty-six, where Liz and her family lived. It was fun babysitting for Tammy, who was two, even though Daddy took the three dollars when she got home. Then, last Friday, her daddy told her he had another job for her. Tammy's daddy was going down to Austin for the weekend, and he'd let her go along to look after Tammy.

"Pack a little bag with your pj's, and go with him," her daddy had told her.

It was exciting to get a chance to go all the way down to Austin by herself. For her, it was like a wonderful, grown-up vacation. The funny thing was, she didn't even have to babysit—when she got in Drake's car, his baby and his wife weren't there. It was just the two of them.

"Where's Tammy?" she asked him. "Where's your baby?"

"She's with her mommy," Drake said. "You're my baby now."

Well, Liz thought, it would be the easiest three dollars she ever made. Maybe she could even keep some of it for herself. Maybe she could even buy a dress, so the kids in her seventh grade class would stop whispering "*Pea*-nut! Poor *pea*-nut!" when she walked down the hall. Her family never had any money, but now Daddy complained about it more than ever. Mr. Zimmerman, who ran the June Bug, would bang on the door each month and Daddy would make excuses about why he didn't have the rent. Daddy said it was winter, and the slow season for boarding houses, and Mr. Zimmerman would just have to wait.

At least Mr. Zimmerman was nicer than the bill collectors who'd started showing up at the door just before they left Bethany, Oklahoma, in the middle of the night. Those bill collectors scared Liz to death. They looked meaner than her daddy. One of them told Liz he was going to break her daddy in two if he found him. She really wanted to watch him do that, but she never got the chance.

Mother had just had her fifth kid, a new baby named Mindy, so there were seven people in the family now: Mother, Daddy, Jimmy, Maryanne, little Chuckie, Liz, and the new baby. And there they would live, all seven of them, in that seedy one-bedroom efficiency with two double beds, for the next two years. It was so crowded there was hardly room to breathe: tiny kitchen, smaller living room, a hall, a bedroom, and one bath. Liz slept in the hallway on an old crib mattress, and the other kids shared the two double beds, two to a bed. Mother and daddy slept on a small fold-out couch in the living room; in the night, they'd get up and parade around in their underwear and take pictures of each other doing things and they looked so funny and so awful at the same time. In the morning, Liz would find those awful pictures scattered on the floor, and she'd hide them so the little kids wouldn't have to see.

Mother got a job at a fancy restaurant, and she came home late with her pockets jingling and doggy bags full of steak and lobster. The kids couldn't have any. That was Daddy food. The kids ate corn soup, potato soup, macaroni soup, and hot dogs. Daddy couldn't work. He didn't want any old meatball job, he wanted something suitable. So he just stayed home.

That's why Liz needed this job.

It was after dark when she and Drake got to their motel room in Austin, and he let her in and then went out for a drink. She crawled between the delicious, clean sheets on that big motel room bed and fell asleep. A little while later, Drake woke her up.

"Hey, lady, I've got some orange pop for you," he said. "Here, go ahead—drink some. Take this aspirin, too. It'll make your headache go away."

She didn't have a headache, but she took the aspirin anyway. In a little while, she started feeling so warm and sleepy and tingly she could hardly sit up, so she lay back on the bed and closed her eyes. She hardly noticed when Drake started gently stretching her out across the bed and taking off all her clothes. When she opened her eyes, he was leaning over the bed taking pictures with a tiny camera. She wondered in a sleepy sort of way why daddies always liked to take pictures like that. Her eyes drifted closed, and then she felt him climbing on top of her, pushing inside her. He was kissing and touching her all over, gently, caressingly.

"I love you, baby," he said. "You're beautiful! You're so beautiful!"

She could hardly believe it. He said he loved her! Nobody had ever told her that, except Michael. Sitting in seventh grade that Monday morning, her mind was on the wing like a bird in the sky. She could still hear those words: "I love you, baby . . . you're so beautiful . . . I love you . . . !" She'd always remember those words, even if Drake did tell her to "run along home now, like a good little girl," when they got back to the June Bug. Even if she'd seen him hand her daddy some money and some pictures. "I love you, baby . . . I love you . . . !" As soon as she could, she promised herself, she'd find somebody to make her feel that way again.

Baby, I love you. I love you!

"Did you find someone to make you feel that way again?" Dr. Walton asked.

"Yeah—it was only a few months later. A guy named Henry Nelson. The Third." She smiled faintly, remembering. "Sort of a strange little man with dazzling black eyes, who dressed like a beatnik. He was staying at the June Bug boarding house, and once we met, we were in bed as soon as possible."

"Did your parents know?"

"The father raised a huge stink at first—Henry was twenty-one, and I was only fourteen. 'You're still a minor, and that means you're *mine!*' he'd scream. But then, all of a sudden, bingo! Henry was wonderful, nothing was too good for him, and we were going out on our first date together—with Daddy's blessing. I couldn't figure it out, but I didn't care. I never did figure out what he was up to, until it was too late."

Liz didn't care why her father let her go out on that first date with Henry Nelson the third; she just grabbed at the faint chance for happiness. She and Henry drove down to Chinatown and ate with chopsticks and walked through the crowded, crooked streets under the paper lanterns and talked about everything and laughed and talked some more. Liz loved him because he was the only person in her life who would let her talk. One by one, the other girls crept out to take a look at this tall, dark man in the black turtleneck, with the gentle black eyes that seemed to understand so much, and they all approved. Penny Lavender loved it when he had her try on an expensive brocaded Chinese gown, and then bought it for her. She felt like one of those paper lanterns, filled with air and light, tilting in the sky.

Me-Liz loved him, too, because he listened and his hands were gentle. Not long after that first date, Henry Nelson made love to Liz on a creaky motel room bed, but Me-Liz was not there for that. In her own mind, she was a virgin and always would be. That's why, when Henry began showering them all with gifts—cocktail dresses and little sparkly shoes and tinkly wine glasses wrapped in tissue paper—Me-Liz became the keeper of the hope chest. She was never to be married. The hope chest filled up with lovely things, but they were never to be used. The hope chest had a lock on it, just like her virginity.

229

Henry treated them all like princesses. When they were with him, everything else disappeared. All the horror and the dreariness and the darkness and the pain just disappeared. They could be somebody. He allowed them to *be*. And when he really did ask them to marry him, they said yes aloud only once, but in their hearts they said it a thousand times.

It ended as abruptly as it began. One day she skipped school so they could spend the whole afternoon together. They'd just climbed into Henry's big brass bed when there was a knock on the door. When Henry opened it, there stood three policemen and—to Liz's amazement—her mother.

"You're under arrest for statutory rape," one of the cops told Henry, who was standing there with an incredulous look on his face, wearing nothing but a sheet.

Her mother dragged her back home and put her on restriction for weeks, drearily washing and drying and rewashing and redrying every single dish and utensil in the house, until she got so sleepy she fell off the chair and then she got hit. Her parents wouldn't tell her what had happened to Henry. But a few weeks later, she found out. She ran into Henry's friend Buddy at the store, and he told her that her daddy had finally sprung his trap. Henry, it turned out, was rich—or at least rich enough for her daddy. He'd been following the two of them around for weeks, waiting until he knew for sure they were having sex. Then he went to Henry and demanded money. He threatened to call the cops if Henry didn't pay—after all, Liz was a minor. Henry punched him in the nose. And now her daddy had gotten even. Henry might even wind up in jail.

Weeks later, when Liz saw Henry driving by in his little white Volvo, she flagged him down.

"I'm so sorry about what happened, Henry! I'm so sorry!" she sobbed. "Isn't there any way we can start over?"

"It's no good, Elizabeth," he said. "It's all over."

And then he drove away.

"How did you respond to this?" Dr. Walton inquired gently. "It's a terrible, rather monotonous pattern, isn't it? Every good thing eventually goes bad."

"I responded by throwing Michael out of my life," Liz said flatly.

"Michael?"

"Yeah, Michael. He kept telling me things were going to get better, and they never did. They got worse. He kept telling me I was strong, and I wasn't. He kept telling me God loved me, and He didn't—otherwise why would my life be so miserable? I finally figured out that Michael was a fraud, and I threw him out."

"Isn't it a bit odd that you blamed *him,* and not your parents?"

"She couldn't control her parents, but she could control Michael," Kitty interjected. "At least, she could control whether or not he was able to appear to her, or to any of the others. Michael told Liz he could only appear if she allowed it. That was part of his physics or something. If Liz chose to shut him out of her life, there was no way he could get back in until she let him in."

The words caught in her throat, and for a moment she was silent. That was years and years ago, but now the fearful loneliness of Liz's decision swept over her again, a sick, scared nausea, an illness more than a memory. She was fourteen years old, and alone in a universe devoid of all life.

.

"Liar!" Liz shrieked, throwing herself across her crib mattress on the floor in the dirty hall, weeping bitterly. "Dirty stinkin' liar! Fraud! Faker!"

Michael lied and played mean, dirty tricks, just like Daddy did. She'd finally figured out that nothing he said was true. All those wonderful things he told her were just glittery, empty promises to make life more bearable. They were like promises of water to a man dying of thirst. They were dirty lies. They were sand in the mouth.

Well, she was going on from here alone. Screw him! She'd be better off without him anyway. Living without Michael would just make the bad things easier to take. She wasn't going to trust anybody, or expect anything of anyone anymore. No one could betray her that way again. Nobody could hurt her anymore.

And it was true: in the weeks and months after she threw Michael out of her life, the bad things *were* easier to take. If you didn't care what happened to you, it didn't matter what happened. One day her daddy hit her in the stomach with an iron and she was bleeding from the mouth for days, but she didn't care. She didn't tell anyone. If she died, so what?

Living without Michael made it easier to lie or cheat or do whatever she had to do to avoid the fist and the punishments. She didn't care. Her daddy had taught her to lie with the best of them. What did he expect her to do with that knowledge? Liz could lie as easily as she could breathe. She got through school with lies. She got around the beatings with lies. She got out of the house with lies. She got out on dates with lies. She came to live in a whole twisted little world made of lies.

She was pretty and smart and she had a mother and daddy who loved her and took such good care of her! They lived in a normal house in a normal world. Everything was wonderful. She got this black eye because she fell. She broke her finger because she caught a football the wrong way. She split her lip when she ran into a door.

Once Liz told her guidance counselor at school that her father was tying her up and beating her with a coat hanger. He went right to her daddy and asked him, and he denied it. Of course he denied it! Then, of course, he beat her. The only good part was that at least he'd stopped trying to have sex with her. It was as if, now that she was growing up, she was no fun anymore. He couldn't make her afraid like he used to, and it was the fear that turned him on the most. The *fear*. She had no more fear to give him—she felt only disgust.

Liz could see things more clearly now that Michael was gone. She could see clearly that both her mother and her father were insane. The only way to survive the madness, she decided finally, was to go mad right along with them. To become a part of it, too. When the bill collectors called, she lied for Daddy almost without thinking. When somebody from the school called with bad reports about the kids or herself, she would pretend to be Mother. And if the house was a mess, it got cleaned up fast or she would lose her temper and hit the kids herself.

Then she realized it. She was becoming just like them. She was becoming her mother and daddy. And when her stomach started bleeding with ulcers, just like her father, she knew the cycle was complete.

My God, she thought, *I'm him*!

Chapter 27

Early in January, a sudden thaw followed by a freeze encased Tompkins County in ice. It was as if winter had fossilized the world in glass. Roofs and chimneys glistened. Tiny details of things—buds, blades of grass—wore grave clothes of ice, like little mummies. Outside Dr. Walton's office in the rambling Victorian house on Forest Avenue in Ithaca, ice-glazed elms tinkled faintly when they stirred in the wind. But inside the house, where the steam radiators clanged and hissed against the cold, he and his most curious patient left that material world of ice, snow, and the present time far behind.

"Eventually, your father stopped abusing you sexually," Dr. Walton mused, peering across at her intently. "But what sort of relationship did the two of you develop as you got older? What happened in high school?"

"That was weird. The weirdest," Liz said. "During my senior year in high school, Daddy suddenly realized his daughter was turning into a beauty. One day I'm worthless, a tramp, a whore, and the next day I'm Marilyn Monroe. He started dressing me up like a lady, buying me lavish, expensive, grown-up clothes—low-cut cocktail dresses, nylons, black push-up bras, lacy underwear. 'You're so beautiful,' he'd say. 'Let's go out and get you some clothes.' Then we'd leave Mother at home and drive down to the garment district in Dallas and go on a spree. It was like, all of a sudden, he was having an illicit affair with me, or dating me, or something."

"Did he make any sexual advances toward you?"

"No. The sex had stopped years before. But after he got me all dressed up like a Barbie doll, he'd take me out dancing to some glittery hot spot, or take me out to a posh restaurant for dinner. He'd tell people who were serving drinks that I was his secretary or 'somebody I'm seeing.' "

"How did you respond to all this attention?"

"I didn't feel flattered. I felt suspicious. Wary. We all did. I knew it was a big fake, a charade, and it would end when he wanted it to. But, for the time being at least, I decided to go with the flow. Why not? It was better than getting hit."

"How long did it last?"

"It lasted until the beauty pageant. He read about this pageant in the local paper and he just absolutely insisted that I enter. The winner would be crowned Miss Highland Park, you know, and she'd go on to compete in the Miss Texas and Miss America pageants and all that. Penny liked the idea—she'd been taking modeling classes at Sears—but Me-Liz thought it was tacky. I guess it was Liz who finally agreed to do it."

It was so bizarre! Now, suddenly, Daddy longed for Liz to be a beauty queen, Miss Highland Park, riding the float down Main Street and waving her wand over the crowds like the fairy godmother of suburbia. If people only knew what her life was like! If they only knew what had gone on in that house all those years! All through high school, all Liz ever wanted was to be normal. To her, normal life was a fairy tale. She didn't want to be a beauty queen, she just wanted to be average. Whenever anyone asked about her home life, she'd take stories she'd heard from twenty different kids and just average them out. Then she'd tell that story. She didn't know what normal life was, except from what she'd heard from other people or seen on TV, so she had to make it up.

After her daddy got a job at a grocery store, they'd moved out of the June Bug Boarding Home and into an ordinary-looking house on an ordinary-looking street, just like everybody else. But nothing changed inside that house; things just got worse. Mother and Daddy started having people over at night, and they'd always lock a special door that sealed off the whole back of the place from the kids' bedrooms up front.

Sometimes, when Liz went in to use the iron the next morning, she'd find pictures scattered all over the floor. She didn't even want to look at them. She didn't want to know who that Oriental girl was, hanging naked from some kind of rope and chain device suspended from those eye screws in the family room.

Sometimes Daddy would lock himself into that back part of the house and not go to work for days. She could hear him back there, yelling and howling like an animal, and things going *thump* against the wall. A bad smell—Daddy's smell—started seeping out from under the door.

How could she tell anybody about *that?*

Liz entered the pageant in January, 1967.

Her father began shuttling her around to all the various functions associated with the pageant, not in demure little skirts and blouses, but preposterously overdressed for the occasion—in low-cut dresses and nylons with seams down the back. She'd be wearing gobs of makeup that her mother would apply on her face. The same mother who up until now wouldn't allow her to wear lipstick.

All the contestants were asked to make public appearances at fundraising events for the pageant, sponsored by local businesses. One night not long before the pageant, Liz was asked to attend a "gambling night" sponsored by the Kiwanis in University Park, a neighboring town. Her chaperone led her into a small auditorium that had been converted into a miniature casino, with crepe paper and balloons, and a variety of legal betting games laid out on tables. Almost the moment she walked into the auditorium, Liz noticed a tall, rangy Mexican man standing across the room. He was returning her stare.

"Who's that Mexican guy over there?" she asked the chaperone.

"That's the auctioneer. There's gonna be an auction tonight, too." He looked over at her suspiciously. "You are not to get involved with anyone, you understand? You're a queen contestant, and I'm your chaperone."

She'd been unlucky enough to draw a chaperone who took his job with comical seriousness. But throughout the evening, Liz and the Mexican auctioneer kept trying to maneuver closer to each other through the crowded room. He seemed as attracted to Liz as she was to him. During the auction, she sat in the audience in the second row, but it was clear the auctioneer's mind was not on his job. He kept staring at her so blatantly that people began to snicker and glance her way. Finally, during a break, she asked someone to slip him a note: "Meet you on the front porch—quick!"

Liz made some excuse to elude her chaperone and met the auctioneer on the porch. They looked at each other shyly for a moment, full of awkward fascination.

"I'm Domingo," he said, holding out his hand. "Domingo Garcia. People call me 'Mingo.' I've kinda had my eye on you."

"Yeah, I know," Liz said. "You weren't hiding it very well. I'm Elizabeth Meyer. I'm in the pageant."

"I know. I saw your picture in the paper. I'm working on the pageant, you know—I'm in the Kiwanis."

"Oh, really? You mean . . . you mean I'll be seeing you around again?"

"If there's any way I can arrange it, you'll definitely be seeing me again."

They both laughed.

"Hey," he said suddenly, "Wanna get out of here awhile? I've got a twenty-minute break."

"Love to."

Domingo helped her into his little white Mustang and they went for a spin around town while they talked. He was twenty-five, he told her. He lived in University Park with his family, and worked in an appliance store. He knew a lot of businesspeople around town, through his work with the Kiwanis. He wanted to make something of his life. He was an up-and-comer. And he was very interested in her. She tried to make it clear, without exactly saying so, that she felt the same.

But her daddy wasn't going to have any of it.

A few nights later, when Domingo showed up at the door to take Liz out to dinner, her father greeted him with a solid wall of ice.

"You have no business dating my daughter," he told Domingo. "I don't care if you're with the Kiwanis or whatever, you're not welcome in this house. I don't want to ever see you here again. Don't come back."

But Liz and Mingo didn't give up. She liked this man—he was handsome and kind and he treated her with respect. He listened. They kept on talking furtively on the telephone, and seeing each other in secret. One afternoon they arranged to meet at her house when her parents were gone. Unfortunately, moments before Domingo arrived, her father came home. He was standing in the front hall when Domingo's white Mustang pulled up in front of the house, and without hesitation he flew out the door, met Domingo coming up the sidewalk, and decked him on the spot.

"Stick with your own kind, you filthy Mexican!" he screamed, and was about to deck him again when Domingo jumped back in his car and sped away before things got any worse. Liz went immediately to her room. Everything had gone bad with Henry Nelson, and now it was going bad with Domingo. Just then her little sister Mindy came wandering into her room to see what all the commotion was about.

"Did I ever tell you about the time our own parents put us in an orphanage?" Liz asked her suddenly. She knew that Mindy was too young to know. She knew that Mindy would run to her parents to find out if it was true. And she also knew what would happen then.

"That's not true! That couldn't be true!" Mindy said, beginning to cry. "Our parents wouldn't do that to us!" And she ran down the hall to ask them if it was true. Liz sat on the floor of her room, surrounded by half-finished centerpieces for the coronation ball, waiting for the explosion.

In a dim, unconscious way, Liz was seeking punishment. She was addicted to her parents' punishments. She needed their negative affirmation. Whenever she felt she had done something bad, her first reaction was to go find Mommy and Daddy and do something to make them punish her. It was Liz who had internalized all the guilt and blame, and she who needed the humiliation that only they could give. A few minutes later, she heard her father's footsteps thumping up the hall.

"What kind of trash are you talking now?" he demanded. "What kind of lies are you telling Mindy? You're a liar and always have been! You know damn well nothing like that ever happened!" He backhanded her across the face. "Look at all I've done for you—look at all these dresses! Look at all these clothes! And this is what I get for it? Dirty lies?" He hit her again, this time with his fist. "And now you're taking up with some dirty Mexican!"

He hit her again. Wham, wham, wham! His rage would start to cool and he'd stalk out of the room, then he'd turn around and come back in again and start pounding on her some more. She just took it. After all, she deserved it. When it was over, both her eyes were blackened, her lip was split, and her nose was bleeding.

And the pageant was only ten days away.

By the day of the pageant—March 4, 1967—Liz's face had begun to recover. The puffiness and discoloration around her eyes had begun to subside, and the lip had started to knit. Her mother made her an appointment at the beauty parlor to get her hair done early in the afternoon.

It was Penny Lavender who performed that night. For the talent part of the competition, she did an art demonstration, showing the audience how to do a quick portrait using colored chalks and an easel. The bathing suit competition came after the talent contest, so Penny slipped into her suit backstage. There was something the matter with it, though—standing behind the curtain, peering out onto the spotlit stage, she kept tugging at the bottom edge to keep it down. Why wouldn't it stay down?

"Everything's going to be fine," whispered one of the pageant organizers, standing behind her. "Just relax! It's your turn now."

She gave Penny a gentle push out into the light. With poise and confidence, Penny strode out the raised runway, which extended off the stage into the auditorium. She'd learned how to look and walk like a model in her classes at Sears, and she was proud of it. She felt calm and otherworldly. She was a blonde marble goddess, cool as stone. She was lovely, she was perfect. She was a thing of mist and air. When she reached the end of the runway, she turned calmly on one heel, and then—for a moment she could hardly comprehend it—suddenly the bottom edge of the bathing suit rode up, and one buttock plopped ingloriously out into view. She was standing there showing her bare behind to six hundred people. All over the auditorium, there was an audible gasp. Then, far in the back, she heard one male voice hoot with laughter.

She recognized the voice immediately.

It was her father.

In a flash, all the glory and romance of the pageant dropped away. One instant, she felt like a beauty queen, serene as a goddess; the next, she felt like someone who'd just told a dirty joke at a funeral. Crude, shunned, disgusting. How could this possibly happen? What was going on? What was she going to do? Alone in the spotlight, she felt stunned and confused for a moment, her body filling up with shame, and then she just disappeared, like a wisp of smoke. A moment later, Liz was there, completing the turn and hurrying back down the runway. It was as if the physical sensation of shame was a chemical signal that called her out. She recognized shame and humiliation; that was her cue.

When Liz slipped behind the curtain, she was fighting off the tears. In the half-darkness, she peeled off the bathing suit and fumbled into her formal for the final line-up. Then she knelt down and took a closer look at the bottom edge of the suit, just to make sure. The seamstress who had made alterations in the suit had put in a row of tiny stitches along the bottom seam to keep the elastic snug. But laying there in her hand, she could see that someone had crudely jerked them out, one by one.

Chapter 28

S o I take it you didn't win the pageant?" Dr. Walton inquired
mildly, eyeing the small dark-haired girl with the heavy-lidded
eyes seated in front of him.

"No," said Penny Lavender, without looking up.

"Was that a blow to you?"

She didn't answer. She didn't know how to. All that came back to
her now was a feeling of unspeakable sadness. Instead of answering the
psychiatrist aloud, Penny stood on the edge of the wildflower meadow
in her mind, and she sang a sweet, sad, faraway song all to herself.

"Did you continue to see Domingo?" Dr. Walton asked finally.

"I eventually married him," Liz responded. "We had . . . kids . . .
together."

Dr. Walton considered this new information quietly.

"Did you ever tell him about what was going on with you—about
missing time, for instance?" he asked.

"No. I tried to once or twice, but he never seemed to hear it. Besides,
I didn't really know how to explain it myself."

"Did you ever tell him about this vague notion you had that there
was some 'secret' you needed to protect?"

"No," said Liz, firmly. "We never told anybody about that. See, it

239

was weird: we all knew that the secret had to be protected at all costs, even from Domingo, but none of us except Kitty even knew what the secret was. We had lots of secrets about our past that we never told him, or anybody, but the Big Secret was a secret even from ourselves."

"I assume the alter personalities 'came out' in Domingo's presence?"

"Oh, sure."

"Well, what happened then?"

"You see, Ralph," Kitty cut in impatiently, "It was Liz who fell in love with Domingo. She was the one who got engaged to him. Sometimes he'd come into the room when Penny or Me-Liz was out, and they'd instantly withdraw, like a spider pulling in its legs when it's touched. They weren't engaged to him, after all. Only Liz was—and they felt they had no business being there. They also understood, in some vague way, that they were to protect the secret, and going away would help. No one was to know, not even their own husband. The secret had to be protected. Even if they didn't even know what the secret was."

After they decided to get married, Domingo rented a little apartment on White Rock Boulevard, not far from the June Bug Boarding Home, for $125 a month. Liz, Me-Liz, Penny, and the others moved in by themselves. Domingo refused to move in until after the wedding—he considered himself a religious man, even though he never went to church, and he intended to go to the altar a virgin. He was also proud, old-fashioned, and Latin, and insisted on being his fiancée's sole provider. He was only making eighty dollars a week at the appliance store— he had to buy her wedding band at a pawnshop—but still he refused to let her work.

The others felt proud and pleased with themselves. Now they were grown-up engaged ladies, with their own apartment and a coffeepot and a man who loved them. They were out of that hateful house, and free of the parents, at last. After the fiasco of the beauty pageant, they had moved out of that house forever. They'd finally had enough. It didn't make any difference if the parents approved or not: one day they just packed up three boxes with everything they owned and walked out. They didn't even leave a note.

The new apartment was small but clean, on a shabby commercial strip across the street from a Tarot reader's temple. The Tarot reader was their landlady—a dark-eyed gypsy woman who always wore a turban and ropes of jewelry made of gold coins. Domingo trusted Liz enough to send her over with the rent check each month, and Liz loved going in that place. She thought she'd never seen anything so pretty. Everywhere you looked there was sparkly brocade and velvet tapestry and picture pillows in piles. Towering over the Tarot temple, glittering like Christmas, was an enormous neon sign of a gypsy lady moving her hands over a deck of magic cards. At night, alone in bed, Liz and Me-Liz and Penny would stare out the window at the neon gypsy moving her hands kindly around those cards that contained all the sorrows and mysteries of the universe.

Domingo arranged the wedding service. He paid for a package deal at a place in Austin called the Temple of the Bells, because it sounded like fun and it was cheap. It wouldn't be a church wedding—they didn't know the church might not even consider it a wedding at all—but they decided to go for it anyway. On a sunny afternoon in August, two months after her graduation, they drove down to Austin and got a room in a motel over a garage. Liz was dazzled by the lights, and she was excited and proud of herself. Maybe now things would be all right. She was free. She was grown up. And she was about to be married to a handsome, tender man who loved her.

The service was scheduled for the next morning at eleven. They got up that morning, had breakfast, packed everything in Domingo's Mustang, and were downstairs checking out when a man burst into the motel office.

"Hey, there's a fire out here! There's a car in the garage on fire!"

They went tearing outside, and there, surrounded by curious onlookers, was Domingo's car, engulfed in smoke and flames. The car had everything in it—all their money and traveler's checks, all their clothes, everything. Liz's heart sank. Mingo didn't say anything. He just watched as the fire department blasted the smoking wreck with their hoses. The only thing they had left was what they were wearing: she had on a yellow dotted-Swiss wedding dress, a mini, and he was wearing a suit.

"Well," Domingo said, "At least we look good!"

They both laughed, a little nervously. She gave him her hand, and together they walked down the street to the Temple of the Bells. They were going to get married, no matter what.

The "temple" was as a small roadside affair done up in a western motif, with a rough brick floor, raw wood beams and pews, and stucco archways trailing masses of fake vines and flowers. Hanging from the rafters, row upon row, were thousands of little golden bells. In the back of the chapel sat an enormously overweight, enormously drunk couple who had apparently just gotten married. They were all dressed up in sequiny white cowboy outfits, with white hats and white boots, and they seemed to be having a fabulous time. They were shouting and talking and whooping and hugging each other.

"Hey, you guys gettin' married?" the man howled when Liz and Domingo walked in. "It's great! Fantastic! You oughta do it more often! Hey, you alone? Who's gonna be your best man? Who's gonna be your maid of honor? Ain't you got no witnesses? You gotta have witnesses to get married. Who's gonna be your witnesses?"

"Well . . . I don't know," Domingo said uncertainly. "I didn't know we had to have witnesses. Is that some kind of law or something?"

"Oh, yeah. Gotta have witnesses. Hey, why don't we do it? We'll do it! We'll sign the papers for ya!"

So two drunken strangers in white cowboy outfits became their witnesses. The justice of the peace who ran the place appeared—an old man with a bald head, wire-rimmed glasses, and one wild eye that seemed to drift and float around the room. He had them sign some papers and then stood them in front of a makeshift altar piled up with plastic philodendrons. His wife, standing in the corner, turned on a record that played the *Wedding March* over and over. Behind them, at the back of the chapel, the freshly wedded couple in cowboy outfits started having their first argument.

"We gotta take your kids out to dinner after this ceremony," the lady was saying. "They come all this way, and they're hungry! They're probably tearing that motel room apart by now!"

"Aw, no, honey," the man whined, "I ain't waited all this time for nothing! Let's get us a room! We got a honeymoon to start!"

"But *ho*-ney! The kids! What are we gonna do about the kids?"

Meanwhile the justice of the peace was droning through the ceremony. Finally he said, "And do you, Domingo, take this woman to be your lawfully wedded wife?" Domingo hesitated a second. The man's bad eye seemed to be floating up toward the ceiling; it was hard to tell who or what he was looking at. Finally Domingo said, "I do?" Then he took the pawnshop wedding band, held it up to her finger, fumbled a moment, and dropped it. The ring bounced once and rolled out of sight. In the back of the room, the witnesses stopped arguing and then they came bounding up to the front of the chapel. Everybody, justice of the peace included, got down on their hands and knees and began searching for the ring. Two mile-wide rears covered with sequin-spattered white satin rodeo pants lumbered in and out of the pews.

"Got it!" the cowboy called out a few moments later, when he found the ring in a sand-filled crack between the bricks on the floor. They all got back on their feet, laughed a little, and picked up the ceremony where they'd left off. Domingo slipped the ring on her finger, and then the justice said, "Do you, Elizabeth, take this man to be your lawfully wedded husband?" And even though the floating eye was drifting toward the window, she said "I do," and they were married.

It was August 27, 1967.

"Well, what shall we do now?" said the cowboy brightly when the service was over.

"My car just burned up," Domingo told them. "It had all our stuff in it, all our clothes, all our money, everything. We've gotta find some way to get out of here. I gotta be at work at eight o'clock tomorrow morning."

It was amazing how quickly the cowboy couple disappeared when he said that. And then Liz and Domingo were standing outside the wedding chapel in the hot Texas sun, all dressed up, with nothing between them but loose change and a wedding certificate. They spent the rest of that afternoon in a motel lobby while Domingo called friends back in Dallas, trying to get somebody to wire him enough money for a bus back home. It was dark before the money came through, and they caught a Trailways bus for Dallas. They never even went back to find out what happened to the car.

They spent their wedding night on the bus.

That fall, only a few months after they were married, Liz started throwing up almost every morning, and she realized she must be pregnant. Although she had some terrible secret doubts about having children, Domingo badly wanted a child—a male child—and in the end she'd gone along with it. Well, she thought, when you got married, you had kids. That's the way it was. She'd gone to see a doctor around the corner from their apartment, and he told her that if they wanted a boy child, she'd have to take these little blue pills, and if they wanted a girl child, they'd have to take these little pink pills. The pills cost ten dollars a week, but they decided it was worth it. Every morning, Liz took a little blue pill.

Liz went to Sears and bought a layette. She started fixing up one of the two bedrooms for the new baby, and inside a feeling of warm joy and anticipation began to grow like a seed. But the nursery was never used. A few months later, they moved out of the apartment, into a "guest house" on the property of one of Domingo's well-to-do friends. The $125-a-month rent for the apartment was just too much, and the new place was only fifty dollars a month. The guest house was actually a converted garage—a dark, single room with a bathroom, one bed, a kitchen chair and table, and a single unit that served as sink, stove, and refrigerator. The place was so small they couldn't unpack most of what they owned, so a quarter of the space was taken up by unpacked card-board boxes.

By then, Liz was almost six months pregnant, and she felt nauseated and exhausted most of the time. Maybe it was just the pregnancy, she thought. But there was something else, too. In a vague, dark way, sometimes she thought she might be mentally ill or something. She just couldn't seem to shake the blues. She felt drained. She didn't have the energy to fix up the place, clean the dishes, or pick up after Domingo. For days, she just lay in bed staring at the dark, crowded room. It had begun to smell like dirty socks and sour milk, but she just stared at it and didn't move.

The Mexico trip only made things worse. One of Domingo's Mexican relations was having a baptismal party in the little border town of Neuvo Laredo, so one weekend he and Liz drove down there for the festivities. It was just after the party had ended that an ancient woman approached her. Speaking through one of Domingo's relatives, who spoke both Spanish and English, the woman told her that she could tell Liz was infected with bad spirits. She told her she wanted to help protect the baby from infection. Then the old lady took a safety pin with a little wad of dried goop on it, like a raisin, and pinned it to the waistband of Liz's maternity pants. She mustn't ever take it off, the old lady told her, because if she did the child would turn into a mass of white maggots.

Liz was horrified. How did she know that she wasn't really infected with bad spirits? Maybe that was why she felt this way. Maybe that's what was the matter with her. After that, she refused to take the safety pin off, even when she went to bed.

The guest house was just too small and too depressing, Domingo decided after they'd been there less than a month—there was hardly enough room for the two of them, much less a baby. So he applied for a mortgage and went looking for a house they could afford. He found a little two-bedroom bungalow in a modest neighborhood, and six weeks later the loan went through. Almost before she knew it, Liz had moved into the first house that she'd ever been able to call her own.

It was a pleasant little place with two bedrooms, a kitchen, living room, a patio, and a big backyard nicely landscaped with plants and flowers, next door to a power plant. She took the larger of the two bedrooms and made it into a nursery, and bought a crib. A few weeks later, she gave birth to a healthy baby girl, whom they named Angel Elizabeth. The little blue pills hadn't worked.

Hospital records show Angel Elizabeth Garcia was born at 5:45 P.M. on June 14, 1968, at Parkland Memorial Hospital in Dallas.

Liz loved the baby. And she began to feel happy in her own small way, in her very own house, until the "inspections" began. There was no other way to describe them. Out of the clear blue, completely unannounced, her parents began showing up at the door to conduct military-style reviews of the house. They had discovered where she lived, and now seemed to consider her home a rightful part of their territory. They would roam through the place making sure everything was up to their standards of cleanliness and order—what a joke!—poking in dresser drawers and linen closets, and if everything was not just the way they wanted it, they would demand that she clean it up before they left. It was as if, now that they couldn't control her in their own home, they were going to control her in hers.

But for the first time in her life, Liz began to fight back. All the anger that had been boiling up inside all those years began to escape, like a scalding jet of steam.

"This is my house, not yours!" she screamed at them one day when they appeared for an inspection. "You have no right to come barging in here and do this to me! Of course the house isn't spotless—it's not a museum, it's the place I'm trying to raise a small baby all by myself!"

"You're not going to bring Domingo into this family thinking we raised you as a pig!" her father yelled back, his face two inches from hers. The same father who'd called Domingo "a filthy Mexican" less than a year before now seemed to consider him an adopted son—and consider Liz a tramp.

It took every ounce of courage that Liz had not to cry or back down. Nobody had ever told her she had the right to do or be anything, and she wasn't completely sure she did. When Domingo got home from work that night, she told him what had happened.

"Liz, I think your parents just want you to keep the house a little cleaner, that's all," he said. "Don't get so worked up about it! You really ought to keep the place cleaner, you know. You ought to be more grateful."

Maybe she *didn't* have the right, she thought. Maybe she should be more grateful. Still, in her heart, she felt a helpless rage and an unspeakable new loneliness. Even her own husband wouldn't support her. It was as if Domingo was now in league with her parents against her. Her father had put him under his spell. He had poisoned his mind against her, and now she was alone. Well, she thought finally, that's just the way it was. She was powerless to do anything. This was life. This was the way things were.

There was no way to escape.

Chapter 29

For a dizzy moment, Liz thought she was waking up at home in her own bed. But it wasn't like waking out of sleep, and she wasn't in bed. She was standing up, fully dressed, inside some kind of kiosk in a shopping mall parking lot. She felt confused and disoriented, like a top that has just spun to a stop. There were stacks of yellow film-processing packages piled on a counter, and a little tower of receipts impaled on a spike.

Liz caught sight of a sunlit reflection of herself in the window, and she sucked in her breath with a gasp. She was wearing an enormous, frizzy white Afro wig, a red miniskirt with black nylons, and black patent leather half-boots. It was a style of dressing that was all the rage in Dallas in 1968 . . . but *she* never dressed like that. She didn't even own any clothes like that. What was she doing here? Where did these clothes come from?

A man in a pickup pulled up to the kiosk and shoved a package of film through the slot.

"Hi, sunshine," he called out. "Can I get these pictures back by Wednesday?"

She just stared at him. Did she have a job here? Is that what it was?

She fumbled for the handle of the door, snapped it open, and took off walking, fast, across the parking lot, leaving the door ajar behind her.

"Hey!" the man yelled after her. "Wait a minute! What did I say?"

An illuminated sign—Parkway Shopping Center—towered over the low-slung mall. She was three miles from home. It would have to be a long, fast walk, she thought anxiously. This time she might get caught. This time, it would be hard to explain away. What if Domingo was home when she walked in dressed like this? Maybe . . . well, who knew what was going on? It didn't really matter. She was used to it. Probably happened to everybody. Life didn't go in a straight line, from one thing to the next; it was all broken up in pieces, with funny blank spots in between. She refused to wear a watch because that was her way of covering up the blank spots, but sometimes, like now, the blank spots were too big to cover up. And they seemed to be getting bigger and bigger. Other people wore watches, she thought. Weren't they afraid of blank spots? She felt tired. When she got home, she'd just take off these clothes and go to bed.

Suddenly, the thought hit her like a hammer in the brain: Where's Angel? Who has my baby? As she broke into a kind of loping run down the sidewalk toward home, the strangeness of what had just happened—even that it had happened at all—evaporated like a mist.

Baby Angel was asleep in her crib when Liz got home. She glanced out the back window and saw the *abuelo,* her husband's grandfather, quietly raking in the backyard. She slipped into the bedroom, peeled off the red miniskirt, black nylons, boots, and wig, and stuffed them under a pile of clothes deep in a closet. She pulled on blue jeans and a T-shirt, got herself a cold glass of milk, and walked out the back door onto the shady stoop. The *abuelo* looked up from his work and smiled, then bent over his rake again.

It was nice having the *abuelo* around, she thought as she settled herself on the back step and took a cold sip of milk. The old man stooped to pick up a tiny scrap of paper, then returned to his raking. He was always raking. He'd turned the backyard into a tidy little paradise already, and he'd only been living with them two months. She'd grown fond of his gentle little habits—his raking, his cup of morning tea, his collections of string and gum wrappers, and (as long as they'd lasted) his language lessons.

Domingo had simply announced one day that his grandfather was coming up from Mexico to stay with them awhile, and the next day, he'd brought this gnome of an old man home from the bus station. The old man was dressed in workman's clothes, and he'd given her a sweet, enigmatic smile when he saw her. He brought nothing with him except a roll of clothes and a paper sack containing odd bits of string rolled up in a ball, a collection of old tinfoil from chewing gum wrappers, and some weird tobacco he grew on his farm in Mexico. He didn't speak a word of English.

Liz had fixed up a bed for him in the baby's room, because that was the only available space, and the old man quickly set about decorating the place with little yellow braids made of Juicy Fruit gum wrappers. They were charms to keep the good spirits in and the bad spirits out, he said. She and Domingo started calling him the *abuelo,* which means grandfather in Spanish. The *abuelo* would get up at five o'clock every morning and make himself his cup of tea and spend the entire day out in the backyard with his garden tools, raking and planting and raking some more.

Some mornings she'd get up early when the house was quiet, and the *abuelo* would be sitting in the bedroom in a rocking chair with his great-granddaughter in his arms, singing and talking to her softly in Spanish. At other times, he would pull a quarter out of his pocket and say to her, "Co-cola?" She'd nod, and then he'd walk down the street and bring back two bottles of Coca-Cola and they would sit out on the back step and share a glass of Coke together, with the baby laying beside them on a blanket.

From the very start, she and the *abuelo* seemed able to communicate without words. They had a way of expressing themselves that was higher and finer than words. She sensed the sweetness and serenity in him, and it calmed her heart, like a hand smoothing the covers on a rumpled bed. Somehow, he seemed to understand how troubled she was, and she knew that. He seemed to feel sorry for her, and he did what he could to help. Sometimes he would take the baby out in the stroller for long, long walks, just so she could be alone.

He'd started giving her little language lessons in the backyard. He would take her by the hand and point out green things and birds and snails and tell her their names in Spanish. If she didn't know their names in English, she'd take Domingo out there when he came home from work and he'd tell her the English words. Little by little, she began learning gardener's Spanish.

Then her father found out.

"I don't want you turning into a damn Mexican," he told her. "If these people are going to live in the United States, they're going to have to learn to speak English, not the other way around. Don't let me catch you doing that again."

She took another sip of milk and stared out at the *abuelo* stooping over his rake. She remembered the day last week when he'd understood. They'd been sitting out here on the step together when a big tortoise came lumbering across the yard. Their neighbors kept tortoises as pets, and sometimes they'd escape through a hole under the fence. The *abuelo* had pointed at the tortoise and said "*tortuga*," then looked at her and smiled. She didn't repeat the word back. Her heart had been full of sadness. She'd cast her eyes down for a long time, and when she looked up again he was staring at her intently. His face was full of understanding, and his eyes were full of tears. He'd nodded. It was as if he knew.

Liz sipped the last of the cool milk. "*Tortuga*," she whispered, so low no one could hear.

"Which personality was it who woke up in the photo kiosk?" Dr. Walton inquired, gazing at her pensively.

"It was Penny who started work that day," Kitty responded. "She loved to dress up like that. But it was Me-Liz who woke up there."

" 'Waking up' out of the blue someplace, with no idea how you got there—that must have been a rather unsettling experience, to say the least," Dr. Walton mused. "But hadn't things like this been happening all your life?"

"Yeah, sure, that stuff happened to all of us," Kitty explained. "But now she was grown up. Now she had a husband and a child. Now she was being forced to recognize that something was terribly, terribly wrong. Wasn't it obvious? Yet somehow, for all those years, she'd succeeded in denying it, blanking it out, forgetting it."

"So there were other blackouts during those early years of the marriage?"

"One other time it was Liz who woke up by the kiosk. She was lying in the back of a parked bread truck, making love to the driver. The guy's name was Dennis. He was wearing a white uniform. She sat up, collected Penny's clothes—you see, it was Penny who seduced the driver, but it was Liz who woke up in the truck—gave him a little peck on the cheek, and then she climbed out of the truck. He said, 'Bye-bye, baby.' And then she walked home."

"You mean . . . you just walked away, as if nothing out of the ordinary had happened?" Dr. Walton asked, incredulous.

"Look, doc—some of them had been having these blackouts since they were little kids. They were only beginning to realize there was something weird about them. Besides, they were experts at denial. I guess you could say they still are."

"Did the blackouts become more frequent as time went on?"

"No, not really," said Kitty matter-of-factly. "But the stress got steadily worse. They started falling into these black holes of depression, and they couldn't get out. They couldn't stop crying sometimes. They couldn't remember anything. They had no energy, no sense of love or joy in their lives. They felt so alone! Something was terribly wrong, and they didn't know what it was. Then, overnight, the rest of Domingo's entire family moved in. It was insane—eight people in a two-bedroom house! Then Liz discovered she was pregnant again. The stress was unbearable. She was shaking apart at the seams."

Nobody ever asked her permission, or even bothered to explain why; one day Domingo's whole family—four people, in addition to herself, Domingo, the *abuelo*, and the baby—simply moved in. It was the spring of 1969, and overnight the little house was stuffed to the rafters with unpleasant people she barely knew, most of whom hardly spoke a word of English. There was Marguerite, Domingo's mother, who was forty-six but nevertheless pregnant by a merchant seaman. There were his nine-year-old twin sisters and his older brother Vincent, an incorrigible teenager who had been repeatedly thrown out of high school.

Marguerite immediately commandeered Liz and Domingo's double bed. She was pregnant, she said, and in her condition she deserved it. She even moved the TV from the living room into what was now her bedroom. Marguerite was clearly the undisputed matriarch of this big, disorderly Latin family, and everybody—including Domingo—did whatever she said. Liz and Domingo moved to the living room couch, and everybody else threw down pillows and blankets wherever there was room. The *abuelo*, who didn't like sleeping indoors in the summer, made a bed for himself on the screened-in porch and tried to keep out of things. He knew what it was doing to her. He made his own little place out there, with his gum-wrapper chains and flowers and little jars and bottles of things he had collected.

One day toward the end of November, Liz looked down at her stomach while cooking and realized she was pregnant. *Very* pregnant. By the looks of things, she was probably five or six months along. Five or six months! How had that happened? It seemed like only the day before her belly had been smooth and flat, and now, the next thing she knew, she was only a few months away from due. She had never lost that

251

much time before! The next day she went to see a doctor, and he concluded that she was not five or six months pregnant, but seven. She'd be due in January.

In a matter of weeks, Liz's pregnancy progressed to the point where she could no longer sleep through the night on the living room couch. She'd be up in the night pacing the floor, and when Marguerite got up in the morning, she'd slip into her old bed and try to get a couple of hours of sleep. But when Marguerite found out, she put her foot down. That was *her* bed now, and she wouldn't allow Liz in it. Domingo did nothing. So Liz threw pillows and blankets in the bathtub and began sleeping there.

Liz went into labor on schedule, one afternoon in January, while standing at the stove. Domingo drove her to the hospital, and she was taken to the labor room and was in labor for a couple of hours when a technician wheeled in a flouroscope and took a couple of X-rays of her abdomen, then disappeared. Moments later, he came back in and shut down all the equipment. Her doctor walked in with a look of amusement on his face.

"False alarm, sweetheart," he said. "You're not full term after all—you've got twins in there!"

"You've gotta be kidding!" she said, as a feeling of panic and exhaustion swept over her. "You've gotta be kidding! How much longer do I have to go?"

"It looks like you're only about five months along. They're big, healthy babies. Unfortunately, I think that means you're going to need some hospitalization. They're so big we thought you were already term."

If she was this big already, Liz thought, how big was she going to be before the babies came? Well, she concluded finally, at least she *hadn't* lost all that time. She might have twins, but at least everything else was "normal." Things weren't really as out of control as she feared.

The doctor gave her medication to stop the false labor and sent her home. But as the pregnancy progressed, she grew steadily sicker. She developed something the doctors called pre-eclamptic toxemia, with seizures, fainting, kidney problems, and high fevers. She would lay on the couch with a blanket wrapped around her and just shake. In early November, to her great relief, Domingo's family had found another place to live and moved out, and she got her bed back. But the pregnancy was not going well, and in April, she spent a week in the hospital. She got very ill again and spent another week in the hospital at the beginning of May, shortly before she was due. On the thirteenth of May, 1970, her doctor allowed her to go home for the weekend to see her family, as long as she promised to stay in bed and not get up except to go to the bathroom.

Domingo brought her home and made her comfortable in bed. Since she was feeling relatively well, he'd decided to take the baby and go night fishing with some friends—they were going to leave in the wee hours of the morning and be back home by dawn.

"If you need anything, the phone is right by the bed and the lady across the street said she'd help out," Domingo told her. "You feeling OK, babe? Sure you'll be all right?"

"Yeah, I'm OK," she said. "I feel fine. Don't worry about me."

Domingo had gone out to the car with another load of bait buckets and fishing poles when the phone rang. She rolled over to reach for it, and suddenly her water broke. Almost immediately, it seemed, she started having powerful contractions.

"Call the hospital right away!" she gasped when Domingo came back in the house for another load. "I'm in labor real hard!"

Domingo called the hospital and then grabbed a sheet, ripped a hole in the top of it and fitted it over her. He helped her struggle into the front seat of the station wagon and then he took off like a shot, headed for Parkland Memorial Hospital, thirty minutes away. This wasn't anything like the way her first baby came—this time she'd gone from zero to heavy labor in a matter of minutes. She was going to have these twins in the front seat if Domingo didn't hurry!

"You gotta stop! You gotta stop!" she gasped. "I gotta lay down in back!"

Domingo pulled off the expressway, ran around the back of the car and made a place for her among the bait buckets and fishing poles and greasy auto parts, and helped her climb in. Then he took off with a jolt. A bucket of bait slopped over her sheet. Something cold and greasy rolled against her face. It was happening so fast! These babies were desperate to be born, and it didn't matter where she happened to be. Domingo squealed into the hospital emergency entrance, two nurses helped her onto a gurney, and before she even got upstairs, she gave birth to the first child.

"It's a girl!" one of the nurses told her as she lay on the gurney waiting for the elevator upstairs. "It's over now, just relax. You did great!"

"No, wait, listen," Liz gasped, "I've got another one coming! I've got twins! Domingo, tell her!"

"No, you've had your baby," the nurse insisted. "That's the after-birth you feel. Just relax."

"Look, I've been coming in here for months! Ask Dr. Goldberger! I've got twins!"

"Yeah, that's right, she's got twins," Domingo said.

Suddenly the nurse understood. When they got off the elevator on the fourth floor, she wheeled Liz into a delivery room, and another nurse came in and slipped an IV into her arm. She started cutting the grease- and bait-covered sheet off her body with a pair of scissors. Liz felt the labor pains coming on again, squeezing her whole body like a vice, then letting up again.

"How can people live in such filth?" she heard the nurse muttering under her breath. "Grease, dead fish—God, what a stench! You're a pig! A filthy pig!"

At that moment, time stopped. The words were a slap in Liz's face, an assault, a humiliation. Wracked with pain and spread-eagled across the delivery table, she was utterly defenseless against them. So she just went away. It was Me-Liz who stepped in to take the next contraction. And the next. And the next. She was thrilled by it all—she had always wanted to have a baby of her own, and this way she could do it without ever having sex. Even when the baby refused to be born and the doctors had to use some kind of suction device to assist its descent down the birth canal, even then she could stand the pain. It was all worth it. To her, the birth of her only daughter was a miracle.

It was a virgin birth.

Hospital records show that the twins were born an hour apart, at 1:15 and 2:15 A.M. on Mother's Day, May 14, 1970, at Parkland Memorial Hospital in Dallas. They were identical, healthy girls and weighed seven pounds, fourteen ounces each. Liz and Domingo named the first one Rita Louise, and the second one Ramona May.

It was funny, but afterward Liz never could remember anything about that second birth. The doctor told her later that it had been a difficult delivery, because the baby was posterior, but all Liz cared about was that her little girls had been born healthy and it was all over. She was too exhausted to think of anything else. She was still suffering from the symptoms of toxemia, and she'd lost a lot of blood; she felt as if her body had been ripped open, and that it would never heal. She didn't think she could ever go through this again.

She stayed in the hospital eight days. Domingo took the twins home to her parents until she was discharged, but Liz didn't care—she was too exhausted to care. For her, it was a relief. They returned the twins to her as soon as she got home, and at first, she had plenty of help with them. Her sister Maryanne and neighbors came over to help, and someone brought over a tiny portable washing machine. The hospital provided them with a year's worth of diaper deliveries. But once the congratulations and newness wore off, the help disappeared and the drudgery set in. She had three infants in diapers now, and sterilizers for the baby bottles were going constantly. Dishes and laundry piled up. She was on her feet from dawn until long after dark, and up two or three times during the night. She felt continuously on the edge of exhaustion, longing only for sleep. She couldn't seem to get her spirits back, or her physical health. Sometimes she just couldn't stop crying.

She didn't know anything about all the fighting that was going on between Penny Lavender and Me-Liz. Both of them felt they had a claim on Ramona, whom everybody had started calling "Mona." It was Penny who'd had the job in the photo processing kiosk, and she was convinced the children's father was not Domingo at all but Dennis, the man in the bread truck. She even called Dennis up at work one day.

"I'd just like you to know that you're the father of twins," she told him.

To Me-Liz, Mona didn't really have a father—all she knew was that *she* was her mother. She loved being her mother, and she came out as often as possible to take care of her. After all, she was responsible. She understood in a confused sort of way that the other children were her responsibility too, but they weren't really hers. In reality, Me-Liz didn't know much at all about mothering. Her image of what a mother was supposed to be came mostly from television shows, like "Father Knows Best" and "The Donna Reed Show." She liked to fix her hair up like Donna Reed, and imagine herself on TV as she was changing Mona's diapers or making her bottle.

Liz remembered nothing of those occasions. In a vague way, though, she did understand that there was some kind of great turmoil going on inside her. Sometimes, lying in bed at the end of the day, all she could remember was turmoil, as if she were looking at one of those little glass globes that you shake to make snow descend on a miniature winter scene. All that pretty, sleepy white snow, fluttering down on the people and the houses and everything that had happened to her, until her whole life was buried and all she could see, or remember, was the snow.

There was only one relief from the drudgery, once a month. Doctors at Parkland Memorial had expressed great interest in the babies, because they were conducting some kind of a psychological study of twins. Penny had agreed to participate. Once a month, she'd load up the car with strollers, diaper bags, bottles, and all the paraphernalia she needed for the day, leave Angel with a sitter, and drive Rita and Ramona down to the hospital. She loved the chance to get prettied up and out of the house for a day. She was a good-looking single woman, after all, and getting out into the real world, if only for an afternoon, was like a holiday in the Bahamas.

She was curious about the twin study, and watched the psychologists in action a few times. Sometimes they'd study the children's behavior and facial expressions when they were together, and other times they'd separate them and film from behind a curtain while the youngsters played alone. But most of the time, Penny just sat in the hall for the two or three hours the testing took, relieved to be alone and silent for just a little while. It gave her a chance to collect her thoughts. And one day, when she was sitting out there, she decided she should take this chance to talk to one of the psychologists. Maybe they could help her. Maybe they could tell her what was the matter with her.

When she got home that night, she hesitantly asked Domingo's permission to do it.

"Look, Liz, I can't afford that!" he exploded. "I mean, I'm already working my fingers to the bone just to afford this house! How am I supposed to pay for a shrink? Besides, babe, I think you're just tired and overworked. I mean, you'll get over it. Really. You will."

He wasn't really angry—but her parents were, when Domingo told them about it.

"What do you mean 'you've got a problem,' you 'need to see somebody'?" her father asked her scornfully. "Domingo is working his butt off just to pay all your medical bills, and now you want to make him pay more so you can have a little chat with some guy with a goatee? You're just feeling sorry for yourself. You're just being selfish. You have no consideration at all for Domingo. Besides, no daughter of mine is going to a psychiatrist!"

But Penny went anyway, in secret, paying for her visits with grocery money. She was sent to a man named Dr. Silverberg, who listened quietly with his fingers laced together while she haltingly explained what she thought was the matter with her. Then he smiled benignly.

"Mrs. Garcia, I know it's awfully difficult getting through this period. Having three small children in diapers is about the equivalent of climbing Mount Everest without oxygen! I know: we've got five of our own. But I feel strongly that what you're going through is ordinary, postpartum depression. After-baby blues. It's amazingly common—I see young mothers like yourself all the time, believe me. The good news is that eventually it just goes away by itself."

"But doctor, it's more than that," she pleaded. "It's . . . it's like . . . I don't know, I just feel so sad. I feel so depressed all the time. Sometimes I can't even remember what I did that day."

"Those are classic symptoms, Mrs. Garcia, believe me. I've heard them a thousand times. You've got to remember that it will pass in time. You've been through hell, I realize. But look on the bright side: at least you have three healthy girls. A lot of couples can't have children at all, no matter how hard they try. They'd envy you. You're lucky."

He wasn't listening to her at all. He was just giving her feelings a name, as if that explained anything.

One day a month later, Liz woke up in the back of a car parked on the shore of a lake, making love to a Latin man she'd never seen before. She sat up abruptly. She pulled on her red miniskirt, black tights, and black patent leather half-boots. The man, who appeared to speak no English at all, hurriedly pulled on a white lab coat with a little badge that said "Ed Diaz, Radiological Department, Parkland Memorial Hospital." He looked at her in confusion for a moment, then climbed into the front seat, started up the car and drove back to the hospital.

In the hallway, he kissed her and went his way, and she went upstairs to get the twins.

Chapter 30

I'd like to talk about the car wreck, if you're willing," Dr. Walton announced at the beginning of their session on the afternoon of January 27, 1986. He seemed wary, on edge. "I know it's difficult. Do you think you're up to it?"

Liz loosed an enormous, weary sigh.

"Yeah . . . I guess so," she said.

"I'm frightfully sorry about it, Elizabeth. I hope you understand that. Losing your family that way, so suddenly, so violently—it would take a healthy person years to recover from something like that. A whole lifetime, perhaps. I think it's critical that we confront this experience, and learn to live with it."

He looked at her gravely.

"Do you think you're ready to talk about it?" he repeated.

"Well, I don't know what there is to say," said Liz, blandly.

"When the wreck occurred, how old were the children?"

"I think it was the twins' first birthday. Mother's Day. Angel was three."

"Did the marriage continue to disintegrate after the period we've been discussing?"

"Yeah. We had a fight. A big fight on Easter morning. I threw

Jell-O in Domingo's face and then he chased me out to the driveway and bashed my face in the cement. We split up not too long after that. Me and the kids lived in dumpy apartments. We finally got evicted and ended up living out of the car. I was feeding the kids crackers and ketchup. Things were a mess. Everything was coming to pieces. Then Domingo and Me-Liz moved back together for a few weeks, and that's when . . . you know, that's when it happened. The wreck and stuff."

"Maybe you could just tell me the story. I know it's difficult."

She sighed.

"It was the twins' birthday, as I said, Mother's Day. I don't remember the year. I was gonna have a party. Went to the store to get some stuff—a Pin-the-Tail-on-the-Donkey game, balloons, decorations. But I felt . . . ill . . . and everything looked funny. I felt weak and unsteady. The kids started blowing those little party favor things in my face . . ."

Her voice trailed off.

"And?"

"I thought I was going crazy. I hadn't been feeling well. I was dizzy. I thought I saw the floor rippling, lights flickering."

"You mean you were having visual hallucinations?"

"Yeah, I guess you could say that."

"Then?"

"Then I came home and I . . . I guess I . . . I got scared. I felt like I was splitting apart. The babies' crying went right down in my brain, like broken glass. They kept crying and crying and wouldn't stop. I covered my ears and they wouldn't stop. I couldn't stand it anymore. I was coming to pieces. I could hardly stand up. I went in the bathroom and sat down on the seat and I just rocked and rocked and rocked. I was holding my arms tight because I was . . . I was terrified I was going to hurt them."

"Hurt the babies?"

"Yeah."

"And then?"

Long pause.

"Then I was living in Minneapolis, in a nice house near a lake. I was living with a man named Eric. He worked for the power company, I think."

"Wait just a minute. You mean you don't remember anything between that moment, sitting in the bathroom in Dallas, and living in Minneapolis?"

259

"No. Look, I'm sorry, Ralph. I can't help it. That's all I can tell you."

"But you've been doing so well until now! You've been able to recover almost everything about your past, and the others' past! Your recall has been extraordinary. Now you can't remember a thing for a period of, what? Four to six months? A year?"

"I can't help it, Ralph. I'm sorry."

Her eyes were desperate, pleading.

"Then how do you know there was an accident?"

"What do you mean?"

"How do you know your husband and children were killed in a car wreck?"

She hesitated a moment.

"I . . . something about a phone call. I got a call from the . . . I remember they said Domingo and the kids had been . . ."

She sighed again.

"I've been feeling pretty lousy lately, Ralph. I've been having the cold sweats at night. I lost six pounds in the past couple of weeks. I've been coughing. Dr. Scott thinks I might have bronchitis, but probably I'm just smoking too much—I'm up to three packs a day now."

"Are you aware that whenever we try to deal with difficult material, you start talking about your medical problems?"

Liz didn't answer for a moment.

"I feel nervous. Exhausted all the time. But the funny thing is, I can't sleep. I'm too tired to sleep."

"Elizabeth, I want to talk about the loss of your husband and daughters. Do you think we could continue?"

For just a moment, a shudder of absolute panic rippled through her.

"How do you know they were killed in a car wreck if you don't remember it?" he asked again.

"I got a call, I think. Some drunk . . . they got hit by some drunk on the expressway."

"Who was it that called? The police?"

"I . . . I don't remember."

"Did you go down to the police station?"

"Uh . . . I don't know."

"Was there a wake?"

"I don't know."

"Do you remember the funeral?"

"No."

"Seems very odd, doesn't it? That you can't remember the funeral?"

"Yeah."

"Let's see now, Liz, when was this? I'm always so confused about dates when you start talking about your past. Could we pin it down in time? Do you have a death certificate, maybe?"

"No. Not that I know of." She sighed again. "What if it's not bronchitis? What if it's something really terrible? What if it's lung cancer or something?"

Suddenly a terrible cry ripped through her.

"I don't know! I don't know, Ralph! I can't remember! Sometimes I hear voices. I hear voices in the night and they say '*You killed them! You killed them!*' But Ralph, I just can't remember! I can't remember!"

She stared at him blankly, like an animal transfixed by onrushing headlights.

"They're not gonna send me to jail, are they?"

Then she covered her face with her hands and just shook.

All that winter, during the long months of therapy, Kitty Rosetti had been listening quietly to every word that was spoken in Dr. Walton's office. Even when she'd allowed Liz or Penny or Jess to occupy the body, she'd watched and listened nonetheless, crouched just behind the rim of consciousness. And Kitty had heard every word that was spoken in the office that snowy January afternoon. More and more, she was convinced that it was Liz who was holding them all back. She knew that Liz had a world-class talent for evading the truth. She knew all about Liz's remarkable ability to manufacture medical problems, as a smoke screen against facing the pain of her past. And she was convinced that this woman whom she so despised was incapable of helping herself any longer. In order to be healed, in order to become whole, everything had to be remembered. That's what Michael had said.

And the only way to get Liz to face the truth of what happened to Domingo and the children, Kitty decided, was to provide Dr. Walton with indisputable evidence, and get *him* to tell her. Liz would have to be backed into a corner, with no way out.

When Liz got home from therapy that day, Kitty promptly emerged. She began putting together every bit of documentary evidence she could find, rummaging around in boxes to locate marriage licenses, divorce papers, insurance papers, photographs, and letters. Then she stuffed it all in a big manila envelope and mailed it to Dr. Walton, with a cover letter:

261

Dear Dr. Walton,

I've kept this stuff put away for quite some time, but I feel that it may be appropriate that you see it now. The photos have been collected over time, so as not to confuse her. There are pictures of all of us . . .

We have much work to go through about this accident business. We must be careful not to let the others know before it's fully out. The reason it got out of hand was because it happened in bits and pieces and was taken so out of context. This was experienced by four people, not one, you see . . . Please don't show the documents to the others, but only to me until they get used to it—*to* knowing, I mean. I can help with as much as I can. I have memory, but I am not responsible for their decisions. We must work together on this. I will fill you in on what happened and when their family memories are missing I can help. I can tell you now that the babies and husband are not dead. But, it would be better for her if they were. She can never go back. Not if she really loves them, and soon she will realize that her ethics will be challenged beyond belief. Stand strong by her and so will I. Her goodness will shine through. She is innocent of murder.

KITTY ROSETTI

Ten days later, on February 10, Kitty got up early for her first session with Dr. Walton. She had, of course, been out dozens of times during the long months of therapy—but she had never fully *revealed* herself. When Kitty occupied the body during therapy, she'd kept her natural flamboyance on such a short leash that Dr. Walton never seemed to notice she was even there. Like all the others, Kitty was a master at self-concealment.

Now, however, the time had come for Kitty's coming out, and she was flushed with excitement. She put on a yellow turtleneck sweater, a muted gray and yellow thirties-style Pendleton jacket, and gray wool slacks. Jeff drove her to the appointment, and when she arrived she immediately asked the secretary for a full account of the amount of money due. She knew that Liz, as usual, had simply let the bills go unpaid. As usual, she had to clean up the mess that Liz had left.

When Dr. Walton opened the door to the waiting room for Liz Castle's afternoon session, she could see immediately that he was momentarily taken aback. Kitty was happy to see him—and very happy for him to see her.

DR. WALTON: *She shook hands with me very firmly, as if she were meeting me for the first time, and she held onto my hand for a few seconds longer than necessary. She said in a loud, confident voice, "Hi, I'm Kitty!" I was quite surprised, because Liz never shook hands. And this woman seemed noticeably taller, a physically bigger presence, than Liz. She was also dressed very colorfully (Liz always wore demure, subdued colors) and she had red hair. I assumed she had dyed it or washed it or she was wearing a wig. This, of course, was the first time I had ever met Kitty. She was outgoing, assertive, flirtatious, confident—in all, very definitely a different person than Liz.*

"So, didja get the stuff I sent?" Kitty asked as they walked in.

"Yes I did," he said, still eyeing her intently. "Quite a remarkable little package."

Liz always sat in the chair facing Dr. Walton, but Kitty plopped right down on the floor, with her back against the chair.

"You know why I sent it?"

"Tell me."

"I want you to tell the girl. That's your ammunition. Just show her that stuff and tell her what happened."

"Well, what *did* happen? You still haven't told me yet."

So Kitty told Dr. Walton the whole pathetic story, right straight down the line, as dispassionately as a police reporter.

"But please be careful," Kitty told him. "See, you've got to understand, Ralph, Liz is very fragile. She's like a little animal made of glass. If I told her the truth, she might have shattered. She might have tried to kill herself, and then we'd all be dead. So I fed her the car wreck story to protect her. To protect all of us. But I'll tell you the good news: she's panicking right now because for the first time, that car wreck story ain't ringing true. It seems phony to her, but she doesn't know why. That makes your job all the easier."

"Why do you think I'm the one for the job?"

"Because, you're a head cracker. You've got diplomas. She respects you. Plus, I just don't have much patience in dealing with that sort of person."

Dr. Walton promised to tell her, when she came in for their next appointment a week later.

Chapter 31

I n the months since Dr. Scott had first suggested the diagnosis of multiple personality disorder, Elizabeth Castle's medical problems had steadily diminished. For the first time in years, she seemed to be approaching physical health. There were times when she'd go for two months running without a treatable medical problem. But on February 12, two days after Kitty's meeting with Dr. Walton, Dr. Scott had his number one patient checked into Tompkins Community Hospital again. This time there was a new and more serious worry: pulmonary tuberculosis.

Liz was not clearly aware that Kitty was stirring the pot the way she was. She just knew that trouble was brewing, and she had to change the subject fast. In the days before Kitty's meeting with Dr. Walton, Liz had been listless, achy, and feverish, and her hacking cough seemed to have gotten worse. Then a chest X-ray had revealed fluid collecting in her left lung. Concerned about the possibility of tuberculosis, Dr. Scott gave her a PPD, the test for TB—an injection under the skin of her forearm. He told her to come back in forty-eight hours to check the reaction, but Jess called him the next day. The area around the shot was very sore, Jess reported, with a red, raised welt the size of a quarter.

264

Dr. Scott asked his patient to come into the office, and when he got a look at the PPD reaction, he seemed visibly startled. He ordered more lung X-rays and CT scans and sent Jess home. That night, Dr. Scott called his patient at home to check on the reaction.

"This is not a normal PPD reaction," Jess tried to tell him, but he was coughing and choking so hard he could hardly speak. Dr. Scott hung up the phone, got in the car, and drove immediately to the house, where he gave his patient a couple of shots to reduce the swollen airways and checked her into the hospital. It looked like Stevens-Johnson syndrome, he told her—a potentially dangerous respiratory reaction to the PPD test, one that strongly suggested she might really have TB. She was in the hospital for four days of tests, and then released on the sixteenth, after being scheduled for more outpatient tests.

On the morning of February 17, Liz was scheduled for a CAT scan of her abdomen at the hospital. That afternoon, she was to see Dr. Walton for therapy. But by the time she walked into Dr. Walton's office that day, a sense of doom was hanging over her like a suffocating cloud. The CAT scan had shown a mysterious mass down near her pancreas. The mass, the attending physician had written, "measures approximately 4 cm [centimeters] in diameter. Tissue density readings show that this is not simply a fluid-filled collection. Initially, I thought this may be a collection of bowel loops since the patient is so thin. I then had the patient walk to change the distribution of the oral contrast and then I repeated the slices [scans]. This abnormality persists unchanged. Therefore, I am quite suspicious that this does represent a mass in the region of the lesser sac. . . ."

At the bottom of the CAT scan report, the doctor had written, "Rule out lymphoma." Liz knew what that meant: Cancer.

"The doctor says we have to do more tests to make sure it's not a lymphoma," Liz told Dr. Walton that afternoon in a flat, mechanical voice. "They think it might be cancer."

Dr. Walton said nothing; he simply stared at her intently with his deep, grave eyes.

"Want me to send you an invitation to my surgery?" she said with a faint smile. "A little card with black around the edge?"

"Listen, Liz," he interrupted, "I wanted to talk again today about the accident. The car wreck. About your children. All right?"

She sighed and looked away.

"Now, I had a very interesting session here with Kitty last week. Do you remember that?"

It was Liz's turn to be silent.

"She told me some things about your past that may come as a surprise to you. She asked me to tell you."

Liz just stared. He pulled out the packet of papers Kitty had sent him and laid them gently on the edge of the desk.

"Kitty told me that the babies were not killed at all. Your children are still alive, apparently. So is your husband. There was no car wreck."

Silence.

"What happened was . . . Liz? Are you listening?"

"I'm sorry, Ralph, I just can't concentrate on this stuff. He repeated this CAT scan two or three times, and he still found this mass down there. Right down in my guts. Right down there. I'm sorry, but this thing really freaked me out, you know?"

"Do you not want to talk about this now?"

"Dr. Pechter, the guy who ran the scanner—he actually gave me the papers to take over to Walt. It's got 'rule out lymphoma,' right here on the bottom. What does he think I am, some dummy? Does he think I don't know what that means?"

Dr. Walton did not respond. She was not listening at all.

DR. WALTON: I made the decision fairly early on not to use hypnosis in this case. But that day I jotted in my notes, 'Should we use hypnosis?' It was clear she was not confronting this material at all, and this might be the best way to get her to face it. Up until this point, I had been leery of hypnosis. She presented with a history that sounded so much like a psychosis that I was unwilling to rule out that possibility entirely. And I'm a little fearful of using hypnosis on someone with such a history. My task is to help people maintain a hold on reality, to stay put together, but hypnosis can sometimes have just the opposite effect on someone with a psychotic illness. It can cause them to decompensate, to fall apart.

But now, after having met Kitty for the first time, I was quite convinced that I was dealing with multiple personality disorder here. I still had some reservations about it, though. Because I did not feel then, nor do I feel today, that this diagnosis adequately expresses everything I was dealing with here. She was not like other multiples I had treated; I could not confidently fit her into a psychiatric category, so I gave up trying to label her.

266

*   *   *

Later that afternoon, Liz took the CAT scan report over to Dr. Scott's office and handed it to him in person. He was leaning up against a file cabinet, but she could see the momentary look of shock that passed across his face when he read it.

"You need to go back in the hospital right away, partner," he told her. "I'm checking you into the hospital tonight."

So he did. Liz was scared of the tumor, but she was glad to be home again—back home in the hospital.

Dr. Walton came to see her in the hospital the next day. He was seated beside the bed when a nurse came bustling in and started piling her clothes and toiletries into a big plastic bag. Liz assumed they were getting ready to release her. But moments later, another nurse came in, wearing gloves and a mask.

"What's going on?" Dr. Walton asked.

"The doctor just got the X-ray results," the nurse told him hurriedly. "He'll be here shortly."

Dr. Walton, suspicious, went out in the hall and phoned Dr. Scott. Moments later he returned to the room.

"Apparently Dr. Scott got the lung films back. He says it looks like you may have tuberculosis after all, and they may have to put you in isolation, at least until they confirm it. I'm sorry, Elizabeth. I really am."

Then he turned on one heel and walked out.

Liz was moved to a different part of the hospital, into a room of her own, like a princess, like some exotic, fast-fading flower. Her attendants had to wear gloves and masks, and visitors were restricted. Nurses and doctors hustled in and out. Tests and more tests. She was in her element. As always, her husband Jeff was concerned and supportive during this latest medical crisis—it was his insurance that was paying for it all—but Liz felt increasingly distant from him. Her home was in the hospital now, surrounded by these masked valets—not with Jeff, in that stifling little cottage by the lake.

One day not long after Liz was moved into isolation, Me-Liz came out. She was alone, sitting cross-legged on the hospital bed, when Michael appeared. He clambered onto the bed, crossed his legs, and reached out and took both her hands.

"I'm going to show you something wonderful," he told her calmly, with his unfathomable smile. "I'm going to give you proof. I want you to relax and close your eyes, because everything that's to be seen can be seen by looking within. Now. Just breathe deep and relax. Feel the warmth spreading out through your body . . . outward and outward . . . calm, calm . . . now you're going to feel the energy growing from within as a vibration . . . feel that? That little humming vibration?"

"Yeah," she murmured. "Yeah." She shivered slightly. It felt like she was on a merry-go-round, just beginning to turn. For a moment she felt a dizzy nausea as the spin picked up speed, but that passed and she felt herself spinning faster and faster, and then she heard a faint murmuring hum or buzz, rising in pitch, higher and higher, until she lost any consciousness of how fast she was spinning at all. She heard Michael's voice, speaking to the very core of her being:

"Whatever is not necessary to the proper functioning of this body, be removed . . ."

For a moment, Liz had a sensation of being nowhere at all. Not just sitting quietly in darkness, but of being nowhere. No vibration. No feeling of energy. No sound. Nothing. Then, faintly, she felt the vibration returning to the edges of consciousness, slower and slower, and heard the sound of a faraway hum descending in pitch, until she woke up in bed. She opened her eyes. She was still seated cross-legged on the bed, holding hands with Michael. Her whole body felt cleansed. Purged. Filled with a sense of physical peace. Michael winked at her.

And then he was gone.

Two days later, on February 20, an ultrasound scan of the abdomen was performed at Tompkins Community Hospital. Dr. Pechter, the same doctor who had done the original CAT scan, did the ultrasound. But this time, he couldn't find the mass. It was gone.

"Anterior to the spleen," he wrote, "no definite definable mass is seen. Because of this finding, I took the patient back to the CT scanner and did 10 cuts [scans] to the upper abdomen correlating to the previously described abnormality. The patient was given oral contrast to flood the gut. No definite mass is appreciated. It must be stated that I really flooded the gut and distended the stomach and proximal small bowel. . . ."

DR. SCOTT: This just shows you what medicine is like: If you do enough tests, you're bound to find something. First he finds a mass, then he can't find it. The guy even repeated the CT scan and he still couldn't find it. This "mass" was probably just a fluid-filled loop of bowel; CT scans can't distinguish between a bowel loop and a mass. Still, at the time of the first scan, she also had a really high white blood count— twenty-five, whereas normal is less than ten. A high white count like that suggests an infection, an abnormality. Well, it was just one of those funny things.

Chapter 32

Liz sat at the kitchen table in the cottage by the lake, staring out into the dreary February snow drifting over the upended rowboats along the shore. She couldn't stop crying bright orange tears. One tear fell on the unfinished letter that lay on the table in front of her, leaving the print of a tiny explosion, orange as iodine. The drugs she was taking for the TB had turned all her body fluids that sickly, medicinal color—as if her whole body were saturated by something utterly foreign to life, something inhuman.

"I woke up crying," she had written in the letter, which was addressed to Dr. Walton. "It's never happened before. I felt like I had been crying for a long time. I found orange spots from my tears on my pillow case and my face was all swollen-feeling, puffy and stuffed up. I took a shower and cried the entire time, dried off, and tried to stop crying. I couldn't. The more I tried not to cry the more I cried. . . ."

Because now Liz knew the truth. There was no way around it anymore. She really hadn't heard when Dr. Walton told her that the children were alive. But not long afterward, Kitty had come to her and she told Liz the whole sad story. It was Kitty who finally pushed open the door, so that light streamed through and Liz could finally remember it all. Kitty took her back to that day, Mother's Day, the twins' first birthday, when she was so scared she was going to do something terrible to the children. She'd tried to put the kids to bed, but they wouldn't go to sleep that day. Mona stood up in her crib and cried and cried, and then Angel started crying, too. The noise of their crying went right down inside her brain, like broken glass. Something bad, something awful was about to happen. Something was ripping apart. She grabbed her head with both hands and fell down on her knees beside the bed, and the children kept crying and crying and crying. Outside the window, she could hear mariachi music, and two women arguing in Spanish.

She got back on her feet. She got the kids out of their beds and led them into the bathroom. There was a bottle of shampoo on the edge of the tub, so she put it in the medicine cabinet. There was a bottle of aspirin on the sink, so she put it away.

"Now I want you all to sit down on the rug and be very, very quiet," she told them. Her voice was shaking. It sounded like someone else's voice. "Mommy has to lock the door for a minute, but it's only a game and I'll be back to get you very soon. I want you to be very, very quiet and don't be afraid."

She closed the bathroom door and locked it.

Then she called Domingo at work.

"You have to come home, *now*," she pleaded. "Now!"

"Hey, calm down, babe! What's the matter? Are you OK? Are the kids OK?"

"Look," she sobbed, "I can't explain, but you've got to come home right away!"

Something was ripping apart. Something bad, something awful, was about to happen.

"But Liz, hey, I'm at work, babe! I can't just leave here! We're short-handed today. What's the matter, anyway?"

"Now! You've got to come home now!"

She slammed down the phone and walked into the kitchen. She took the pile of party things on the table and began putting them back in the bag. Suddenly she heard a high-pitched scream from the bathroom, and she ran to the door.

"Mona climbed on the sink and she fell off!" baby Angel wailed. All three of them had begun to cry and scream in there. It sounded as if Mona might really be hurt. Liz struggled to unlock the door, but something was the matter with it; it wouldn't budge.

"Open the door!" she yelled. "Push the little button on the door, Angel! Unlock the door!"

271

"I can't do it, mama! I can't do it!"

She ran into a hall closet and fished a little hatchet out of her husband's toolbox, to bash the door open, to save Ramona. Inside the bathroom, all three of them were screaming and crying at the top of their lungs.

"Angel, listen to me!" she yelled through the door. "Put the twins in the bathtub and climb in with them, do you understand? Get in the tub and close the shower curtain! Do you understand?"

She couldn't tell what was going on in there. The screams were going all the way down inside her brain. She raised the hatchet and it went *thunk* in the door. The sound of it terrified the children, and they screamed even louder. *Thunk, thunk, thunk!* The door began to split around the lock. Wood chips flew up into her face. Suddenly, the hatchet glanced off sideways and opened a gash in her hand. Blood spilled down the white door. Blood spilled on her blouse.

Blood! So much blood!

At the sight of it, Liz shrank away. Abruptly, Me-Liz came out. She was horrified and confused. What was she doing with this axe? What was all this blood? Why were the children in the bathroom, screaming?

"Angel, Angel, what are you doing in there? Why can't you get out?"

"We're stuck, Mama! The door's locked! Mona hurt her head!"

Me-Liz struggled to open the door, but she couldn't do it. She began to weep in frustration and terror, beating on the door with her hands, leaving little splats of blood with every blow.

It was at that moment that Domingo came home from work.

He burst in the front door and came bounding up the stairs, and when he saw her standing there crying in her blood-spattered dress, holding the hatchet, with the children shrieking and crying in the bathroom, he stopped dead still. His eyes widened. He grabbed the hatchet out of her hand. Me-Liz shrank away in terror at the look on Domingo's face, and then Penny appeared, sleepy and confused. What was going on? Why was he looking at her like that?

"You monster! You monster!" he shouted at her. "Get the hell away from here!"

Penny stumbled into the darkened bedroom. She sat down on the edge of the bed and held herself around the waist, and she began to rock. Then Liz came back. She was incapable of comprehending what was going on. She was numb. She couldn't seem to think at all. She just stared down at the blood on her clothes and rocked and rocked and rocked. She heard Domingo forcing open the bathroom door, heard him gently calming the children, heard him shepherding them into their bedrooms. Finally he came into the bedroom where she sat, shut the windows and drew the blinds. He stood in front of her in the dark room, and when he spoke, his voice was icily calm.

"Elizabeth, I cannot deal with this any more," he said. "This is it. This is the end. If you do not leave this house immediately, I'm going to call the police and have you arrested for trying to murder the children. Now take your purse, take your car keys, and get out. *Get out!*"

Murder the children! Murder the children!

Bright orange tears streamed down Liz's face, remembering those words. Those words had been burned so deeply into her brain that for almost fifteen years she had never been absolutely certain that she *hadn't* left three tiny bodies on the bathroom floor.

"You put the kids in the bathroom to *protect* them, Liz!" Kitty insisted. "You were afraid you might hurt them, so you did the only thing you knew to protect them! You put the shampoo and the aspirin away so they wouldn't poison themselves! You didn't fail as a mother— you did the very best you could!"

But Liz was disconsolate. She *had* failed. Even if she hadn't tried to kill the babies, she had abandoned them. Abandoned her very own babies, on their first birthday! On Mother's Day! That meant she was as bad as Mommy and Daddy. She was as bad as those people whose hearts were a black, evil void. She was evil. She was a wreck, a ruin, a failure. She belonged in an institution, or in jail, or in hell. Shame on her. Shame, shame on her for treating her children like that.

"The children have been cared for and loved and they lack nothing," Kitty told her. "I took care of the divorce with Domingo a few years ago, just before Penny married Sandy Lentz. Domingo was glad to hear from me, because he wanted to remarry and his new wife wanted to adopt the kids. The children are looked after, Liz. They have a new mother now. They're safe."

But Liz could not seem to stop crying. She tore her hair, she wailed, she grieved. She had failed, she had failed, she had failed. For a few days after she first found out, she became so violent that she scared Little Andrea and Little Elizabeth. Then she got quiet. For Liz, quiet was deadly. Once the truth soaked through to her bloodstream, it flowed through her veins as silently as poison.

Now, alone and sick, she sat at the kitchen table in the cottage by the lake and she envisioned herself walking naked out onto the snowy lake and laying down on the ice to die. She had abandoned her babies. She'd never even said goodbye. It was then that she remembered the pills. The house was a regular roadside pharmacy by now, and all she'd have to do was line them up and swallow. No problem. No cries for help, no multiple personality problem, no medical tests, no lies, no shame. Just the sweet bliss of sleep.

A sense of certainty and gentleness came over her when she got up from the table and walked into the bathroom, where all the pills were. She took down the little plastic prescription bottles one by one, took them back to the kitchen, lined them up on the counter. Such relief. She opened one jar and felt a momentary sadness because they weren't capsules. Capsules were easier to swallow. She put on the teapot to make some hot chocolate to use to take the pills. Jeff would find the body when he got home from work. Such quiet . . .

Suddenly, Kitty exploded into the body.

"Hey, snap out of it!" she yelled. "Think about what you're doing! You have no right to kill us all!"

Alarmed and indignant, Kitty took charge. She recognized that Liz's suicidal fantasy had crossed some indefinable threshold; the woman was serious. She was a danger to herself, and therefore a grave danger to all of them. If she killed the physical body, they all died. And if she lived, but refused to accept responsibility for what had happened to the children, none of them could become whole. Everything had to be remembered, and accepted, before they could become one. That's what Michael had said.

Kitty grabbed the pills, walked into the bathroom, emptied them all into the toilet, and flushed. Then Kitty, the crisis counselor, and Jess, the medical doctor, sat down at the kitchen table and began doing a psychiatric evaluation of the patient. Liz hung her head, filled with shame. She couldn't even succeed at killing herself!

"Where are you?" Kitty demanded.

"I'm at home," said Liz in a low, dreary voice.

"Where is your home?"

"Aurora, New York."

"What day is this?"

"Tuesday."

"What's the year?"

"Nineteen . . . nineteen . . ."

"Who is the president of the United States?"

"Richard Reagan."

"We feel that you are not capable of making decisions that are healthy for you right now," Jess told her in a calm, kind voice. "We can help you take some of this off your shoulders. We know of a place you can go where it's safe and quiet, and you'll be well taken care of."

"What if I don't wanna go?" Liz shot back, suddenly bristling with suspicion.

"We'll call Dr. Walton right away and get you checked into Tompkins," said Kitty.

Liz was silent, considering.

"The other option is to explore these things in safety and privacy," Jess said. "You don't need to go to the hospital. There's a better place we could send you."

They both smiled at her. Of all the others, Liz had always been the most resistant to counseling, the most stubbornly self-deluded. She lived in a hysteria of fear and denial. To face the truth about the children—to *accept* the truth—she needed to be force-fed it one drop at a time, as if the truth were some terrible, wonderful drug dripping into her veins through an IV needle. She needed prolonged hospitalization, with round-the-clock nursing care, in a locked ward of the mind. She needed to be sent somewhere deeper than "going deep," down to some intensive care ward of the unconscious, where she couldn't hurt herself or anyone else. It was a dramatic, drastic measure, but it was the only way Kitty and Jess felt they could make Liz accept the truth. There was also something else, of a more spiritual nature, that Me-Liz understood about all this: This woman would have been eternally incomplete if she did not accept this knowledge before she died. Since all spirits are eternal, the best gift they could have given her, for eternity, was the knowledge that her children lived.

"Would it make you feel any better if I brought Michael?" Kitty asked Liz gently. "Could Michael come for a visit?"

"Yeah . . . yeah, that'd be OK," said Liz. And then Michael was there, standing beside her, in his dark hat and dark coat.

"Do you want to go now?" Kitty asked.

"Yes," Liz responded firmly. She lifted her chin and shook her head, so that her mousy bangs fell away from her eyes. Michael motioned for her to sit down on the kitchen floor, and then he and Jess and Kitty seated themselves around her.

"Close your eyes, my child," Michael said. "The world is within. First we'll just go for a little practice spin, OK?"

"Yes, Michael. Yes."

And then she could feel them going into the spin. She could hear Jess and Kitty calming and soothing her. "Relax, little girl, relax!" Jess was saying. "It's just a game!" She heard the hum again—low and steady, like a high-tension line—all around her. Something amazing was happening to her, to them, as she spun. She heard voices, many voices, all singing and chattering confusedly. Yet for just a moment she felt . . . free . . . and whole . . . and at peace . . . for the very first time in her life. She had never felt this way before! She had no idea it was possible to feel this way! It was as if she were spinning free of her battered old broken-down body, spinning into the very air. She heard voices—so many voices!

"Have you come this far to die?" Jess inquired kindly.

"Do you deny us our right to live—we who have worked so hard to survive?" asked Me-Liz, with a trace of anger in her voice.

"I have a right to be!" Kitty insisted.

"What about me?" asked a tiny, childish voice.

"Me, too!"

"You can't kill me, bitch; I won't allow it!" Kitty railed.

"I am! I am!" shouted someone else.

"It's time!"

And from inside came a feeling, so many feelings, all at the same time. "How could this be?" she wondered. "*I* scream, *I* cry, *I* curse, *I* rage . . . *I* laugh, *I* love, *I* feel joy, *I* feel whole, *I feel one!*" It only lasted a moment, but she felt it. It was there and then it went away, but she felt it. To be whole! To be one!

When the spin peaked, for a moment she passed into a kind of nothingness, and then she began descending as the spin slowed, the hum dropped in pitch, and then finally it disappeared. She opened her eyes. Her face and ears felt hot. Michael was seated in front of her on the kitchen floor. It was late afternoon, and twilight was descending through the snow-lit air. Out the kitchen window, she could see a billowing curtain of snow filtering through the trees. Suddenly her heart felt heavy and sad, after that fleeting ecstasy of weightlessness. The shame and sickness came rushing back into her heart, like the ocean reclaiming a hole dug in the sand.

"I want to do it again," she told Michael, without a trace of hesitation in her voice. "I want to spin out of here, and I want to do it now." Because when she was in that spin, not only was she safe and at peace for the first time in her life, but she also felt very clearly that she was not there at all. She had escaped her own body. She was gone. She had vanished into some strange wholeness that was not her at all. It was the ultimate suicide.

Michael looked down at her gravely.

"Are you quite sure, my child? Is this really what you wish to do?"

"Yes," she said firmly.

"Do you know of any reason why you should not?"

"To the best of my knowledge, no, Michael. I want to go now. I am too grievous an error to stay."

"So then. We will go a little further this time—not all the way into the farandola, but further and deeper than you've ever gone before. It's only a kind of sleep, my child. Don't be frightened."

He took her two hands in his, and together they went into the spin. Orange tears, happy tears, streamed down her face. She could hear Kitty whispering "Goodbye, goodbye—we will meet again!" She could even hear Little Elizabeth and Little Andrea, faintly, laughing with joy. On the tape player, she could hear Penny's favorite music, George Winston's *December*—a loping, melancholy piano line, full of wistfulness and longing. Michael pulled her into his arms as the spin accelerated. She had the sensation this time that they were spinning not just level with the ground, like a merry-go-round, but on the horizontal, diagonal, and vertical—multidimensionally, like an electron. A sensation of great heat and light swarmed up around her, taking on a kind of mass, a luminous mass, as it picked up speed. She felt so calm, so at peace! As they spun, Kitty could see them turning into a pearly, luminous galaxy of lights that brightened to an intense glow, steadied there a moment, and then began to decelerate, the light and heat and mass fading down all together until it hung like a wisp of smoke in the air and disappeared.

Only Michael was standing there when it stopped.

Liz was gone.

JEFF CASTLE: I came home from work one night in February and she had the window open about four inches. It was freezing out, down in the teens, and snowing. I said, "What in the world is going on here? Why is the window open?" She said, "I had to turn the heat back and open the window because it's so hot in here!" I noticed then that it actually was comfortable in there. And I got into bed with her that night with the window still open, all that cold air coming right in the house, and the room stayed comfortable all night. Her body was very hot—it was like a radiant heat, like when someone has a sunburn and you touch their skin.

Now, this whole thing was very bizarre to me. The furnace was coming on during the night—it had to be, to keep the pipes under the house from freezing—but it was not turned up. Yet it was warm in there. Sometime, I think it was the next morning, she explained to me about this "spin" she had gone into the night before, and the metamorphosis that she was undergoing and so forth. She told me that she had gone into one of these spinning things that she described to me in detail one other time, that allowed her to begin the fusion of the personalities, and that this technique was causing internal heat that was escaping, and it took many hours afterward for all the heat to escape. Apparently she'd just finished doing this, right before I came home. Her explanation was very unsatisfactory to me, as a scientific-type person. Still, I'd just experienced something that was hard for me to explain. Bizarre. Pretty bizarre.

Chapter 33

For the first time in more than thirty years, Little Elizabeth and Little Andrea crept out into the thin spring sunshine. They were pale, sickly looking children, back-alley children, with sores on their legs and black filth in the creases of their skin. In the ragged grass around the cottage, they found tiny green things unwrinkling into the light. They made collections of sticks and acorn caps. They played in the dirt. They petted the cats, Skinner and Freud. They watched green frogs jumping into the road. Little Andrea ate a worm.

Kitty and Penny and Me-Liz and Jess, the adults, watched over them tenderly. Just to see these children rediscovering their childhoods, three decades postponed, made them feel rejuvenated. They basked in the returning sun. For the first time in their lives, all of them had begun to feel like a family. They could see and hear each other now. They laughed and talked and played. They spent lots of time at Penny's pond, and taking long walks in the woods. Jess built bunk beds in Penny's log house, so the children could sleep there. Little Andrea abandoned her gray cave, and the old paper bag she'd been sleeping on for all those years.

There was a new sense of stability and peace about their comings and goings now. When any of them wanted to go into the outside world—that bizarre and perplexing parallel dimension—their crossing-over was no longer a panicky explosion into consciousness. It was more like walking into the next room.

The physical body they all occupied was now healthier than it had been in years. In the weeks and months since Liz was spun out, nearly all of her medical problems seemed to have vanished as well. It was as if Liz's sad, battered body had vaporized along with her. Except for weekly visits to the chest clinic, and occasional blood tests to make sure the TB drugs weren't causing liver damage, their visits to Walt Scott's office were mainly social.

For her part, Liz was in a place where she could neither hear nor see the outside world. She was a cocoon, a mummy. She was like the prize of the hunting spider, blinded and paralyzed by the sting, trussed up, tucked away. She was free of pain and free of time. Sometimes Jess and Kitty would go to check on her, and they could see her lying there—not a body at all, but an oblong mass of gray, muddy color—in a paralysis of contemplation, somewhere deep in the underground of consciousness. But she was not unconscious. She was conscious of herself, and of the knowledge that her children were alive. Drip by drip, that single piece of knowledge slipped into her veins, accumulating in her tissues until she could no longer deny it.

The others had much less trouble accepting the fact that the three girls were alive. In fact, there was a good deal of discussion among them about whether or not they should go back to Texas and try to find the children. In the end, though, they all decided against it. By then, the twins would have been sixteen years old, and Angel eighteen—almost a grown woman. They'd have been raised all those years by an adoptive mother whom the others had never met. To reappear in their lives—a multiple personality patient still in therapy—would have caused so much grief and confusion it would have been hell for everybody.

With Liz spun out, and the others at play in their safe interior worlds, it was Kitty who was out most of the time that spring of 1986. Her home life with Jeff Castle—a man she did not love and to whom she was not married—grew increasingly strained. Liz had been a wonderful cook, but Kitty was more inclined to warm up a TV dinner. Kitty wasn't much on housework either. She refused to clean bathrooms or vacuum, or put her hands in dishwashing liquid. Her hands did not belong in a sink, she told Jeff.

One night she and Jeff had a long talk that lasted well into the night. Kitty told him about the "new situation" in the house: his wife, Liz Castle, was gone. She wasn't there anymore. Now she, Kitty, was in charge, and things would be different. For one thing, she was not about to go to bed with him, because that would be dishonorable. They hadn't actually had sex in years, but now she refused to even sleep with him. She wasn't his wife, after all—she wasn't *anybody's* wife. Jeff listened calmly and carefully to it all, and then offered to convert the laundry room into another bedroom so Kitty could sleep there. But Kitty took that as a towering insult. She couldn't believe he felt she would be comfortable sleeping in a laundry room—her, Kitty Rosetti! A $1000-a-night opening star! She told him she was going to move out, as soon as she could find a place. Jeff didn't protest.

JEFF CASTLE: The weekend before her birthday [May 10], I told her I'd taken the weekend off to help her celebrate. But she just panicked. She freaked out. She told me then that my wife wasn't there anymore. She said Liz had tried to commit suicide and she—Kitty—wasn't going to allow that to happen, and eventually she got rid of Liz. She had spun her out of existence, and she'd never come back. She tried to make it very clear that Liz was gone and would not return. She was very emphatic about it. She had gone into the spin and all that and she had spun right out of the picture. My immediate reaction was, "Whatever I can do to help you, I will. I don't have a lot of money but I'll help you in any way I can." Well, we didn't spend that weekend together. In fact, she tried to set me up with one of her girlfriends.

Kitty told me that she was very much in love with me, but she couldn't go to bed with me because it was like going to bed with her sister's husband. I don't believe a word of it, though. Kitty did not like me, never did. Maybe it was an excuse or maybe it was a lie she made up later. Maybe later she thought it would be good to think that she did love me, it would be easier for her to deal with the fact that she treated me so terribly. I mean, at the end she treated me very nastily—she thought she was being nice to me because she wasn't being mean to me, but it was all a put-on. She was cruel. She was not telling me what was going on in therapy. We were hardly seeing each other. Big changes were taking place in her personality. She wasn't even coming to bed with me. That house was not a pleasant place to be.

My way of dealing with all of this was to treat her like a single person, not many different people, and I was the only *one treating her that way. I didn't want to get caught up in the hysteria of the situation.*

Everyone else—Walt Scott, Walton, all her friends, like Edie Zenns and Isabel—all they heard was the spectacular, the bizarre. But I am the one who had to come home to her every night after work. I was the one who had to carry on everyday life with her. That is what I gave to her. Here was one place where she didn't have to put on a show—if she wanted to become Kitty she could, and I didn't question it. And Kitty and I had some terrible arguments. I did not like Kitty. But I never even tried to say, "Well, that's Kitty." When I was arguing with her, I was arguing with Liz. One person. My wife. And I would recommend the same approach to anybody else who has to live with a multiple.

It was important that all of them know they had a home here. They could be safe here. I wanted to give her the security. I wanted her to know that whoever came out of this therapy, whoever that person was, it didn't make any difference to me—that I was going to love that person, and we'd see what happened after that. See, early in the therapy, Liz knew that something was going to happen so that she was no longer going to be here—she knew that. But what she thought was that one of the personalities would take off and just leave town—and then five years down the line she'd just pop out again and not know where she was. She'd say to me, "What would you do if five years from now I call you from Poughkeepsie, and have no idea how I got there?" She was scared this was going to happen, and she was also scared about what my reaction would be if all of a sudden she would reappear. We discussed this many times. It was my idea that after the fusion we were going to start a whole new life together as completely different people, in a sense. What actually happened, of course, was quite different.

Throughout April and May, as a fine green spring swept over the forested hills above Cayuga Lake, it was Kitty who was going to the weekly sessions with Dr. Walton. Both of them felt they were making great progress. Kitty felt comfortable telling him about what had happened to Liz, about the farandola, about Michael. Dr. Walton did not rush to judgment, like all the other doctors and psychiatrists she'd seen in her life, except for Walt Scott. Nor did he automatically accept everything she said. He simply listened. Kitty understood that her work with Ralph Walton was crucial to the task of becoming whole. But she also understood that Michael's love and guidance were equally important. She spent an hour a week in therapy with Ralph Walton, and the rest of the time, so to speak, in therapy with Michael. It was as if these two men who looked so alike, one material and one immaterial, had taken her by each arm and were leading her like a bride to the altar.

282

Among the others, there were many great and heated discussions about this matter of integration—the goal of therapy. It was a terrifying prospect, in many ways. What did that really mean, anyway—"integration"? Did it mean that they'd all be melted together, like old crayons, and poured into a new mold? Would they become some kind of weird group mind, like in science fiction stories? Or would they die? Would they all be killed, and only one survive? If so . . . who?

Of all the others, Jess was the most resistant to the idea of integration. He was terribly worried that, in fact, it would mean death for the women and children in his charge. Dr. Walton had told him this was not a typical case of multiple personality disorder and therefore it was impossible to predict the outcome of integration. Should he involve these helpless creatures in this potentially tragic adventure? If he did so, wouldn't that be a violation of his medical ethics, as a doctor (or at least, someone who aspired to be a doctor)? What could be worse than agreeing to something that would result in the death of a patient?

Me-Liz was the biggest advocate of integration. She cherished a humble faith in life after death, and to her, what Dr. Walton was preparing them for was death and resurrection. She would die, and live again. Think of it! To rise out of her white grave clothes, torn apart, transformed, made new! It was an unspeakable gift from the Creator, and one so awesome, so terrifying, so holy, that she hardly dared to breathe its name.

Penny and Kitty were confused about integration. Intellectually, they were all in favor of it; but on some baser level, they resisted. Penny put her trust in Michael, who had told them all it was their destiny. And she felt responsible for passing on this message to the children, who did not share Me-Liz's faith. They were scared that they'd be put in a box and buried. Penny even made up a little song about integration, to calm them in the face of what they could not possibly understand. Some nights she would borrow the key to the Lutheran church and let herself in alone to play the piano and sing the youngsters that sweet lullaby:

I'll be loving you, my little ones,
I'll take your hand and up we'll run
and Michael's there, he waits for us
and sings our song
and smiles for us!
So children come, let's look up now

283

we'll touch his hand and see our friend
and he'll be lo-ving us!

One afternoon in May, during their weekly session, Dr. Walton and Kitty returned to the awkward question of Kitty's responsibility for the car wreck story—the Big Lie. They'd been seeing each other every week for almost nine months now, and their relationship had grown into an honest and durable friendship.

"What I've never understood is why you persisted so long in this lie," Dr. Walton told her. "If you knew everything, and you really cared for the others as much as you say you do, why didn't you let them know the truth?"

"I was just doing what was best for them," Kitty told him. "They couldn't handle it."

"Do you think you've always done what's best for them?"

"Most of the time, yeah. Sure."

"So you think you knew better than they did what was best for them?"

"Hey, Professor, lighten up! I'm not responsible for their problems, or their decisions!"

"But what I'm getting at, Kitty, is that you must accept responsibility for your actions. I don't think you've done that. You've got a blind spot when it comes to yourself; you always pass off your problems on the others. Don't you think you had anything to do with their pain and sadness over the years?"

For the first time in a long while, Kitty was silent.

"I do feel bad sometimes, Ralph," she admitted finally. "Sometimes I do feel terribly responsible for all the bad things that happened. God, what a mess we made of our lives!" For a moment her upper lip trembled, as if Kitty Rosetti might actually break down and cry.

"When I think of Liz stumbling around in that gray fog of hers, so scared and confused all the time, so sick and depressed, and deep inside not being sure she *didn't* murder her own kids . . ."

Kitty paused, struggling to regain her composure.

"But I was just trying to protect them, Ralph! I'm not perfect! I was doing the best I could!"

"Well, it's certainly not your fault that the others exist," Dr. Walton said gently. "You didn't create them. You're a victim."

"I have been victimized but I am not a victim!" Kitty shot back, suddenly flushed with anger, rising out of her chair. "It is my conscious decision whether I want to continue to be a victim or not, and

I don't! I refuse to be victimized for the rest of my life! I won't let myself be jerked around like Liz was! I *won't!*"

Dr. Walton, momentarily stung by this outburst, eased back in his chair.

"I think you're absolutely right, Kitty," he said. "You're not a victim unless you choose to be. It's a deliberate choice, just like taking responsibility for your actions is."

"Look, Professor, I get what you're driving at. You want me to admit I really messed up their lives by telling them some big story. But if it wasn't for me, we'd all be dead by now! I wouldn't even be here!"

"I don't think lying is ever a solution to anything."

"It wasn't a lie! It was a . . . it was . . . I was desperate, can't you understand? And then after you create the situation, there's no way out of it, so you just go on, and you figure ways to block it out and not deal with it, and day after day it gets bigger and bigger, until finally I knew that if I let Liz find out she would kill herself, and kill us all! What kind of a solution is that?"

"Not much of one, sure. But yours wasn't much better, Kitty; it was bound to fall apart eventually. All lies do. We're here to figure out a solution that's going to last for the rest of your life."

Kitty stared at him, tears welling up in her eyes.

"Don't you understand how hard it's been for me, Ralph? Don't you understand how many times I felt like killing myself too? How confused I was, how scared? Don't you understand how lonely it's gotten in here? God! Dear God, *won't anybody ever love me?*"

Suddenly Ralph Walton came up out of his chair and in one motion wrapped his arms around her in a hug that seemed to encompass everything about her. For a moment Kitty was utterly astounded. She didn't even know what this was—to be accepted like this, to be . . . loved. She felt his fingertips gently brush the nape of her neck, where her hair hid a three-inch vertical surgical scar—that hateful mark, that imperfection, that failure. Nobody, not a single human soul, had touched that spot since the surgery almost two years before. He seemed to touch her there knowingly, as if he were forgiving her for having that mark. He forgave her imperfection, when she could not forgive herself. For a moment, Kitty was so overwhelmed by emotion she vanished, and the others rippled in and out—Jess, Me-Liz, Penny Lavender, even the babies—so that each one of them had a chance to blissfully absorb a piece of that hug.

To be loved! To be loved!

Kitty staggered out of Walton's office that day with her heart in a swoon. For days afterward, she felt herself caught like a leaf in some churning undertow of ecstasy and despair. She sent Dr. Walton a letter in which she wrote: "Something is happening that I've not experienced before. I'm not sure what it is, but as much as it fills me with joy, with it comes an equal ration of sadness and a feeling of humiliation; because I know somehow that it is wrong to feel this way. . . . I'm going to have to go deep for a while longer to try to figure it out. . . . I really can't identify what I feel. . . ."

She didn't know it, but for the first time in her life, Kitty Rosetti had been shaken by real love. It was just her luck that it had finally come her way just as she was getting ready to die.

Chapter 34

One rainy Saturday in the middle of June, just as the late afternoon light was failing, Michael came to Kitty and told her that it was time.

"You must prepare the way for the others," he told her. "I wish to ask you to go into the spin with Liz now. Just the two of you, alone. It's time for her to go, for good."

Excitement and terror shuddered through Kitty's heart all at once.

"You two!" Michael smiled. "You're like opposite extremes of the same thing. That's why you can't stand each other. And that's why you'll be so good for each other—because balance is essential to the spin. You'll balance each other like the light balances the dark."

Liz had always been the most in need of comfort, so perhaps it was fitting that she go first, Michael said. She'd only been wakened from the spell of sleep for a few weeks now, and she still seemed drowsy and confused. She was that way when Jess and Kitty first brought her back from her subterranean chamber far below the rim of consciousness, her body still vague and muddy, like a smear of discolored light. Just as they had after her suicide attempt, Jess and Kitty had started running a psychiatric evaluation on her, to determine if she was functional.

"Where are you?" Kitty had demanded.

"Uh . . . I'm not sure," Liz said, glancing around the room.

"What's your name?"

"Elizabeth Katherine Castle."

"Count backward from fifty-nine," Jess said.

"Uh . . . fifty-nine, fifty-eight . . . fifty-seven . . ."

"What day is this?"

"I don't know."

"How do you feel?"

"OK, I guess. Sleepy. Is that you, Kitty?"

It was natural that Liz felt a little disoriented, Jess and Kitty had realized. She'd been in the deep freeze for weeks, for one thing; and further, she'd never been to this house before. She'd been asleep when Kitty moved out of Jeff's house and into this new place at the beginning of June. She liked it well enough, though, as soon as she got up and around. They all liked it up here. The house was a secluded little two-bedroom place on a hill near the outskirts of town, dating back to the mid-1800s and overshadowed by a maple tree of mythological proportions. A long time ago a man was supposed to have hanged himself from that tree, but to the others, that tree was a benevolent guardian, keeping all bad things outside of its enormous circle of shade. They felt surrounded and protected in that house. And they all felt there was something of great significance about the move here—something portentous, magnificent.

Kitty liked the solitude, and the fact that it put an end to the pretense of her "marriage" to Jeff Castle. Yet she also understood it was the right place for the unfolding of the great event toward which Michael had been guiding them for months. Michael seemed to approve of the place, too. In fact, he was there as much as any of the others were. There were times when Kitty would be out sunning in her bikini and Michael would show up. Or Jess would be out back mowing the lawn and out of the corner of his eye he'd see Michael kicked back on a lawn chair, and he'd turn off the mower and walk over and sit down and they'd talk.

Michael explained that they were all reaching the point where their energy systems would be able to rise and expand at the same rate, so that the farandola—the great event—could take place. This was no small task, he told them, since they were of different ages and sexes, different IQ levels, different intellectual outlooks, different chemistries. None of them entirely understood what all this really meant, but they joyously prepared for it all the same. Everyone, even the babies, simply understood that this was to be the culmination of all their lives. Michael had helped each one of them individually to understand and accept the truth about their past, and to be at peace with that truth. He had helped Jess and the babies to calm their fear of whatever was going to happen next. He and Dr. Walton had helped each of them love and accept their fundamental selves. Not "I love the way I fix my hair," but "I love that I'm compassionate." Not "I love that I'm a great carpenter," but "I love that I'm a worthwhile individual." And he had helped them all understand that they must now swear allegiance to a greater goal than their own individual lives—the goal of wholeness.

Self-acceptance, joy, and calmness—they were all necessary before the spin could take place. But there was something else, too: you have to name what it is that you wish for, Michael had taught them. Anything is attainable as long as you can name it; as long as you can train your mind and consciousness to identify what it is that you want. Naming was the final thing that had to be learned. In a joyous, comfortable, natural way, in the little bedroom upstairs or on the secluded back patio, Michael began taking them deeper and deeper into the spin—training their minds to focus on this goal, teaching them to feel free and not to fear it. Out on the back patio, he'd take the little ones into a low, slow spin and they would laugh delightedly, like kids on a merry-go-round ride.

They laughed and laughed.

They didn't know this was the way they would die.

That rainy afternoon in June, when Michael told her the time had finally come, Kitty understood immediately where she had to go. The farandola was to take place at the Baptist camp, on the ragged hillside above Jeff Castle's cottage—the high place near water that Me-Liz had seen in her visions. She didn't know why; she just knew. From here at the new house, the hillside was a three-mile walk through the rain. Kitty laid out her red umbrella and yellow rain slicker by the door, but her heart felt lost. Suddenly a sense of unutterable sadness swept over her. A tumble of things spilled out of her memory like children's toys, in no order at all. She thought of the others creeping out to warm themselves around the fire, down in Baja, when they were abandoned in the desert all those years ago. How scared and lonely they felt that night! She remembered waking up in a car somewhere one time, with snow on the windshield. She was naked and confused. She had no idea how she got there. She remembered waking up in hospitals. The locked neurological ward. Probes going into her spine, into her brain. "DI-AGNOSIS: Psychomotor seizure disorder of unknown etiology . . ."

How Eric Rosetti used to explore her navel with his tongue sometimes. How gently he would stroke her into flames. She thought of the litter of their lives: three failed marriages, some crummy furniture, old photos of people she couldn't remember, three children who were not hers.

Touched by Kitty's sadness, Penny came out and walked away from the door. She put her favorite music on the tape player, George Winston's *December*—that lone piano, misty and gray as a winter afternoon. The others began flashing in and out, filled with that sadness, touched by some terror they couldn't name. Liz stumbled into the room, frightened, confused. All these years, she had been working so diligently toward her own death, but now that her death was imminent, she panicked. What was the matter with her, that she felt this way? Why did all the others seem so joyous, while she felt only fear?

Liz's memories tumbled out as well, as wind-driven rain pattered against the east windows. A sad little girl tied to a pepper tree, like a puppy. A dark, secluded house filled with fear. That smell, Daddy's smell, a pissy stench that seeped into the rugs, into the furniture. She and Maryanne hiding under the bed, watching Daddy's feet stumble drunkenly around the room. The aquarium crashed against the wall. "I want an orgasm!" he screamed. "I want an orgasm!" Daddy's smell: the smell of death. In her memory he had no face at all, only a smell. That Mexican lady who told her she was infected with evil spirits, and that she'd have to wear some special goop pinned to her pants or her baby would get infected, too. Maybe she got the bad spirits from Daddy. Maybe that's what was wrong with her. Maybe that's what had always been wrong.

She remembered waking up in a park somewhere, with leaves drifted across the grass, and white swans adrift in the lake. How calm they looked, how stately. Minneapolis, maybe? She didn't know. She had no idea at all how she got there. She just sat on the park bench and cried.

"Mama! Mama! Mona fell and hit her head!"

"Open the door! Open the door! Turn the little thing on the door!"

"I can't, Mama, we're stuck in here and Mona hurt her head!"

Thunk, thunk, thunk! Blood on her hands, blood on the white dress. Blood on the door. And now . . . and now it turns out that they lived. Her little girls lived. Yet somehow even that knowledge that had come at such a cost filled her with inconsolable sadness. If she went away now, she would never get to say goodbye to her babies. She finally had them back, and now she would never get to say goodbye. . . .

On a sudden impulse, Penny sat down at a tape recorder that was lying near the door, punched "record," and began to talk and cry into the machine.

[*On the tape,* December *plays in the background, gentle and sad. Then suddenly Penny's voice breaks in, very melodramatic, shaking with emotion*]:

"What time is this? What place is this? Please, won't somebody tell me? I've tried! I've tried! But it can't come true! Oh, my God! Where is this place? Who am I? Please . . . I'm all alone here! Oh my God, won't somebody help me? Hold me! I'm going away! . . . I cry . . . but nobody hears my words! Hear me now! I'm alone in here! *(Crying)* I'm so afraid! Do I live? Do I die? What time is this? What time is this?"

[*Click. Silence. Then Penny's voice, singing a song she once wrote for Liz—cool, calm and bluesy*]:

> *Sittin' in the sun*
> *on a blanket in the backyard*
> *sippin' on cheap wine*
> *feelin' migh-ty fine . . .*
> *I've come to the conclusion*
> *that you and me both are fools . . .*
> *livin' for us just don't come easy, but*
> *it's clear enough for me to see*
> *you and me got those*
> *we-lost-our-baby blues. . . ."*

[*Click. Kitty sings a few lines, torchy, half-growling, like a late-night strip queen*]:

> *Ohhhhhhh, I love the way I feel!*
> *. . . Mean, mean mama,*
> *mean as I can be . . .!*

[*Click. Little Andrea breaks in, squeaky and pleading. She sounds like a child of perhaps three or four*]:

"Penny, sing the song about me here! Sing it! Pretty!"

[Penny sings sweetly and gently]:

> *And I'll be loving you, my little one*
> *I'll take your hand and up we'll run*
> *and Michael's there, he waits for us*

291

and sings our song
and smiles for us!
He says, "Loving you is why I'm here,
loving you I hold you near,
my little ones, my little ones."
So children come, let's look up now
we'll touch his hand and see our friend
and he'll be lo-ving us! [voice breaks]

[*Little Andrea breaks in again*]:
I wanna sing! I wanna sing, too! I wanna sing about Mi-chael! [*Sings,
falteringly*] *And he'll be loving us . . . straight and tall . . . he's our
friend and loves us all . . . Mi-chael!*

[*Talking*] *Penny, how tall is Michael? He's bigger, bigger! Can I take
the red umbrella? Can I? Penny? Penny, are you there?"*

[*Click. Kitty sings again, very schmaltzy, accompanying a recorded
show tune*]:
Have faith in your dreams
and someday your rainbow
will come smiling through!
No matter how your heart is grievin'
if you keep on believin'
the dreams that you wish
will . . . come . . . true!

[*Click*]

Kitty turned off the machine, and then she threw on the yellow rain
slicker, opened the red umbrella, and left the house. The late afternoon
sky was dark and roiling with rain. Once or twice, as she made her way
down the hill toward town, the sun burst through and let down ladders
of light into the lake. She walked down into town, past the Aurora
Diner and the courthouse—now closed and dark for the weekend—
under the blinker light, and out around the north side of the water.
Liz was with her somewhere, but she could not see her; she seemed to
be dissolving out of the physical realm, or something. Her body and
her face were just a vague, unearthly presence, like a reflection in shiv-
ering water. Kitty walked down the gravel road toward Jeff's cottage,
and then cut up through the marshy scrub to the hillside at the Baptist
camp. By then, it was nearly dark. The rain had slowed to a patter in

the deep grass, and far off she could see lights coming out around the rim of the lake. Thunder rumbled, retreating. Liz had resisted the truth for all those years, but when it came time to walk up that hill, she did not hesitate.

When they got to a little copse of fir trees halfway up the field, Michael came to them.

"It's necessary that Liz feels safe," he told Kitty gently, "so I want her to reside within you until the farandola is complete."

Then he took her hands, and ever so slowly, they began to spin. Kitty heard Michael laughing and then she heard Liz laughing, too, nestled somewhere inside her. It was a laugh of pure joy—the only time in her life that Kitty had ever heard that laugh from Liz. Such lightness! Such delight! It was as if Liz's body itself were the burden she had carried all those years, and now, as they accelerated, the burden grew lighter and lighter until her very molecules began to separate and break free, and she became weightless as an astronaut breaking free of the thrall of earth. Breaking free! Breaking free! Kitty's hair flew outward, like a kid's on a carnival ride, and they went faster and faster until they spun into a whirling galaxy of light and Kitty didn't feel anything at all. She could hear Liz's laughter—increasingly wild, almost delirious—as all the pain and sadness and memories and then finally her very being spun away.

Far overhead, the thunder rumbled again. The spin began to slow, the lights came down, Liz's laughter faded away, and then Kitty was standing under the dripping fir trees in the dark, with Michael's arms wrapped around her. She felt exhausted.

But this time, she knew that Liz's pain was gone for good.

The next morning, Kitty got up bursting with wild exhilaration. She felt supercharged with joy and energy. She threw open the windows. She threw open the front door and then the back door—she had never done that before—so the rain-washed summer breeze could sweep through the house from one end to the other. Today, she was letting the whole world in. It was Sunday, June 18, 1986. Father's Day.

She made coffee and took her TB pills, as the others buzzed in and out excitedly, like children revving up for a field trip. Jess and Me-Liz discussed what they'd seen and felt the night before, barely able to suppress their own awe and excitement. Penny and the babies just chattered and laughed. They felt little apprehension; they were going to see Michael and live in the sky, and what could be better than that?

They trusted him as they trusted God, and they knew nothing bad could happen. Last night, they had been observers; now it was their turn.

It was decided that Kitty should do the walking today, so she bathed and put on white cotton drawstring pants and a blue blouse. Penny took the hands of the children, and when Kitty walked out the door, they danced off to see the wizard. Everything that Kitty saw, they saw. They were there, laughing and skipping down the road, but they could "see through" Kitty, just as Kitty had always been able to see through them.

It was a sunny summer morning, with towering cumulous clouds exploding in slow motion in a blue sky. They walked down the hill through town, past the courthouse, around the north side of the lake, and up through the Baptist camp to the hillside. They sat down on a rickety old picnic table and then, one by one, Michael held each of them close.

"You are important," he told them. "You are necessary. I love you. Your whole lives have been aimed at this point—but remember, just as you have no beginning, you also have no end."

"Are we gonna go live in the sky now?" Little Andrea asked.

"Yes, my child," Michael smiled. "Yes."

Penny sat on the old picnic table with the babies on her lap, their little heads against her neck, singing and whispering and crooning to them with a terrible sense of loss already coming up like floodwater around her throat. She was trying to be brave, but she felt like she was drowning. Her little ones! Her little doves, gone forever! Where were they going? What would it be like for them there? Would they be scared? Would it hurt?

Michael seemed to sense what she was feeling, and he gently squeezed her shoulder as he lifted Little Elizabeth out of her lap and into his own. Then he and Penny sat there on the rickety table for a moment, facing each other, one child in each lap. There was such love and sadness in Michael's eyes. He reached out and clasped Penny's hands. They smiled at each other.

"Ready?" he said.

"Yeah," she grinned, but her voice was breaking.

He squeezed her hand again, and at once she could feel a triggering of energy and hear a high-pitched tone that seemed to come from everywhere and nowhere at once, so that it vibrated the very air. Hands linked, she and Michael began to revolve slowly, around and around, like a pair of tethered balloons drifting lazily in the summer air. The babies giggled. It was the funny ride again! They didn't know this was the end. How could they? They didn't know anything. They barely knew how to talk. They had never even really lived—they'd never even learned to laugh until a few months before, more than three decades after their childhoods were stolen away. These two sickly, defenseless infants, with their pale skin and ringworm sores, stunted and hidden away like circus dwarves for almost forty years, had just now learned what it felt like to be loved. To trust someone. To expect something good to happen. Now, long, long delayed, they began to laugh deliriously, like children, as Liz had laughed, moments before the spin accelerated to light speed in an instant, and they disappeared. They were simply gone.

The next thing she knew, Penny was standing on the hillside with tears streaming down her face. Michael and Jess and Kitty and Me-Liz crowded around her, gently welcoming her back. She was silent. Where had the babies gone? What did they feel like now? What could they see, wherever they were?

Michael squeezed her hand again and then released it. He motioned for Jess, who was standing somewhere behind her, to sit down on the table between Penny and himself. Jess clambered up on the table, trying to cover his terror with a nervous laugh; then Penny sat down beside him. Like Liz, Jess's physical form seemed to be already disintegrating; only his colors were there, not his red ponytail or his long, competent fingers or his solemn eyes. It was as if only some essential essence of him was left, some mass of energy as individual as a fingerprint.

"Let's get this show on the road," he said, with a great show of gruffness.

Penny and Michael clasped one another's hands, with Jess's energy encircled by the hoop their arms made. Then they all began to drift lazily into the spin. Jess shivered with fear and wonder. This was the ultimate experiment. It was beyond science, beyond physics, beyond anything he'd ever heard of! If it really worked, think of the possibilities! If this force, this farandola, could be tapped and understood, think what could be done! Think of the hurts that could be healed—the psychiatric disorders and physical ills that could be cured! Then, for just a moment, Jess felt a flash of terrible sadness. He knew he was never coming back to this life. He knew this was the end. He'd never get to go fishing again. He'd never see dawn come to a misty lake, or see Kitty Rosetti's face. Now he would become part of the Mystery and vanish into the void, like a meteor hurtling off into deep space. He would never be able to come back and tell Dr. Walton all about it. He'd never be able to report his findings to science.

Penny and Michael, with Jess in between, began to accelerate slowly. They whirled around six times, eight times, ten times, gathering speed, until suddenly, with a flash, Jess fused into some wholeness beyond himself and in an instant was gone.

Me-Liz was standing beside the table when Michael came back. He took her hand gently and led her away, down the hillside through the deep grass, like a lover. Me-Liz had always had a special relationship with Michael, a kinship of faith. She had always been the most accepting of him, the most understanding. She was his beloved disciple, his chosen one. He had taken her places the others had never been. Now all she felt was ecstasy; her faith in her own resurrection surrounded her with radiance, like white robes. She was entirely without fear. Me-Liz knew she would die, and that somehow, somewhere, maybe in another time, maybe in another dimension, she would live again. She was prepared to leave the body. She knew that it would be as simple and painless as stepping out of her clothes. Standing in the deep grass, facing one another, she and Michael took one another's hands, and she met his eyes for the last time.

"Goodbye," she said. Her face was bathed in ecstasy. And then she spun out, as easily and naturally as a sunlit dandelion seed drifts out of sight on the wind.

Michael walked back to the table afterward. Penny and Kitty were waiting there for him.

"If it would be all right, I'd like to go next," Penny told him. Her voice sounded weary, sad.

"I don't know, Penny," Kitty interrupted nervously. "I think if I don't go next, I'm gonna lose my nerve!"

Penny assented, with a gentle nod, and then Michael sat back down on the old picnic table. Kitty climbed up into his lap and she buried her face in his chest like a child. She was overcome with emotion. She didn't have to be strong anymore, after all those years of struggle, all that fighting to achieve, all that fighting to keep them alive! Now Kitty could finally give up. She wasn't responsible anymore. It wasn't her problem, or her fault, or her business anymore. Now she could weep, and be weak, and go away forever. Michael wrapped his arms around her, and her shoulders shook with great sobs as together they spun out like a great, glittery nebulae and then Kitty Rosetti, the survivor, was gone.

When Michael came out of the spin, only Penny Lavender was left. All she longed for—all she'd ever longed for—was to go away. Now at last it was time. How many years had she longed to go away! When her father's smell seeped under Penny's bedroom door and she heard him raging outside like some inhuman thing, like some monster, like a thing without a head or a face, she longed desperately to go away. Crouched over those big sheets of wet paper, long ago, in kindergarten, she longed to go away into her paintings. She longed to go away when she sat at the piano with her eyes closed, in that dingy duplex in Oklahoma. She longed to go away even when she lay in her white cabin by the pond, staring at the carvings that told the story of her life. She'd always had to come back, back to the world of pain and sadness, but now she would never come back. This was the final story, the last carving in the bedpost.

Penny climbed up onto the rickety picnic table and into Michael's lap, just as Kitty had done. She was scared and shaking. She was too frightened to speak or even sing—suddenly she was mute, just as she'd been when Sandy Lentz broke her heart all those years before. Michael encircled her with his arms. She felt a dizzy shiver of energy as they went into the spin. She closed her eyes. And then, in a rush of radiance, she too was gone.

Part 3

"Katherine, It's Time."

Chapter 35

KIT CASTLE: I awoke in Michael's arms. I was in the dining room in front of the fireplace in the new house, from which the others had left on their last journey. I realize now that I was naked, but I didn't realize it then. I didn't know how I had gotten there, or even exactly who I was—but I knew who Michael was. I looked into his face and it was like looking into the face of God. He smiled, and his voice welcomed me with my name.

"You are Katherine," he said, "but I shall call you Kit."

"What is Kit?" I asked.

"You are Kit. Kit means Katherine, It's Time."

That first day, I did not understand what he meant by this. All I knew was that I was there and that this gentle being who guided me also loved me. And I knew that I loved him. The first few days of my life, I remember sleeping a lot. I would wake up in Michael's arms, and he would comfort me and make me laugh. I remember that one night—I don't know if it was the first night, or later—he took me out to the swing suspended from the giant maple tree in the front yard. I could hear the wind whistling past my ears as the swing sailed up into the night sky. I could see the bright moon through the branches, and lights coming on down in the village below the hill.

"From now on," Michael told me with a little laugh, "when it's time to be outside, you must always wear clothes."

The next day, we spent hours trying on clothes in front of the mirror. I didn't quite know what went where; I had to turn to magazines and TV for understanding. I recognized the toilet bowl cleaner from a TV commercial, and I began using it every time I used the toilet. I didn't know until later that you didn't have to clean the bowl every time you used it. It was strange: some things I knew, many others I did not. It was like having a selective amnesia. I knew about chicken noodle soup, but I didn't know how to use a can opener. I didn't know how to turn on the stove or tie my shoes. Yet I knew how to light a cigarette, how to speak English, and how a tape player works. I went down to the library in town and checked out elementary school arithmetic books, to teach myself numbers, and simple books about all sorts of other things I didn't understand.

In the same way Michael gave me information about day-to-day life— in bits and pieces, as he felt I was ready for it—so he showed me about the others. As time went by, I gained more and more memory of Little Elizabeth, Little Andrea, Jess, Liz, Me-Liz, Penny, and Kitty. I learned of them little by little, slowly, over time. Michael feared that learning of their histories too rapidly had the potential to damage me psychologically, as it had damaged them. I learned to love and respect these seven individuals unconditionally, for they could not explain their birthright any more than I can explain my own. I do not understand how this can be so, but they are not me, and I am not them. They are gone. I was born on June 18, 1986, in Aurora, New York, into the body of a grown woman. All I know is that now I must learn to live on my own, as a whole, responsible adult, though in many ways I am still a child.

Once I asked Michael what happened to Jess and the girls after they went into the spin on the hill, and he told me something that mystifies me to this day:

"Little Elizabeth was diffused," he said. "Little Andrea was diffused. Jess is now with a medical student in Hamilton, Ontario, Canada. He is to this student as I am to you. Penny Lavender resides in a level where the form of communication is tonal in nature. Me-Liz resides with her 'real father.' Liz resides with her 'real father.' Kitty resides in the area of color that surrounds you. She is not of you, but remains near. It will be necessary for her to make a reappearance for a very short period of time. There is unfinished business. . . ."

As the weeks and months went by, I began to experience friendship and love, and all the positive emotions that lead to these ultimate gifts. I was

302

fortunate to have a ready-made support group awaiting my arrival—the friends that Liz and the others had made for themselves here. They offered me their caring and respect, even if they did not fully understand that I am not the person(s) that they knew. I feel privileged to have been included in their lives. I think of them as my family.

Ralph Walton was a beacon of kindness and support for me in those early days when I still understood so little about this world. I considered him to be kind of my cofather, along with Michael. This man who had loved me into life continued to be there for me when I felt terrified that I could never learn to be whole. Our therapy continued until we both felt it was no longer necessary, but he continues to be a supportive figure in my life.

Shortly before my first summer turned to fall, Michael and I walked the land of the still-abandoned church camp on the shores of the peaceful lake. We had spent the afternoon exploring the special places—the places the others saw in their visions, and where they willingly gave up their identities, the place of my conception. Michael explained that soon I must make my way out into the world, that much would be asked of me, and that I must be ready to accept the challenge. That who I was was more important than where I came from. That the others' experiences must be shared with the world, if only to help one child, one adult, to end the cycle of abuse that can ultimately affect us globally.

"How can I help, Michael? I'm only one person," I said. "I don't know if I have the ability to change the world."

"We all have the ability to change the world, if we only take responsibility for changing ourselves," he said.

"When do I begin?" I asked, as he reached for my hand and led me down the softly sloping hill to the lake. He turned, looked into my eyes and then into my heart, and said, "Katherine, it's time."

303

Stefan Bechtel, an award-winning newspaper reporter, has also worked as a senior editor at Rodale Press and as executive editor of *Men's Health* magazine. This is his first book.

Kit Castle is now living a private life and pursuing her own personal adventure.